The New Airedale Terrier

The New Airedale Terrier

JUNE DUTCHER
and
JANET JOHNSON FRAMKE

HOWELL BOOK HOUSE

New York

Collier Macmillan Canada
Toronto

Maxwell Macmillan International
New York   Oxford   Singapore   Sydney

Copyright © 1990 by June Dutcher and Janet Johnson Framke

Copyright © 1978, 1966, 1962 by Howell Book House Inc.

Howell Book House
Macmillan Publishing Company
866 Third Avenue, New York, NY 10022

Collier Macmillan Canada, Inc.
1200 Eglinton Avenue East, Suite 200
Don Mills, Ontario M3C 3N1

Library of Congress Cataloging-in-Publication Data
Dutcher, June.
   The new Airedale terrier / June Dutcher and Janet Johnson Framke.
    p. cm.
   ISBN 0-87605-007-0
   1. Airedale terriers. I. Framke, Janet Johnson. II. Title
SF429.A6D87   1990
636.7'55—dc20   90-23585   CIP

Macmillan books are available at special discounts for bulk purchases for sales promotions, premiums, fund-raising, or educational use. For details contact:

               Special Sales Director
               Macmillan Publishing Company
               866 Third Avenue
               New York, NY 10022

10 9 8 7 6 5 4 3 2

Printed in the United States of America

This book is dedicated to Gladys Brown Edwards, the First Lady of Airedales, and to the many fanciers who find the "King of the Terriers" their dog for all reasons.

Contents

Acknowledgments

First and foremost we must recognize Gladys Brown Edwards and her work in recounting the early history of the breed and the early Airedale descendants both in England and in their early days in America. But above all we are indebted to her for her clear, concise drawings, which remind the reader that a picture is worth a thousand words. Not only was Gladys a truly great artist, but she also had a way of showing exactly what the words described.

We are grateful to Jan Walker of Issaquah, Washington, for her drawings of Airedales doing many different things. Jan, like Gladys, works in all mediums and is especially fond of both Airedales and Arabian horses. Her renderings of both are sought after by collectors.

The wonderful "Dopey Dale" cartoons are from the cartoon book drawn by Paul Clarke of Australia. He has caught the indomitable spirit of the Airedale, and we are pleased that he will let us share them with you.

With heartfelt gratitude we acknowledge the help of the many persons mentioned here and throughout the book who have helped us put this book together.

The Authors

JUNE DUTCHER got her first Airedale as a hearing aid for her deaf Dalmatian. Tim Tam's excellent hearing would alert the Dal, Chequers, to go on fence patrol and guard duty. Knowing absolutely nothing about Airedale Terriers, June went to work for Terrier handler Daisy Austad to learn about dog shows. Daisy put Tim Tam in show shape, and in 1962 she went from the Open Bitch class to Best of Breed at the Southern California Airedale Association to win the Airedale Terrier Club of America Bowl and the Lionheart Comet Bowl. Starting at the top with a winning bitch made June get seriously involved with the Airedale breed, and as June often tells beginners, when you start at the top and work your way down your competitive spirit forces you to rise again.

Through the years June has been involved with the Airedale Terrier Club of America as a board member and then as secretary for many years. She is still actively managing her Coppercrest Kennel, breeding selectively, showing her dogs and hoping to have another ATCA bowl winner.

JANET JOHNSON FRAMKE started in Airedales in 1969, using the prefix "Stone Ridge." Under the able guidance of Virginia Bensman of Benaire Kennels, she learned to groom and show her own dogs. Over the years she has gratefully acknowledged the help of Park Peters, Gary and Joanne Vohs, Gary Clarke, Sue Criswell, George Ward, Wood Wornall, Peter Green, Ric Chashoudian, Mike and Denise Tobey, Susie Depew, Bill Thompson and Bob Larouech. For the last twenty years, Stone Ridge has had the thrill of breeding, importing, owning or co-owning some of the top winning and producing

Airedales in the country. Janet has bred over one hundred champions, and dogs she has bred or owned have earned thirteen Airedale bowl and numerous Best in Show wins. Her philosophy is that temperament is the first goal of breeding, with good looks being the frosting on the cake.

A director of the Airedale Terrier Club of America for the past fifteen years, she has also served as president of the Airedale Terrier Club of Illinois and is currently serving on the board of that club, as well as being active in Airedale rescue. Janet Framke has judged multiple National Specialty Sweepstakes, including Montgomery County, and had the honor of judging a Sweepstakes in Australia.

1

The Evolution of
the Airedale Terrier

THE PICTURESQUE VALLEY of the Aire River in West
Riding, Yorkshire, was the birthplace of the Airedale—"The King of Terriers"—largest of a sporting clan. Although the exact date is unknown, historical data indicate that it was about the middle of the nineteenth century that
the Airedale was evolved to fit the sporting needs of the residents of the Aire
Valley.

THE CRADLE OF THE BREED

Located less than a hundred miles south of the Scottish border, the Aire
Valley, although heavily industrialized, afforded endless opportunity for sport
involving dogs. Its varied terrain—ranging from bleak grouse moors to
wooded glens, from rocky fells to river lowlands—harbored myriad species of
game: upland birds, rabbits, hare, marten, badger, and otter. In town, during
those mid-nineteenth-century years, were the inevitable rats, fair game for any
Terrier.

The many mills and factories lining the Aire River made the stream
untenable for the otter and the fish that are an otter's prey, so otter hunting
was necessarily confined to the Wharfe and other nearby streams. Properly
done, it required a pack of Otterhounds plus a Terrier or two. Needless to say,
this was beyond the means of the average factory worker, although an occa-

sional sportsman kept a couple of Hounds and, with a few Terriers, could expect to have fair luck along the streams. Water-rat matches, with teams of Terriers contesting for points, were another popular sport. Less creditable, but a diversion that in its way contributed to the working abilities of the Airedale, was the intriguing (if illicit) pastime of outwitting the gamekeepers on estates that were off-limits to the average citizen. And because some shootable fur or feather occasionally "happened along," many of the Terriers of the Aire Valley were broken to the gun and trained to retrieve.

TERRIERS IN EARLY WRITINGS

As far back as the sixteenth century, Terriers were depicted in engravings and paintings, as well as mentioned in writings as a specific type. Although later writings gave the Terrier a rather indefinite description, Daniel in *Field Sports* (1760) wrote: "There are two sorts of terriers, the one rough, short-legged, long-backed, very strong, and most commonly of a black or yellowish color, mixed with white; the other is smooth-haired and beautifully formed, having a shorter body and more sprightly appearance, and is generally of a reddish-brown color, or black with tanned legs. Both these sorts are the determined foe of all vermin kind and in their encounters with the badger very frequently meet with severe treatment which they sustain with great courage, and a well-bred, well-trained terrier often proves more than a match for his opponent."

Sydenham Edwards gives a most enlightening description of the Terrier and his work in the *Cynographia Britannica* published in 1800: ". . . The Terrier is high spirited and alert when brought into action; if he has not the unsubdued perseverance like the Bulldog, he has rapidity of attack, managed with art and sustained with spirit; it is not what he will bear, it is what he will inflict. His action protects himself, and his bite carries death to his opponents; he dashes into the hole of the fox, drives him from the recesses or tears him to pieces in his stronghold; he forces the reluctant, stubborn badger into light. As his courage is great, so is his genius extensive; he will trace with the foxhounds, hunt with the beagle, find with the greyhound, or beat with the spaniel. Of wildcats, martens, polecats, weasels and rats, he is the vigilant and determined enemy; he drives the otter from the rocky clefts on the banks of the rivers, nor declines combat of a new element."

Terriers of the period were described by *The Sporting Dictionary* (1803): ". . . of even the best are now bred in all colors—red; black with tan faces, flanks, feet and legs; brindles; sandy; some few brown-pied; and pure white; as well as one sort of each color rough and wirehaired, the other soft and smooth; and what is rather more extraordinary, the latter not much deficient in courage to the former, but the rough breed must be acknowledged the more severe and invincible biter of the two."

Edwards gave a somewhat similar description but mentioned that the

2

ears varied—some short, some erect, some pendulous, and they were usually cropped. He also said that the white color had been in demand in recent years. The white Terriers were more popular because darker ones were often mistaken for the fox by myopic members of the field, and the Hounds were halloed off the line, or what was more serious, the Terriers were mistaken for the fox and killed by the Hounds—which could readily happen after the Terrier had been in a fox-earth and smelled more fox than dog. Experience showed the white Terriers were relatively safe—hence the predominately white color of the Fox Terrier.

Rawdon Lee, in the "Terriers" volume of his *Modern Dogs* (1903), graphically describes Terrier ways and Terrier days: "Few sporting country districts are, or were, without their own special strain of terriers, in which appearance was of little object as long as gameness predominated. By 'gameness' I do not mean partiality for fighting or cat-killing, and standing being cut up piecemeal without flinching or whimpering, but killing vermin and going to ground after fox, badger or otter—wild animals, and not tame, domesticated or semi-tame creatures. I have seen a dog of great excellence and gameness in a street fight which would yelp and run away when a big buck rat seized him by the nose. The north of England was usually prolific in producing terriers; the working artisans in the manufacturing centers owned them; the masters of hounds who hunted the foxes in the hills and mountains, where horses could not follow, required a terrier that would bolt a fox or worry him in the hole if he refused to face the open. Some had a dash of Bull Terrier in them, others had not."

WORKING TERRIERS

Various hunts—among them the Belvoir, the Quorn, and the Grove—were noted for their working Terriers and had their own special breeds. Although in the 1860s the Smooth Fox Terrier quickly became the darling of the show gods, the other Terriers went their usual ways, diligently working for their living, unadorned by Dame Fashion, and, we must admit, somewhat scorned by her. Even the Wire, country cousin of the Smooth Fox Terrier, was shrugged off as a "working Terrier."

In its restricted sense, the term "working" Terrier means one small enough to go to ground after animals and bold enough to force them to retreat. With the exception of the Lakeland, whose job it was to kill the fox, working Terriers were expected to bolt the quarry, hard as it might argue back, or to "mark" its location by barking so it could be dug out. Such Terriers, to go to earth, necessarily had to be small, so were often outweighed, though not outgamed, by their antagonists.

Although the Waterside Terriers, later known as Airedales, were too big to go to ground, they were good for everything else required of a sporting Terrier. Their special forte was, however, the pursuit of the water rat in matches arranged for the purpose. These highly competitive matches were regular events along a three- to six-mile radius of the Aire River, and on Saturday afternoons when two well-known dogs were pitted against each other, the whole countryside turned out to follow the match, watching the proceedings with the keenest interest. Stakes of from one to twenty-five pounds were posted, and a referee was appointed to score the Terriers. Added zest was given by side bets, a whole week's pay literally "going down a rathole" when a spectator backed the wrong dog.

The Terriers worked both sides of the stream as indicated by their owners, swimming from one side to the other when so directed. When one dog located a "live" hole, it counted two points as a "mark," and both dogs were made to stay back while a ferret was put into the hole to bolt the rat. The rat usually bolted directly into the river, with both dogs going after him like Dollar Days shoppers after a bargain. In his first dive the rat would swim from thirty to forty yards underwater, the Terriers meanwhile anxiously swimming about, necks stretched high, expectantly waiting for the rat to surface. If a dog's owner sighted the rat first, he would whistle or wave to his dog; then both Terriers would take off, each deadly determined to get to the quarry first. The dash was usually to no avail, for the rat would again submerge and torpedo away in another direction, only to cause the same furor when he came up for air. Gradually his dives would get shorter, and the nearest Terrier would send his score up one point by making the kill. Often the dog would, in a well-timed dive, catch the tiring rat under water and bob triumphantly to the surface with the crunched animal in his mouth. Many times a dog that lagged in making kills would catch up on his score by being first to locate the rats, the score for the "mark" being double that for the "kill."

THE AIREDALE'S ANTECEDENTS

Before the evolution of the Airedale can be adequately appreciated, it is necessary to have some idea of the character of the canine ores comprising the alloy that is the breed. The "earth" ancestor of the amphibious dog of Aire was that region's version of the old rough-coated working Terrier, variously known as the "Broken-coated Working Terrier," "Old English Black-and-Tan Terrier," "Rough-coated Black-and-Tan Terrier," and so on; but actually he was not always "rough" nor was he always "black-and-tan." His coat was occasionally almost smooth, sometimes almost wooly, but mostly it was hard and wiry. Color varied from red, through various grizzles and bluish grays, to black-and-tan. Even the last was not the familiar pattern of today with the black saddle and rich tan, but rather more like that of a Manchester—black, with tan points on muzzle, eyebrows, inside of legs, and on feet; and he often had a blaze of white on his chest. Before the many outcrosses were made, he was about the size of a large Fox Terrier—a good twenty pounds in weight. It was not until the interest in the waterside matches grew to large proportions

4

Otter Hounds in the River Aire at Gargrave, near Skipton.

that a lively interest was taken in improving the Terrier's swimming ability and scenting power, and in developing an undercoat impervious to water. The Otterhound, or at least what passed for an Otterhound in those days, had all these wanted attributes, and there is no doubt that the Otterhound, or "Hound for otter," was used for the nick. Holland Buckley even names the man who first made the cross, a Wilfred Holmes, near Bradford, and sets the date as 1853. According to Mr. Buckley, "this produced a dog that was as game and hard as the Terrier and better able, by increased size and weight, to hold his own with the larger vermin that abounded in the country of 'Broad Acres.' Frequent crosses between the Hound and Terrier were made, and the puppies found a ready sale amongst local sportsmen. These were again bred amongst themselves until, in about a dozen years, a variety of these crossed Terriers became established in the localities around Otley, Shipley and Bradford; and the dogs had an excellent reputation all over the County for work and fighting pluck. The question of general uniformity and type was not worried over. These Terriers could nearly live in water, and even in the coldest weather would rather be in than out of water, and in the neighbourhood of Bingley were first called 'Waterside Terriers.' "

From all accounts, there was a regular cat's cradle of crosses in the ancestral mesh of the Airedale; the proximity of the vast flocks of sheep on the moors arouses suspicion that the inherent tendency shown by some Airedales toward herding might trace to a sheepish incident involving a Border Collie or other sheep dog.

The Bull Terrier is another that fights his way into the discussion, refusing to be completely downed in his claim to a boost to Airedale spirits. Some state that the Bull Terrier cross did not occur, while others stoutly maintain that it did. But if it did, it surely must have been an admixture to the "original" rough-coated working Terrier, not the later edition, the Waterside Terrier. Support of that theory is given by Gersbach-Jager's *The Police Dog,* written in 1910: "The Airedale Terrier was developed in the part of Yorkshire lying between the Aire and the Wharfe rivers—a great factory and quarry district. Some fifty years ago the workingmen of that section bred a terrier of about 15–20 lbs. in weight and reddish in color. These dogs, a variety of the old hard-coated terrier, were great fighters, and were used for that purpose. Later the Bull Terrier, also a great fighting dog, was crossed with these terriers to give greater size. The result, dogs up to 30 and 35 lbs. and used for rat-pit matches and against each other. The final step in producing the Airedale Terrier was the crossing of these Bull-and-Terriers with Otterhounds of Wharfe Valley."

This version is quite different from some others, but does place the Bull Terrier cross before the Otterhound invasion, although the dates do not quite jibe with Buckley's. Bull Terriers are also referred to in the article on the Airedale in *The American Book of the Dog,* by Shields (1891), in which a Yorkshireman is quoted: "I owned three (Airedales)—Smuggler, Crack and Ben—and they were as good dogs as I ever saw. Ben was the largest and he would probably weigh some 40 to 45 pounds. They breed them much larger now than they did then. When I had them it was over thirty years ago. Crack was first owned by a Leeds gentleman and weighed not more than 35 pounds when in fair condition. He was matched and fought in the pit, in Leeds, with a Bull Terrier, weight 33½ pounds. Crack was to come any weight; the Bull Terrier was to be 32 pounds only, but they let him in at the above weight. I saw the fight and bought Crack as soon as it was over. Crack outfought him, and killed him dead in 48 minutes, and fought fully as quiet as the Bull Terrier. He had better grit, for if the Bull Terrier could, he would have jumped the pit, I think, but Crack pinned him and held him until he finished him. Either of the other two, Ben or Smuggler, would fight just as keen. The Airedale fights much faster than the Bull Terrier and their thick hair seems to sicken the dog they fight with."

Further mention of the early Airedale was made by this same Yorkshireman regarding the bitch "Floss," who fought a Bull-and-Terrier bitch for three-quarters of an hour. The Bull had the upper hand for thirty minutes, but then "Floss set to and killed her. My men told me that she wagged her tail all the time and never made a sound, though receiving terrible punishment. The Bull and Terrier weighed half again as much as she did." Several bitches named Floss were mentioned in early pedigrees, but it is doubtful that this particular Floss is a close relative, in view of the time—the fights having taken place in the late 1850s or early 1860s.

"Stonehenge" (J. H. Walsh), in his *Dogs of the British Isles* (1884), looked down his aristocratic nose at the interloper from the North, scorning his work and his breeders "whose pockets were not deep," and claiming the dog completely lacked gameness because a few well-chosen correspondents (unnamed) had picked up some Airedales at random and matched them against trained pit-fighting Bull Terriers. The Airedales, supposedly having been made into quick cold hash by the fighting machines against which they were pitted, did not impress Mr. Walsh, so for several years in his writings as editor of *The Field,* he continued to ridicule the breed from this standpoint alone. In spite of Mr. Walsh, it is obvious that some Airedales in particular could fight, and what is more, they fought silently, like the Bull Terrier, thus giving further weight to the theory that such a cross was used.

With Bull Terriers allegedly used in the manufacture of the Airedale, a short tour into their history is timely. Bull- and bearbaiting had been very popular up to the 1830s when they, along with dogfighting, were declared illegal. While the first two bloody pastimes were discontinued, prohibiting pit fighting merely added to its zest and it was continued behind closed doors. Because the Bulldog was too slow, Terrier blood was introduced to that of the Bulldog to evolve the breed known as Bull-and-Terrier. The resulting cross was stated to be "even better adapted for mischievous sport" than either the Bulldog or Terrier. Although the Bull-and-Terrier was game, he was an undeniable mongrel in looks, being short-legged, broad-fronted, thickset, and with a broad, blunt muzzle with considerable layback. But as more Terrier crosses were made and the Bull was buried further back in the family tree, the Bull-and-Terrier gradually took on the appearance of the Staffordshire, though his colors were those of the Bulldog—fawn, brindle, pied and occasionally white. It was about the time the breed progressed from Bull-and-Terrier to Bull Terrier that the first crosses were reportedly made into the Airedale foundation stock.

The Bull Terrier did not take on his sleek appearance as the "White Cavalier" until after 1862, when a breeder named James Hinks crossed the Bull Terrier with the elegant, but now extinct, Old English White Terrier. The resulting all-white, long-headed dogs rapidly won the public's favor away from the broad-headed, old-fashioned type, and for several decades Colored Bull Terriers were not bred—in fact, it was not until after World War I that the Colored Bull Terrier, as we know it today, was reintroduced. If the cross with the Airedale had been made after the Bull Terrier had become dominantly white in color, it would have to have been after the 1860s. Certainly more white would have cropped out in the Airedale in subsequent crosses (as it does in all similar white-crossed dogs) than the blaze on chest and occasional white toes that show up even today. Since minor white markings are also seen in the oldest Terrier paintings, and on Bloodhounds, it would seem that they could have been inherited from some factor other than the Bull Terrier. If this argument holds any water, it might give weight to the theory that any Bull Terrier cross was used before that breed was all-white—i.e., before the late 1860s, at least.

Although some researchers credit the rough-coated Welsh Foxhound or Harrier rather than the Otterhound with assistance in founding the Airedale, the majority agree that the Otterhound cross was more likely. Whether they were purebred Otterhounds, Welsh Hounds or mixed will never be known at this date, but whatever their breeding, they had all the qualities necessary for the work.

The Otterhound is thought to be a direct descendant of the old Southern Hound, ancestor of many English scent Hounds, with a cross to the shaggy Griffon Vendeen, another of the same variety, both slow but sure trailers. A few writers indicate there might be a distant Water Spaniel admixture, some mention the Bloodhound, while an occasional modern writer will put the cart way in front of the horse and claim that the Otterhound descended from the Airedale!

Two other breeds that modern writers try to credit with founding the Airedale are the Welsh and Irish Terriers. However, as breeds, both the Welsh and the Irish were in embryonic stages themselves when the Airedale was being developed, so could not possibly have taken a hand in the evolution of the Airedale, although all were founded on the same basic stock—the old rough-coated Terrier. The first Airedales to be exhibited under the breed name were shown in 1883, the first "Welsh" in 1886, and the first class for "Irish" Terriers was established in 1873. But with all colors, sizes and shapes being shown in the latter, it was merely a class for any Terrier bred in Ireland.

The first Welsh were admitted to the Kennel Club Stud Book in 1885 under "Welsh (or Old English, wire-haired black-and-tan) Terriers." For a while there were classes for Old English and also for Welsh Terriers, and one dog, "Dick Turpin," gained a unique fame by winning in both classes. Later the Old English faded from the scene and the Welsh became the sole representative of the old working Terrier on the show bench until the advent of the Lakeland in 1920. The early Welsh were short-headed, large-eyed and often bowed of front, so some exhibitors found a quick way of winning by crossing Airedales with Wires, and entered these smart-looking, long-headed, black-and-tan Terriers in classes for either (or both) Welsh or Old English. They won for a while, but the admirers of the Welsh soon prevented their winning the club specials, and the old-type Welsh again took over until a later date when it too was "smartened up" by the useful Fox Terrier. While misadventures of the Welsh have no real bearing on the founding of the Airedale, the mere fact that Airedale–Fox Terrier crosses won in the first Welsh classes should preclude any claim that the Welsh Terrier, as now known, played any part in the evolution of the Airedale. That the two had a common ancestor, there is no doubt.

As the Airedale progressed, size became a touchy problem and the following dictum was written into the Standard in 1902: "It is the unanimous opinion of the club that the size of the Airedale Terrier as given in the above Standard (40–45 lbs.) is one of, if not the most important, characteristics of the breed; all judges who shall henceforth adjudicate on the merits of the Airedale Terrier shall consider under-sized specimens of the breed severely handicapped when competing with dogs of standard weight; and any of the club judges who, in the opinion of the committee, shall give prizes or otherwise push to the front, dogs of the small type, shall at once be struck from the list of specialist judges." The strong wording had its effect, few judges wishing to face such a penalty. In later years this emphasis on "large" dogs was taken—for a while—to mean the bigger the better. Fortunately this trend, too, was stopped, although not before some specimens reached twenty-four inches, yet remained within the former weight limit, hence were generally lathy and lacking in substance.

The Irish Terrier, as well as the Welsh, has been credited with playing a part in the evolution of the Airedale, but this seems doubtful; by the time the Irish Terrier itself had developed to the point that it would breed true, the Airedale was well on its way to fame. Use of the Irish in later years, to sharpen expression and improve placement, size and carriage of ears, may possibly have occurred in a few isolated cases, but seems rather doubtful.

The similarity of all of the sons of the old rough-coated "black-and-tan" Terrier is very marked in pictures of early champions. Even the Wire was of the same outline, and except for the cropped ears of the Irish and his fleeter build, it would be difficult to distinguish the breeds from the pictures if it were not for the coat markings. All the breeds had the same faults—they were long-cast, short-necked and (again excepting the Irish) cloddy, with a snipey appearance as a result of lacking facial furnishings. While the smaller breeds could tap other sources to improve the breed quickly if so desired—like the Smooth refining the Wire, the Wire aiding the Welsh, etc.—the Airedale had no other large breed of similar type sufficiently advanced in fashion on which to rely. The breeders had to refine the rough ore themselves, heading toward a known ideal, striving always for Terrier quality on a dog of un-Terrier size. And while trying to breed the Hound *out* of the Airedale externally, they wanted to keep valuable Hound attributes internally.

While the average forty to forty-five pounds of early Airedales seems small in these days of sixty-pound dogs, the news in 1879 of a forty-five-pound Terrier caused disbelief and ridicule among the cognoscenti who contended that a dog which was too big to go to ground was unworthy of the name "Terrier." It is true that the Airedale's size would preclude his going to ground and hence prevent his doing the work that gave the tribe its name of Terrier (from "terra," earth). But the Airedale, as he continued to improve, became all Terrier in type and character so that finally even his first antagonists admitted that he belonged to this distinguished clan.

A TRIBUTE TO THE AIREDALE

Albert Payson Terhune sums up the Airedale concisely in an article in *Nature Magazine:* "Among the mine-pits of the Aire, the various groups of miners each sought to develop a dog which could outfight and outhunt and OUTTHINK the other mine's dogs. Tests of the first-named virtues were made in inter-mine dog fights. Bit by bit, thus, an active, strong, heroic, compactly graceful and clever dog was evolved—the earliest true form of the Airedale. Then the outer world's dog fancy got hold of him and shaped and improved into the show-type Airedale of today. The process was not long, for the newly evolved dogs were quick to adapt themselves to their creators' wishes. Out of the experiments emerged the modern Airedale. He is swift, formidable, graceful, big of brain, an ideal chum and guard. There is almost nothing he cannot be taught if his trainer has the slightest gift for teaching. To his master he is an adoring pal. To marauders he is a destructive lightning bolt. In the Southwest and elsewhere these traits have been made use of by numerous sportsmen. Airedales do the work of pointers and setters and other hunting dogs. For nose and steadiness and snappy retrieving and for finding fallen birds, these field-trained Airedales have given surprisingly good accounts of themselves. There is nothing thrown away in an Airedale's makeup. Every inch of him is in use. Compact, wiry, he is 'all there.' No flabby by-products. A PERFECT MACHINE—a machine with a BRAIN, PLUS. He shows phenomenal powers of brain and instinct found in few other dogs. Fashion can never rule the Airedale out of existence. Too many people have learned to value him above any other breed. He is here to stay. He has won his right to PERMANENCE."

2

Early Historical Development of the Breed in England

UNTIL 1957 it was thought that the first dog show was held at Newcastle-on-Tyne in 1859. However, recent research has shown that Newcastle was antedated at least a decade by Cleveland, which catered to Terriers, Toys and Spaniels. Other shows had been held in the 1840s for the same breeds, with some of the exhibitors having a go in the rat pit with their Terriers after the shows.

THE FIRST DOG SHOWS

The Newcastle event was for Pointers and Setters only, and "The Druid," in *Saddle and Sirloin,* gave what is probably the first critique on a dog show and reported that the show took place in a tent, with the public excluded. Macdonald Daly's column in *Our Dogs* gives further data on this: "A 'peeping Tom' found a hole in the tent and gave his pals a running commentary on what was going on. He reported that the judge, Capt. Percy Williams, was 'king at nowt else but slape (smooth) coats and white 'uns.' To Captain Williams thus fell the honour of being the first of many thousand judges, throughout the world, to have their efforts disparaged by ringside critics!" The dogs in question were Fox Terriers, the entry consisting of sixteen Smooths and sixteen "hairy 'uns."

The same year Newcastle held its much publicized first show, Cleveland also staged a show for gun dogs and Terriers. Birmingham, however, had the first championship show, which was held in December 1859 with classes for gun dogs. The following year Terriers were added.

The dog-show sport was quickly taken up by all classes, for anyone owning a dog that even vaguely resembled some identifiable variety was free to join in, and shows were held at frequent intervals and in every part of England. However, for fourteen years the game was entirely unsupervised. Anything could happen, and usually did, and the scandals resulting from shady practices of certain overeager exhibitors almost caused reputable owners to discontinue showing. In due course the need for a governing body with powers to enforce its decrees became obvious, and in 1873 the Kennel Club was established. A Stud Book was initiated, the first volume of six hundred pages having a listing of 4,027 dogs, but of course there was then no breed named Airedale, so any embryonic Airedales were merely listed as one of the rough-coated Terriers in the "non-sporting" classification. The only other classification was for "sporting" dogs (i.e., gun dogs and Hounds), but in the next volume a separate classification of "Terriers" was given these most sporting of all dogs.

In 1864, Keighly Agricultural Show, the first dog show in the Aire Valley, was held. Included was a class for "Broken-haired Terriers," and at Craven, Otley and Bingley similar classifications followed during the next ten years. Not only were Waterside Terriers entered in these classes, but also competing were Dandie Dinmonts, rough Fox Terriers, Bedlingtons, "Scottish" Terriers, and even the antecedents of the tiny Yorkshire.

It was not until 1879 that the Waterside or Bingley Terriers were mentioned by name. In that year the noted dog authority and author Hugh Dalziel, after judging at Bingley, wrote in his report: "The class for Broken-haired Terriers, the Bingley Terrier par excellence—was an exceedingly good one." In his book published that year he describes the Bingley Terrier as having the appearance of a giant Bedlington or Dandie Dinmont, and "appearing to have a lot of hound blood." In the 1870s the Bedlington and the Dandie were quite similar, differing mainly in size and in length of leg; the Bedlington was far from the Whippet-like dog of today with his crew cut and shaved jaw, and had only a slight arch of loin. Although more on the leg than the Dandie, the Bedlington was more long-cast than "square," so the comparison between the early Airedale and Bedlington is not so grotesque as it might seem.

The publication of Dalziel's comments brought immediate outside interest in the breed but also brewed a storm of protest among its fanciers for pinpointing Bingley as the home of the breed. It was thought that the name "Airedale" was first suggested by Dr. Gordon Stables, who judged these Terriers at Bingley the year before Dalziel, for previous to the latter's comments, the name, Airedale, had not been given the breed in any other connection. At any rate, some fanciers held a meeting in Bingley and decided that in the future the breed should be known as the "Airedale Terrier," and when

Mr. Dalziel judged again in 1880 he mentioned the "Broken-haired Airedale Terrier" in his report. There was still confusion about the name, however, and at the Birmingham show in 1883 the show committee arranged a class for "Waterside Terriers." And for many shows that followed, two or all three names were used—possibly to ensure being right on one of them. During this period Airedales were classified in the Stud Book under "Broken-haired Scotch or Yorkshire" Terriers, and not until 1886 did the Kennel Club bow to the Airedale name.

REFINING THE AIREDALE

Having passed the first "Hound-Terrier" stage, the Airedale had begun to lose some of its coarseness and to give a glimmer of its potential as a show Terrier. John Q. Dogowner was beginning to appreciate this rough-and-ready Northerner, but it was the out-and-out fancier who had visions of "knocking 'em dead" in Terrier competition with this dramatic dog that could dominate the ring through sheer size and magnificence—once it was given the necessary polish.

While the Yorkshire breeders always remembered temperament and working ability along with an awakened appreciation of conformation and showmanship, the Southern fanciers were interested primarily in show points. With this singleness of purpose the latter breeders were able to improve conformation and quality much faster than had been the case hitherto. Fortunately, in the ensuing years character and versatility were not ignored and, in fact, were brought more and more to the attention of the public as the Airedale was used for purposes never dreamed of in his native Yorkshire.

The problem of evolving a smart, though large, Terrier from the amalgamated tribes of sporting dogdom was no easy one, with Hound ears, light eyes, soft backs, and "off" coats being among the eyesores that cropped up in even the best of litters.

The descriptions of parents of the best early winners indicated that the sires were often the large, somewhat Houndy dogs, but the dams were neat, rather small, very hard-coated and sometimes even smooth bitches, fiery and Terrier-like through and through. It was doubtless because of such variation in parents that litters were far from uniform, as Holland Buckley mentioned in his book, *The Airedale Terrier:* ". . . it would have been possible, if one were so minded, to have benched specimens from any one litter in Airedale, Old English Rough-Coated Terrier, Otterhound and Welsh Terrier classes, with a fair chance of winning honours." However, by selecting the best from such litters and breeding Airedale type to similar type, it was finally possible to breed fairly true—although some would always have such faults as large ears or soft coats or be oversized or undersized, as can plague us even today.

Airedale Jerry (Rattler ex Bess), whelped in England in 1888, is credited as the foundation sire of the breed.

Ch. Cholmondeley Briar (Airedale Jerry ex Cholmondeley Luce).

EARLY WINNERS AND PRODUCERS

Wharfedale Rush, a good winner in the first shows, was the large, Houndy type, but Venus III was the neat, Terrier type, Newbould Test was the leading winner for about five years, his colors finally being lowered by Colne Crack at Otley in 1890. Crack, of real Terrier type, was considered the best seen up to that time. Airedales had improved to such an extent by 1891 that a team consisting of Cholmondeley Briar, Cholmondeley Bridesmaid and Briar Test won over eleven other teams, many of which represented the then most popular breeds—Fox Terriers, Dandie Dinmonts, and the "Scotch" Terriers. This win caused much comment and gave the breed a great boost in the fancy.

There is no need to name all the winners of the breed's early days, for many of them did not breed on. There is one line that did, however, and to which every leading sire of today traces in direct tail male down through Int. Ch. Warland Ditto, then for twelve generations back to old Airedale Jerry. The "Adam" of this family tree is actually, so far as is traceable, a dog named Rattler, but since it is his son who made more of a name for himself, it is he, Airedale Jerry, to which credit is usually given for founding this phenomenal line. F. M. Jowett, in The *Complete Story of the Airedale Terrier* (1913), says: "Airedale Jerry, whom I remember well, was a dog who did a lot of winning in the north of England, but was never quite up to Championship form. He was a big, strong-boned dog with a long, typical head and a real hard, wiry coat, but overdone in ears. His sire was a dog named Rattler, who won many prizes, and his dam, Bess, was by Champion Brush, who was by Champion Bruce, so his pedigree goes back to the very first dogs that were exhibited." Just as Jerry was more noted than Rattler, so was Jerry's son, in turn, of even greater fame. This was Ch. Cholmondeley Briar, the sole surviving pup of his dam's first litter. Briar's dam was Cholmondeley Luce, said to be a good-headed one, very Terrier-like in character, with small ears and good coat, but a trifle undersized.

Briar won about 170 first prizes, starting his career at six months. He was the winner of the first challenge certificate offered for the breed (1893), winning a total of nine up to the year 1897, and started the fad for bristly names, most of which just had the "briar" with a prefix. Mr. Jowett gives a good description of Briar: "Ch. Cholmondeley Briar was bred at Queensbury near Bradford, and he was first exhibited in some small local show under the name of Red Robin. . . . He had a beautiful long, clean, typical head, with great power in front of the eyes, nice small ears, lovely neck, and clean, well-placed shoulders, with good, short, firm back and well-set, gaily carried tail. His bone and legs and feet were extraordinary, and as round and firm as an English Fox-hound's, and being well covered with hair, gave him an appearance of immense strength. In color he was dense black on his back with rich golden tan on his legs and quàrters, and his coat was both straight and hard. He had any amount of substance, yet he was all Terrier, with nothing houndy or coarse about him. He was well up to standard weight, and when mature I would say he was a little over. . . . Ch. Cholmondeley Briar will always be remembered by Airedale Terrier breeders, as his name appears in nearly every first-class pedigree of the present day (1913), if it is only traced far enough back, and he stamped his own grand type and character upon his breed in a remarkable manner."

The next in this line is Cholmondeley Briar's son, Briar Test (whose dam was by Ch. Newbould Test), a winner in good company, very similar to his sire, but lacking quality of head. His main claim to fame is as a sire, for Ch. Master Briar (1897–1906) was his son, and here the dynasty developed another branch. Master Briar (out of a small bitch named Betty and bred by A. P. Bruce) was all Terrier in type and quality, and was said to be one of the best-headed Airedales bred up to that time (yet his sire did not become a champion because of a "plain" head). Master Briar's qualities as a "laster" were passed on to many of his get. As a puppy he was described as having a well-shaped head but faulty ears, and as a youngster he did not win well. Even with maturity he was usually beaten by Ch. Rock Salt. However, he kept improving with age—his ears came up and his clean skull not only did not coarsen but also filled up before the eyes, and he became noted for great strength of muzzle.

There are two main lines of descent from Master Briar, that of Ch. Clonmel Monarch and that of Crompton Marvel. Monarch was the favorite of Holland Buckley, who bought him for the Clonmel firm at six months of age. This is Mr. Buckley's description of Monarch, written about 1910: "Probably the nearest approach to the Standard was Champion Clonmel Monarch, who, if he did not absolutely fill the bill, was certainly the nearest approach to the ideal I have ever seen; and this dog has had a great say in the type and character of the modern Airedale: A beautifully balanced terrier, with a long, clean, grandly shaped head, eyes that were ablaze with terrier fire, dark and well-set, muzzle very powerful and with that rare barrel-like formation under the eye which is the hall-mark of only the truly great; his front was irreproachable, with great bone, hard and flat. Legs and feet like bars of iron. He was short in back yet with plenty of liberty. Tail set on gaily at a defiant angle. The smallest possible ears, well-set, and always well carried. The only jarring note in the tout-ensemble of this extraordinary dog was his coat; which although hard and wiry, was—as is not seldom with Champions of this breed—decidedly wavy; a failing he inherited from his sire Master Briar."

Of Crompton Marvel, Mr. Jowett said: "He was a beautiful terrier I always thought unlucky never to become a full champion, as he was full of quality, with beautiful coat and color. He will be remembered chiefly by breeders as the sire of the great show and stud dog Ch. Crompton Oorang, who is the sire and grandsire of more champions and first-class show dogs than any Airedale Terrier living at the present day (1913)."

With the bloodlines of all great modern sires funneling back through English and American Ch. Warland Ditto, we will bring the "Master Briar"

Ch. Midland Royal (Ch. Master Royal ex Madame Briar).

Ch. Master Briar (Briar Test ex Betty).

line directly up to Ditto, then mention some of the other dogs and bitches that contributed to Ditto's background. All of these are repeated time and time again in extended pedigrees of today's winners, as nearly all of today's winning Airedales are strongly linebred to Ditto.

Clonmel Chilperic, although not a champion, was the next dog to pass on the line of Monarch, his sire. Chilperic's greatest son was Ch. Master Royal, a high-class dog that was sold to Joseph Laurin's Colne Kennels in Canada, where he stood at a $75 fee, a large sum for those days.

In England, Master Royal had sired Ch. Midland Royal, who is the next sire to carry this line along. W. J. Phillips, in *The Modern Airedale* (1921), mentions Midland Royal along with the growing interest in the Airedale in the early 1900s: "He is still in my mind as a model of perfection and what I should require in a young puppy with championship aspirations, to this day. His beautiful quality and all-around richness at this age made him other worshipers besides myself. North Country men predicted a great future, their prophesies proving quite correct, although having the great Crompton Oorang as his chief opponent. Royal for many years was a force to be reckoned with. So enamored was the writer with these two great strains, the Cromptons and the Midlands, as embodying all that is great in the Airedale, that he at once decided that here was the foundation for a new kennel, which was afterwards known as 'Tintern.' The stock left by Royal has done much to bring into popularity our favorite, for not only was he a dog of great character, but he also had the size that so many of our winning dogs about this time lacked."

Although Midland Royal sired many good winners, he is now more noted as a "sire of sires." Among the main lines were those of Primrose Royalist, Elruge Monarch and Midland Rollo, who handed the baton on through succeeding generations to Ditto. Midland Rollo's son Requisition is the next transmitter of the line, then his son Wadsworth Royalist, who in turn sired Cragsman King. King was the sire of Cragsman Dictator, a war baby of 1917 who eventually gained great fame as a sire, with Ditto being his most famous son. Dictator, Ditto and Ditto's dam, Ch. Warland Strategy, all were imported to America, with Ditto and Strategy gaining further great honors in the show ring, and all of them making their influence felt in subsequent generations. Strategy was better known over here as "Doreda" Warland Strategy, Doreda being the prefix of her new owner, Mr. Joseph Dain, in Illinois. Imported in 1919, she went Best in Show in St. Louis on her first outing in this country in 1920, was shown with great success during 1920 and 1921, then was retired. Although it deals a blow to our "sire line" story, it is to Strategy rather than Dictator that many breeders credit the excellence of Ditto as a sire, for linebreeding to Ditto brought vastly better results than did linebreeding to Dictator.

Ditto was imported by the Anoakia Kennels in 1922 and on the dispersal of those kennels in the same year, he and several other top Airedales were purchased by Chris Shuttleworth, who had originally brought Ditto over for Mrs. Baldwin. Ditto was advertised by Mr. Shuttleworth as the "World's

18

Greatest Airedale Stud," and he was well patronized by the Western fancy, although the Eastern Airedalers did not care to ship such a great distance and so lost out on his use. Lou Holliday said that when he saw Ditto in 1926, Mr. Shuttleworth told him Ditto's score was then eighteen champions. Just how many were Canadian, Continental, and South African, as well as American, cannot be determined at this late date, but Ditto's English champions (eleven) are a matter of record.

A study of Strategy's bloodlines seems in order, for she contributed much to Ditto's prepotency. And when her full sister, Warland Wingate, was bred to Ditto, his most prepotent son, Ch. Warland Whatnot, was produced. Strategy's sire was Ch. Rhosddu Royalist, a dog that went quickly through to his title in England and was imported to America when well along in years. He made a name for himself as a sire in both countries, with his daughters especially bringing him fame through their produce as well as wins. Royalist, whelped in 1913, was out of Maesgwene Trixie, a consistent winner and granddaughter of Ch. Rockley Oorang (a dog eventually owned by the Colne Kennels in Canada and one of the greatest winners of his day).

Rhosddu Royalist is another line of the Master Royal clan, representing the "Primrose" breeding of W. T. Chantler, who started his kennel in 1887. Primrose Rebound was the sire of Ch. Rhosddu Royalist, and Rebound's sire was Primrose Royalist, by Ch. Midland Royal. Thus both the sire and dam of Ditto trace through the same tail male line—through Midland Royal to the Ch. Clonmel Monarch branch of Airedale aristocracy. There are several other crosses to the Master Royal line in Ditto's pedigree, as well as many to the Crompton Marvel branch of the Briar family tree, mainly through Ch. Prince of York (known in England as Dany Graig Commander), and through the previously mentioned Ch. Rockley Oorang.

Strategy's dam was Warland Enchantress, whelped during World War I and founder of the modern "Warlands," although J. P. Hall, owner of these highly successful kennels, was "in" Airedales from 1895. Enchantress' sire was Cheltenham Cadet (by Ch. Clonmel Cadet) and her dam was Camperdown Flyer (by Brown Jug Perfection, another son of Midland Rollo). Clonmel Cadet was by Petronius, who was by Ch. Master Royal.

Although we have traced the direct male line of Cragsman Dictator (Ditto's sire) from the days of old Jerry, it is worthwhile to have a look "inside" his pedigree, for the "ladies" and the bloodlines they brought in also contributed to the excellence of this line. Dictator's dam was Cragsman Lady Girl, who was by Wadsworth Elite, a son of Tintern Desire (who was in turn a son of Ch. Crompton Oorang). The dam of Cragsman King (Dictator's sire) was Cragsman High Lady, who brought in the line of Ch. Soudan Swiveller, who was sired by a dog considered one of the greatest sires of his time, Elruge Monarch. High Lady's dam, Gray Flossie, was by Leighton (also Leyton) Mainspring, by Ch. Crompton Oorang, and Flossie's dam was Leighton Peggy, by Ch. Midland Royal.

Dropping down again to the dam of Dictator (Lady Girl), we find that her sire (Elite) was out of Laval Queen, a daughter of Requisition and full sister to Wadsworth Royalist, and thus a granddaughter of Midland Rollo. Lady Girl's dam was Bramshall Queen, whose dam, Harrington Kitty, was by Tintern Desire, and Queen's sire was Culminton Tyrant, by Springbank Radium. Even a casual glance through this breeding will show that the blood of Ch. Clonmel Monarch and Crompton Marvel is compounded again and again, and would probably show more such concentration of bloodlines if some of the "dead ends" that are not traceable at this distant date could be taken back to their source.

Ch. Clonmel Marvel, easily confused with Crompton Marvel of the same approximate era, was used often as a cross with bitches of the Master Briar line and was very helpful in correcting the soft or linty coats sometimes encountered in that family. It was the Clonmel Marvel–Master Briar cross that produced Ch. Clonmel Monarch; his sire was Ch. Master Briar and his dam Richmond Peggy by Ch. Clonmel Marvel (by Clipper ex Cholmondeley Mona). W. L. Barclay described Marvel in the 1919 Airedale Club Bulletin: "Clonmel Marvel probably weighed 47 pounds. He had the hardest coat, bar none, I have ever had my hands on. He was black on body in his early days in England, but went red on the body, so that when he finally went down to defeat under his grandson, Clonmel Monarch, he was as red all over as an Irish Terrier. His eyes might have been darker, but he was deep-chested, well ribbed up, grand at the quarters, and stood on strong, straight, heavy-boned legs. He probably had a clean head as a puppy, but when I first saw him his head had gone coarse and we would today call him plain-headed. His ears were better than other dogs of that time but that is all that could be said of them. He had a very heavy muzzle and long punishing jaw almost devoid of whisker. The hair on his face was rough, but I cannot imagine that great old terrier with a long white linty mess of soft whisker about four inches long hanging all over his muzzle."

The other "Marvel" was Crompton Marvel, who, like Monarch, was by old Master Briar, his dam being Woodland Judy, by Ch. Rock Salt, a grandson of Briar Test. Unlike Clonmel Marvel, whose influence was mainly through bitches bred to the Briar-line sires, Crompton Marvel set up his own dynasty, which rivaled that of Monarch in quality and numbers. W. J. Phillips said that "Crompton Marvel is probably one of the best of the uncrowned Airedales that ever lived. That he did not obtain the coveted title of champion was more by bad luck than anything else. Built on ideal lines and bred from the best possible strains, he quickly made a name for himself at stud at a very early age. One of the great dogs to claim him as a sire was Ch. Crompton Oorang. After one defeat as a puppy, at Birmingham National, this Lancashire product never looked back—he won the coveted title of champion, and as a sire proved even better worth by his wonderful consistency in breeding. A few of the best of his progeny are: Ch. Dany Graig Commander (now Prince of York), Ch. Crompton Performer, Ch. Rockley Oorang, Tintern Desire, Ch. Clonmel Imperious, Ch. Rebound Oorang, etc."

20

Mr. Barclay further described this line in the 1923 Club Bulletin: "In reviewing the get of Crompton Oorang it is hard to know where to begin. They came to America in shoals. . . . Ch. Rockley Oorang was the most consistent winner of any of Oorang's sons and probably had the greatest number of wins to his credit. After a most successful career on the English bench Rockley Oorang was sold to the late Joseph Laurin of Montreal. The dog spent some time in the Colne Kennels before being shown in the United States. As I remember him he was a short-backed dog, standing on straight legs and feet, weighing about 48 pounds, rather greyish in color, tan markings not too distinct, and having large ears. He had a good muzzle, good length of head, and dark eyes. One of the best known of Ch. Rockley Oorang's get was Ch. King Oorang, who was a good one. He had strong positive good points rather than a lack of faults. He was black in body color with a rich tan. He had a very long head with about the right amount of whisker and had strong straight legs and good body. He was a very big specimen but gave the impression of great activity as well as substance and strength. His ears were well carried and his quarters were especially good. Although larger than most of the Airedales shown at that time, he was all terrier and won a large number of prizes in England before he arrived in America. . . .

"Although probably Crompton Oorang's best son, Prince of York was not his greatest son. Tintern Desire, whose name lives in the pedigrees of succeeding generations, will be remembered long after Prince of York is forgotten. Tintern Desire, by Crompton Oorang ex a Midland Royal bitch, was one of the first bred by Mr. Phillips, now so well known as a writer, breeder and judge of Airedales. Desire is described as a large, strong-boned dog on racy lines, a nice length of neck, a front of the best, a long clean head and real terrier character, with very dark, well-placed eyes. He weighed about 52 pounds. As a sire of Airedales he can stand in line with the best half-dozen that the breed has produced."

IN SUMMARY

While these old-timers may seem of little consequence with the passing of time, they nevertheless have had their influence on modern Airedales—some set the type, others the character, they all had good points and bad points, but help the breed along they all did. Their names are repeated time after time in all Airedale pedigrees. And in modern strains of show quality, in all lands, the name of Ditto is "dittoed" right down the column of names, further intensifying these bloodlines.

So ingrained is the hunting instinct in the Airedale that big-game hunter and Best in Show winner have the same ancestors, and some are even litter mates. All the hunting strains and multipurpose Airedales that combine show quality with hunting and other working potentials trace to Ditto, and consequently to the noted dogs mentioned in his background, while such strictly utility strains as the modern "Oorangs" trace over and over again to Ch. Rockley Oorang, Elruge Monarch and Tintern Desire.

The best known of the combined show and utility lines is that of Lionheart, representatives of which have won many Groups, Specialties and even Bests in Show, yet have made an enviable record on big game as well as on upland game and waterfowl. This line has the further distinction of producing many obedience workers, some of which are also champions, holding all degrees including that of UDT. This one strain in itself symbolizes the versatility of the "show" Airedale.

3

Early Days in America

THE FIRST AIREDALE known to come to America was Bruce, a hard-boiled customer brought over by C. H. Mason, well-known dog expert from Bradford, Yorkshire. Although he left no purebred descendant in this country—there being no Airedale bitches here at the time—Bruce is nevertheless in the pedigree of everyone's Airedale, for he was the sire of Ch. Brush, who sired Bess, the dam of none other than Airedale Jerry, root of the family tree. Bruce was the old-fashioned "fighting kind," and the last heard of him was that he was sold for $21 at a dog auction at the American Horse Exchange. But Bruce was good enough as an individual to win first in the class for Rough-haired Terriers in New York in 1881.

The next Airedales to be exhibited were two listed as "blue-and-fawn" in color, belonging to Mr. Lacy. Mr. Mason's book *Our Prize Dogs* (1888), which contained critiques of many of the dogs exhibited in the East at that time, mentions a lone Airedale named Tatters, whelped in 1885 and owned by Dr. Al Watts, that was winner of the Miscellaneous Class at Boston in an entry of nine very miscellaneous dogs. As with all the dogs in the book, Mr. Mason pulls Tatters apart piece by piece, with occasional praise of visible virtues, winding up with the comment: "A useful-looking second-class dog." Obviously no booster for the Airedale, Mr. Mason went on to say: "Here is a breed almost unknown in America. It is more than probable that a good specimen of the breed has not been exhibited here, and prospect of improvement is not bright." Other writers of the period reflected Mr. Mason's opinion that the breed would probably not become popular, mainly because of the shaggy appearance of these then-untrimmed specimens.

Eng. & Am. Ch. Cast Iron Monarch (Walnut King Nobler ex Lady Conjuror).

EARLY AMERICAN-BREDS AND BREEDERS

From breeding operations started at Charlotte, Virginia, in 1897 came the Brushwood Airedales by Broadlands Brushwood (Best of Breed at the New York show in 1898), and very distinct from the fashionably bred "Monarchs" and "Marvels" of a few years later.

Other early sources of American-bred Airedales were two kennels in New York—that of J. Lorillard Arden, and about a year later that of DeWitt Cochrane. Both showed with fair success, but it was not until Mr. Arden bought Ch. Clonmel Marvel and Ch. Clonmel Sensation from Holland Buckley that the star of the Airedale in America began to rise.

Then the well-known horseman Foxhall Keene brought over Ch. Clonmel Bed Rock and Ch. Clonmel Coronation. And Theodore Offerman had many a successful season with his York Kennels, housing the imports Ch. York (previously Dumbarton) Sceptre, Ch. York (previously Tone) Masterpiece, Prince of York (known in England as Dany Graig Commander), Ch. Bolton Woods Briar and Ch. York the Conqueror. Among the homebreds of the York Kennels were Ch. York the Hayseed, by Masterpiece, and Ch. York the Haymaker, by The Hayseed. William S. Barclay, noted for his articles in magazines and club bulletins, bred many of the Wyndhills founded on Monarch blood that appear in the pedigrees of today's winners. Among them were Ch. Wyndhill Tackle, Ch. The Gamecock and Wyndhill Vandal (who sired three champions although he never gained the title himself). Mr. Barclay's daughter, Caroline Strong, still breeds Wyndhill Airedales today.

Russell Johnson bred the good bitch Red Hackle, and also Ch. Red Sunlight. The latter, bred to her grandsire (Monarch), produced Ch. Red Raven, the dog considered to be the best American-bred son of Monarch.

Lynford Biddle purchased the imported bitch Dumbarton Vixen, who produced Ch. Babs to Ch. The Gamecock, and Babs bred to Ch. The Chorister produced another great American-bred, Ch. The Norseman. Another product of this strain was Ch. The Riding Master (though he was sired by the imported Ch. Endcliffe Crack).

Boston was the other main area in the East in the thick of the early Airedale wars. Arthur Merritt, originally from Northern England, imported several good Airedales, the most famed of which was Ch. The New King, in whose honor the New King Bowl was named. The early Boston area Airedales resembled Rock Salt in type, just as those in Philadelphia favored that area's leading sire, Clonmel Monarch. And The New King, a son of Ch. Rock Salt, was no exception. The New King nicked well with Clonmel Monarch bitches, thus pulling the two Briar Test lines together, as Rock Salt was by Rock Ferry Test, who was by Briar Test. This line has not survived as a sire line but is in the blood of certain families through the dams.

A Boston breeder who started early in the twentieth century and long maintained an interest in the breed was George West, whose best-known Airedale was probably Ch. Vickery Soubrette, sold to the Vickery Kennels and campaigned by them. This bitch, Best in Show at the Eastern Dog Club Show in 1914, was winner of the New King Bowl six times.

In Canada the Colne Kennels of Joseph Laurin made history with their imports and sales of innumerable puppies. Mr. Laurin, then vice-president of the Canadian Kennel Club, introduced the breed to Canada in 1899, and he never balked at paying a high price for a good Airedale, paying $7000 for four Terriers imported in 1901. He spared no expense to further the interests of the breed, bringing over the best of both sexes, not only great winners but also proven sires and dams. Among the imports were Willow Nut, winner of over 130 first placements and sire of more than seventy-five winners; the famous Ch. Dumbarton Lass, winner of fifteen championships (this was before challenge certificates were issued) and dam of many noted winners; Ch. Colne Lucky Baldwin (brother of Crompton Marvel and Ch. Rock King); Ch. Master Royal, who gained his fame in England rather than after importation; Ch. Mistress Royal; Ch. Freeman Terror and many others. But the one best known in the later days of the kennel was Ch. Rockley Oorang, who also gained his renown as a sire mainly from his English-bred stock.

Ch. Rockley Oorang was bred in Yorkshire, England, in 1905 by Sid Perkins, who sold him to Mr. Roper. After campaigning the dog to the heights of Airedale glory, Mr. Roper sold him to Colne Kennels. Later, Mr. Perkins established his Rockley Kennels in Toronto, Canada, and the first Airedale he imported was Llangollen Nellie in 1911, this bitch having a litter by Ch. Crompton Oorang shortly after her arrival in Canada. Nellie formed the foundation of the Rockley strain in Canada, a strain that had a strong influence on American as well as Canadian Airedales from coast-to-coast. The fame of the Rockleys reached its peak during the 1930s, and among the later importations (1936) were Tri. Int. Ch. Cotteridge Brigand, subsequently sold to Holland, Ch. Warland Wondrous and Ch. Warland Warboy, one of the last imported (1941). The influence of the Rockley Airedales on American bloodlines is inestimable, with Ch. Rockley Roasting Hot accounting for twenty American champions. The bitches were equally good as producers and winners—the sensational Ch. Rockley Riot Act producing three champions, and her sister, Ch. Rockley Hidden Treasure, six. Both, by the way, were sisters of Rockley Roasting Hot. Their dam, Rockley Glitter, founded a many-faceted family of American Airedales, all among the big-time winners. Ch. Greenburn Infractious, a good winner in the 1940s, was straight Rockley-bred, his pedigree in the third generation listing Brigand, Warboy and Wondrous. He was, however, bred by the Greenburn Kennels, not by Mr. Perkins, and the blood of the foregoing Airedales was doubled, since his parents were full brother and sister.

The Eleanores of Mrs. Loree, the Gingerbreds of Mr. and Mrs. Perry, the modern Lionhearts of Lou Holliday, many of the Trucotes of Mrs. Smit (later Urmston), some of the Airelines of Charles Ryan, the "First Mate" branch of the Maralec Airedales, many of the Tedhursts and some of the Freedoms are strong in Rockley bloodlines. Many more trace to Rockley-

Ch. Maralec First Mate (Maralec Bingo Boy ex Maralec Surprise) won well during the early 1940s, including a Best in Show under Hubert Doll, Tom Gately handling.

Ch. Warland Warboy (Ch. Warland Wattotstuff ex Blue Flash) won Best in Show handled by Phil Prentice.

Ch. Fallcrest Harry (Tri. Int. Ch. Cotterridge Brigand ex Fallcrest Charm), shown with his handler, Tom Gately.

imported dogs and bitches, if not to Rockley-bred stock, as in the case of Eng. and Am. Ch. Warbreck Eclipse. But this is the "air age," so back to the early 1900s.

We can only touch lightly on the early days and refer readers to the many books on the breed written from 1910 to 1921 for detailed information on breeders and winning dogs. So far as possible, we will try to name those—both people and dogs—influential in the breed at the time, but whose strains have had an effect on today's Airedales, rather than just those who won the most prizes.

W. E. Baker, author of *The Airedale Terrier* (1921), took up the breed about 1905, and his Tanglewood prefix became well known. Ch. Tanglewood Una and the excellent brood matron Brosna Bacchante, whose produce was among the winning Airedales as far away as California, were among the best of his early stock. Andrew Albright, Jr., made his contribution to Airedale history with his imported Ch. King Oorang and Ch. Tintern Royalist and owned several good bitches. George Batson, who for a while owned some of the York dogs in partnership with Mr. Offerman, later imported Ch. Soudan Swiveller and Ch. Soudan Stamboul, both widely represented by their get in the Far West as well as in the East. These two dogs were later owned by William Wolcott's Kenmare Kennels, which also obtained or bred such top ones as Soudan Sapphire (known in England as Ch. Springbank Diamond), Ch. Kenmare Sorceress, Ch. Primrose Royston Tess and Bothwell Sorceress (daughter of Kenmare Sorceress).

Earle Woodward was one of the earliest and one of the most successful breeders in the Chicago area. His Ch. Earlwood Warlock is still remembered not only for his wins in breed competition, but also for taking Best in Show at the great International event in Chicago. Although he was well patronized at stud, Warlock's line does not survive in direct tail male today. Francis Porter's Abbey Kennels housed some of the best Airedales of the time, including Ch. Freeman Terror, Ch. Clonmel Isonomy, Ch. Abbey King Nobbler (a great winner and sire but another whose influence is found in female rather than sire lines), Ch. Springbank Sceptre, Ch. Clonmel Command and Ch. Clonmel Imperious. Fighting it out with the Abbeys were the Vickerys, who bought Ch. Prince of York, Ch. Tintern Royalist and many others, plus the superior bitch Ch. Vickery Soubrette.

In the Far West one of the earliest breeders was R. M. Palmer, whose book *All About Airedales* is a classic on the working Airedale. Mr. Palmer, who owned Ch. Matlock Bob (by Ch. Midland Royal) and Ch. Lake Dell Damsel (a daughter of Bob), stressed working ability along with show points. The Lake Dell Kennels were in Washington.

Other Western breeders who took up the Airedale before 1915 were George Downer and James Keefe in Montana. The former was the breeder of Ch. Kootenai Radiance and Int. Ch. Kootenai Chinook, who was eventually owned by the Vibert Kennels in New Jersey and advertised as "The most widely known Airedale Terrier in the world." Mr. Downer bought the magnif-

28

icent sire Elruge Monarch to head his stud, and although this lost the dog to Eastern use, he was of immense value in leavening the quality of Western Airedales. Mr. Keefe's prefix was Mountain View, and he bred many good ones whose names can be found in extended pedigrees of modern Airedales. Crack Oorang, a son of Crompton Oorang out of a Midland Royal bitch, was advertised at stud by the Chief Kennels in Montana. Among his kennel mates were Chief Chinchinoo (by Elruge Monarch) and Chief Kootenai (by Ch. Prince of York). An imported dog, Marshall Tinner, headed the Flathead Kennels in Montana, which like others in that state emphasized hunting ability while giving plenty of publicity to prize-winning ancestry. Also located in the big-game area of Montana, though a few years later, were Lou Holliday's Lionheart Kennels. This strain proved to be a foundation strain of the West Coast Airedales and is still an important line today, so it will be traced in detail later.

Airedales were well represented in Oregon, also, and Ch. Red Raven (mentioned earlier) headed the kennels of Dr. H. V. Adix in Estacada, bringing Monarch blood to the West Coast. Other lines in the kennels were those of Crompton Oorang and Master Royal.

Among other Westerners who brought the "varmint dog" to the attention of the big-game hunters was S. C. Dietz of Colorado, whose stock was of Elruge Monarch, Clonmel Monarch, Tintern Desire, Crompton Oorang, Midland Royal and other leading lines. C. P. Hubbard, although having his main kennels in Iowa, had another in Wyoming. He was one of the very earliest pioneers to introduce the Airedale to the public as a big-game and general sporting dog. Ch. The Gamecock was purchased by Mr. Hubbard and was of material aid in building up a good working strain.

C. W. Buttles, first publisher of *The Kennel Review*, was an early breeder in Missouri, and his Elmhurst Kennels produced many a fine show dog, importing several also. In Ohio, the town of LaRue was made famous by the Oorang Kennels founded by Walter Lingo mainly on the Crompton Oorang line—the "Oorang" being taken from that dog's name. This strain will also be detailed in due course.

Airedales were far from rare in Texas and the Deep South in the first decade of this century and became progressively more numerous as the years went on, with many big kennels located there and some of the best imports and strains represented.

Frederick C. Hood's Boxwood Kennel fits in between the early and the intermediate days of the first decade or so of the new century, and one of its early champions was Young King Nobbler. But the climax of this establishment's career was the homebred Ch. Boxwood Barkentine's Best in Show win at Westminster in 1922.

Bulletins of the Airedale Terrier Club of America in the 1920s gave the impression that Airedale activity was largely confined to the Eastern seaboard and a few states east of the Mississippi, as the shows reported were those wherein club challenge trophies were offered and, of course, Westminster. The foregoing has shown, however, that Airedales were well distributed all over the country. All over the North American continent might be more exact, for the Airedale flourished from Alaska to and including Mexico, and entries were heavy in shows from Washington to Texas and from California to all points east.

The breed was well on its way upward and onward by its second decade in this country and nearly every big Eastern show saw the latest "greatest Airedale ever bred" making its American debut, usually from a boat conveniently docking a day or so before the show. The wins of these dogs were far from discouraging to other exhibitors, but only gave them the idea to bring over another super Airedale and see if it could knock the spots off the latest sensation. This spirit persists to this day and Airedale exhibitors still find it refreshing to bring over a current winner from England. A good example was Harold Florsheim's Eng. Ch. Westhay Fiona of Hatham. This bitch, coming over just in time to win the Group at her first show, then went on to win the Terrier Group at Westminster in 1957.

Although Fox Terriers, both coats, hold the records of Westminster wins, Airedales have fared well among the larger breeds. Ch. Kenmare Sorceress started the parade in 1912, with Ch. Briergate Bright Beauty following in 1919, Ch. Boxwood Barkentine in 1922 and Ch. Warland Protector of Shelterock in 1933. The last win is probably responsible for pulling the breed from the lowest ebb of its depression back to sound footing. At any rate, 1931 had shown the lowest registrations of Airedales since 1907, but they mounted steadily after Protector's win until they are now back in the multiple thousands.

ESTABLISHMENT OF THE GREAT KENNELS

The early teens saw great kennels founded from coast-to-coast. The most famous of the California kennels started during this period was Anita Baldwin's Anoakia Kennels, which at one and the same time housed Ch. Tintern Tip Top, Whitebirk Tyrant, Cyprus Cadet, Int. Ch. King Oorang and a couple of Anoakia-bred dogs. Later, Chris Shuttleworth took over the Anoakia Kennels, and with Ditto heading his stud, showed under the name Chrisworth.

The Criterion Airedales of George Binney furnished foundation stock that lives on in modern strains, and established about this same time were H. M. Robertson's kennels. Mrs. Greggains' Flashlight Kennels won well up and down the coast, especially in the 1920s with Warland breeding. Later Mrs. Greggains had several spectacular wins with her Ch. Flashlight Protector, a son of Ch. Warland Protector of Shelterock. The Flashlights furnished much foundation stock on the coast, especially in the San Francisco area, and among other good points were noted for beautiful coats and rich coloring.

Dr. Frank Porter Miller bought the Canadian-bred Ch. Colne Master Oorang, winning many of the top spots with him as well as with Fancy of

Anoakia. In 1921 George Binney's Criterion Kennels featured Ch. Warland By Product, a son of Ch. Neville's Double of Primrose ex Warland Enchantress, who was the dam of the immortal Int. Ch. Warland Strategy and Warland Wingate (dam of Ch. Warland Whatnot). George Harker's Bighorn Kennels in San Fernando made canine headlines both in hunting exploits and in the show ring, his "head man" being the versatile Lionheart Politician. Irving C. Ackerman made room among his Wires long enough to take in the big-time winner Ch. Criterion Warland's Double and stop his sale to the East. Double, later sold to the Estancia Kennels, had the honor of going Best in Show at Long Beach as well as several lesser events.

The Portola Kennels imported Warland Whizbang and his dam, Ch. Warland Waterlily. Lily was by Ch. Warland Whatnot, while her son was by Int. Ch. Flornell Mixer, both of which were highly successful sires in England and in this country. Lily and Whizbang were later sold to Texas.

Ruel Riley, on the advice of Lou Holliday, purchased Ch. Dendale Tantalizer, a son of Ch. Cragsman Dictator. Tantalizer was very influential on the coast and was a good winner. Several of the dogs bred by Dr. Warta's Pappio Kennels in Omaha were owned in California and did very well—as they also did in the East—Pappio T.N.T. taking Best in Show at Santa Clara.

In 1926 Lou Holliday moved his Lionheart Kennels to Southern California and before long the "Lionhearts" dominated the West Coast scene with their many wins. These kennels featured the bloodlines of Elruge Monarch through Dakota Bri and others, such as Killarney Sport. Dave Hicks did well with his Pepper Tree Kennels, and his Pepper Tree Don, a son of Ditto, contributed to the foundation of the modern Lionhearts by siring Ch. Lou's J.M.

In Central California Dr. A. P. Deacon was well known for his hunting Airedales. His printed testimonials on bear dogs, 'coon dogs, cougar dogs, and various types of gundogs—all Airedales—apparently paid off, for he mentions selling 237 Airedales in 1922 all over America, Alaska, China, Canada and the Hawaiian Islands. About this time Chris Shuttleworth was doing a bit of exporting too, selling one dog to a British army officer stationed in India, and a brace of Airedales (including two by Ditto) was shipped to President Obregon's kennels in Mexico.

Skyline was one of the best-known kennels in the Portland area. Washington had its share of breeders also, Ray Sheldon being heard from most often.

George Ainsworth's Morning View Kennels of Havelock, Nebraska, bred top Airedales with regularity. Heading his stud force was Dakota Bri, whose get became widely known throughout the West.

Denver had many Airedale enthusiasts, with Edward Allen leading in the 1920s with Ch. Rose Bri, a Group winner who consistently placed high in Airedale classes from the coast to Texas. Rose was by the Canadian-bred Ch. Ruler's Double, first shown on the coast, then purchased by Ted Dealy

Ch. Matador Mandarin (1929).

Ch. Tiger of Deswood (1938).

Ch. Aireline Bombsight (1943).

32

of Dallas, Texas. Traced back several generations, Airedales from Mr. Allen's kennels will be listed in the pedigrees of many of today's winners, especially those on the West Coast.

The Marathon Kennels in Wisconsin owned Ch. Clonmel Cadet, a dog especially noted for his classic head with powerful foreface. Cadet is in the ancestral branches of Warland Strategy's family tree, and his sire, Petronius (by Ch. Midland Royal), was a full brother of Leighton Peggy, great-granddam in the direct tail female line of Cragsman Dictator.

The Midwest was the site of several powerful kennels in the 1920s. The Briergate Kennels in Illinois owned Ch. Rex Persaltum, a much-used sire of the period who later went to Virginia. The Caswell Kennels in Ohio showed many a top Airedale, and their stud dogs were headed by the great Ch. Tintern Tip Top, purchased from Anoakia. The Davishill Kennels in Kentucky took the measure of import and homebred alike in the Eastern shows, taking several Bests in Show. Among the homebreds of Davishill that made Airedale history were Ch. War Boy of Davishill, Ch. Man o'War of Davishill, Ch. War Bond of Davishill and the greatest of all, Ch. Warbride of Davishill, Group winner at Westminster and runner-up for Best in Show at that event. Ch. On Guard was another Ohio dog that was used extensively throughout the country. The Briar Croft Kennels in Ohio had great dogs at stud, such as the famed Ch. Rhosddu Royalist, Ch. Boy, Ch. Briar Croft Authority Nut Brown, Ch. Briarcroft Perfection, Ch. Briar Croft Elms Knight and Briar Croft Flornell Imperator. Nut Brown won at Westminster and the parent club specialty in 1923; Perfection (by Wawasee Whinbush Maxim) won the summer Specialty in 1924, with feminine honors taken by a kennel mate, Ch. Briar Croft Sweet Memory (by Ditto), and Perfection also won the parent Specialties in 1925 and 1926.

The Doreda Kennels in Illinois owned the great sires Eng. Ch. Doreda Craigmillar Prince, Eng. Ch. Doreda Cragsman Kingsway and Cragsman Dictator, who, although untitled, outsired both the other two. A. L. Zeckendorf, well known for his "Freedom" Airedales, first took up the breed when in Michigan but later moved to Connecticut, and his dogs were well to the forefront from then on.

Dr. Thatcher's Cliffdale Kennels in Texas stood various imported dogs at stud, including Stockfield Desire (a son of Ditto), who came to the United States by way of Canada. The Thornbrook Kennels in San Antonio owned the imported dog Narrowdale Nimrod, litter brother of the great Int. Ch. Polan Maxim.

Tennessee was also well up in Airedale news as a result of the excellence of the Chickasaw Kennels. Their stud dogs included Int. Ch. Craigmillar Prince and Ch. Elmhurst Emperor, but their Airedale that will go down in history is Ch. Doreda Kathleen McCaura, purchased, as was Prince, from the Doreda Kennels. Kathleen's most famous son was Clonmel Monarque (by Ch. Warland Whatnot), and she was also the dam of Ch. Chickasaw Sunny Kathleen. G. L. L. Davis's Daystar Kennels in Missouri bred many a good one, and confused the "Davis" mix-up further by buying one or two of the "Davishill" prefix.

Sheldon Stewart's Shelterock Kennels started on the road to Airedale immortality about 1925, the year in which their Ch. Geelong Defiance was Winners at the Specialty. Through importation of the very best dogs and bitches, and a well-planned breeding program, the "Shelterocks" were on the top for nearly two decades, making spectacular wins. As their Ch. Warland Protector of Shelterock has a place in modern sire lines, he and his most sensational son, Eng. and Am. Ch. Shelterock Merry Sovereign, will be mentioned later. C. Rasmussen's Hekla Kennels were begun in the early 1920s, and Hekla brood matrons have earned the kennel a place in the sun by their produce that "bred on."

Harold Florsheim started his Harham Kennels about this same period, importing many good dogs—possibly more than any other exhibitor—and also breeding dogs that have contributed to the excellence of the modern American Airedale, as well as making history in the show ring. Barbara Strebeigh's Birchrun Kennels were also founded at this approximate time. Although at first her kennel did not attain the heights noted by the major exhibitors of the period mentioned, Barbara herself, as officer of the Club and especially as editor of the Newsletter, did more for the breed in America than has any other one person. Her lively comments and work on the Newsletter brought together all Airedale breeders, who up to that time were starved for news, not just show results, but interesting items about breeders and dogs. And not show dogs alone, but hunters and pets also. As if this were not enough, it was the importation by Barbara (and Mrs. Tuck Dell) of Bengal Sabu that not only took the Birchrun Kennels to the aforementioned heights in show wins, but resulted in a major change of top-winning bloodlines in this country, almost eclipsing the long established American lines. Of this, more later.

4

American Bloodlines
to the 1960s

THE CUSTOM now is to give the name of the countries involved when using the champion prefix from one or more countries other than the United States, but in this chapter we will use the term "Int." for "International Champion" on the older dogs originally designated by that prefix. While most were English and American champions, some were Canadian, South African, Indian, Continental, etc., and as we are not certain of the countries concerned on some of these widely traveled dogs, we have left the old terminology. Modern winners will be given specific titles when known. Also, in respect to the older sires and dams, information as to champions produced was often taken from advertisements, stud cards or write-ups, and where the totals do not tally with the number of known American champions, it can be assumed that some of these were of Canadian or European origin.

MOORHEAD MARQUIS LINE

In reference to the lasting qualities of English-bred sire lines and the incomprehensible fading away of the American-bred lines, it is interesting to note the following comment from a 1926 *American Kennel Gazette:* "Another new one was the English champion *Flornell Mixer,* which, rumor says, was one of the highest-priced Airedales ever imported. Airedales are one of the breeds in which America can hold her own with England, so a fancier should watch his step and not throw away a big sum in importing Airedales. We generally win with homebreds. Flornell Mixer won the limit class and went Reserve Winners. He is the property of Mrs. Stanley Halle. . . . The open and winners class was won by Ch. Briarcroft Perfection, which looked better than last year. He also took the medal for Best Airedale. In his present form he is good enough to compete with the best terriers of all breeds. It is not often one sees a better terrier."

Apparently the writer did not know that Perfection's sire. Wawasee Whinbush Maxim, was one of those imports on which money was thrown away. Nevertheless this line did not breed on at all in the sire line, while that of the "high-priced" Mixer is the one that carries on the Moorhead Marquis branch from Ditto. Shortly after the foregoing show, Mixer won the title of Best Airedale at the Sesqui-Centennial show in Philadelphia in an entry of sixty-seven judged by Russell Johnson.

The next dog of this line to be imported was *Int. Ch. Walnut Challenger,* brought over by Fred Hoe. Challenger was Best of Breed at Westminster and won the Specialty in 1931 and 1932. He sired *Ch. Eleanore's Knight,* a successful sire of champions but whose uncrowned son *Maralec Bingo Boy* was destined to become outstanding in this respect. Bingo Boy founded his own line, to which the majority of this dynasty's champions trace. His son, *Ch. Maralec First Mate,* was equally sensational as a sire but also was an outstanding show dog. Among other outstanding wins, he was Best of Breed at Westminster in 1947. Bingo Boy's dam was Miss Hot Trix by Ch. Rockley Roasting Hot, while First Mate's dam was Maralec Surprise, also by Roasting Hot. The Challenger line is doubled here in the background of Surprise—Eleanore's Princess (dam of Surprise) being out of a daughter of Challenger. Also in this breeding is the American-bred line of Ch. Willinez Warrior Bold, a very good one.

CH. WARLAND WHATNOT LINE—CH. WARLAND WATERMAN BRANCH

Another grandson of Ditto imported at the same time as Flornell Mixer was *Ch. Warland Waterman,* a son of the main transmitter of the Ditto line, Ch. Warland Whatnot. Waterman, brought over by Louis Bader of Dover, Massachusetts, was Winners at the 1927 Specialty and Best of Breed at Westminster, and also won the New King Bowl at the Eastern Dog Club show. A son of Waterman, *Ch. Wrose Cargo,* was imported in 1928 by the Penny Ponds Kennels of Long Island, and his claim to Airedale immortality is through his siring *Ch. Wrose Anchor,* the latter the sire of the tremendously successful Int. Ch. Warland Protector of Shelterock. The line breeding to Ditto is interesting in the case of Anchor: Cargo's dam, Wrose Marchioness, was a daughter of Ditto, while Miss Gabrielle, Anchor's dam, was by Flornell Mixer ex Singram (by Marquis, a son of Ditto). Since Whatnot's dam, Warland Wingate, was a full sister to the dam of Ditto, there is a still greater concentration of the bloodlines delineated in the history of Ditto.

Now we come to the immortal *Int. Ch. Warland Protector of Shelterock*, whose dam was Warland Sprite, who was by Clee Brigand ex Seacot Soubrette (a daughter of Whatnot). Soubrette's dam, Seacot Sylph, was out of Warland Watchful, a litter sister of Whatnot, and Sylph's sire was Cragsman King's Own, by Cragsman King. Clee Brigand was a litter brother of the more famous Int. Ch. Clee Courtier, and a grandson of Whatnot via Clonmel Monarque. Brigand's dam, Clee Charming, is out of Warland Stella, by Ditto.

Protector was bred in England by J. P. Hall of "Warland" fame and was purchased as a puppy by S. M. Stewart's Shelterock Kennels. Together with Covert Dazzle, his scintillating kennel mate, Protector was campaigned in England under the guidance of Bob Barlow for about a year, during which time they, as a pair and separately, won eighteen championships in Great Britain, twice Best Brace, best of all breeds in show, and Protector was runner-up for BIS at Crufts.

Mr. Stewart's dream of "breeding a real 'flyer' " literally came true when he mated Protector and Dazzle, producing *Int. Ch. Shelterock Merry Sovereign*. Whelped December 27, 1934, he won his American title in 1936 at consecutive shows in a period of twenty-six days. He was the leading American-bred Terrier, all breeds, for that year, and placed in twelve Groups. This record convinced Mr. Stewart that the English should have a chance to see a first-class American-bred Airedale (though of English breeding), so he did the then unprecedented thing of sending him to England to "have a go," fully cognizant of the setback the quarantine period might have on the dog. Merry Sovereign came out fighting fit, in magnificent condition, and scattered famous dogs to the right and left on his way to the title of "Best Exhibit in Show" at the huge Kennel Club Show at Olympia in London. He again won his championship in successive shows and was runner-up for Best in Show at Birmingham, England's oldest championship show, which averaged an entry of about three thousand dogs at that time. Although the tail-male line of Merry Sovereign is eclipsed by other lines in America, he was a very successful sire of brood matrons—his blood being in the background of many of the best Airedales of England and America through the dams. There are two main lines from Warland Protector in this country, but considering the twenty-five champions sired by this dog, the line, so far as tail-male is concerned, is lagging. Only reference to pedigrees of brood matrons brings out the great influence Protector has had on the breed.

CH. WARLAND WHATNOT LINE—CLONMEL MONARQUE BRANCH

Clonmel Monarque was a great stud force but, like his grandson Walnut King Nobbler, never became a champion—in fact, he was rarely shown. That he was widely used as a sire was a tribute to the excellence of his get, six of his sons and daughters gaining the title, with others carrying on the line as sires or producers with remarkable success. Clonmel Monarque, who was whelped in 1921, was one of Whatnot's first sons, the latter having been whelped in 1920.

Monarque's greatest claim to fame at this date is through his son *Ch. Clee Courtier,* sire of thirteen champions as well as two untitled dogs that did more in the way of continuing the line than did some of the more famous winners. The uncrowned Clee Brigand, older brother of Courtier, founded a line in England but did the greatest amount of good to the breed through his daughters. Courtier was a magnificent show dog, and as J. Ethel Aspinall said in *The Airedale Terrier,* he seemed to exercise a dwarfing effect on certificate winners of other breeds, as witness his many Best in Show awards. He won a total of fourteen CCs at England's largest shows, including Crufts.

WALNUT KING NOBBLER LINE

The most fabulously successful of the Courtier lines is that of *Walnut King Nobbler.* This dog was whelped in 1930 and was bred by Major J. H. Wright, whose Ch. Murose Replica brought him more fame fifteen years later and whose Ch. Holmbury Bandit was a great sire of the 1940s. Nobbler was originally named Holmbury Good Lad but renamed under the "Walnut" prefix of his new owner, Sam Bamford. Nobbler was the sire of seventeen English and nine American champions as well as some that acquired their titles in other countries, and several were in the "international" category. Nobbler's dam was Holmbury Brunette, who was by Neadwood Captain ex Taff Queen (whose sire was Ch. Mespot Tinker). The latter was A. J. "Towyn" Edwards's most famous dog and his stud card gives him credit for siring sixteen champions, of which eight were English.

WALNUT KING NOBBLER LINE—TRI. INT. CH. COTTERIDGE BRIGAND BRANCH

Much of the success of the Nobbler line is through his son *Tri. Int. Ch. Cotteridge Brigand,* founder of a branch responsible for more American champions in the fifties than all other lines combined. Brigand was imported to Canada by Sid Perkins, and the few litters he sired there before being sold to Holland gave even more fame to the "Rockleys." While the Cotteridge Brigand line was much less influential in England, its dominance in American bloodlines cannot be denied. Brigand's full brother, Ch. Aislaby Aethling, however, contributed heavily to English lines. Brigand's reputation as a sire could have been made by the one litter that produced Ch. Rockley Riot Act, Ch. Rockley Roasting Hot and Ch. Rockley Hidden Treasure, for Roasting

Hot founded the line that produced 97 of the 130 champions of the Brigand dynasty, and the two bitches also founded strong families of their own.

Ch. Rockley Roasting Hot was purchased by Mrs. Eleanore Loree of Summit, New Jersey, and although he had a good show record, it was not as outstanding as that of Riot Act. Whelped April 19, 1937, Roasting Hot gained his title while still under a year of age. What enduring fame he may have lacked in the show ring he made up for as a sire of twenty-one champions.

Roasting Hot's leading son is *Ch. Eleanore's Royalty of Lionheart,* this branch producing fifty-four champions in the last decade, with Ch. Roy el Hot Rock and Ch. Eleanore's Brigand being the other main contributors. Royalty was bred by Mrs. Loree and purchased as a young prospect by Lou Holliday. It is as a sire that he will best be remembered, but he made a fine record in the show ring, being one of the Airedale elite to have an all-breed Best in Show win to his credit, many Group placements, and a Specialty Best in Show. The Specialty Best in Show win took place in 1947, the first year the Ch. Lionheart Comet Bowl was on offer for winners of the Southern California Specialty. And it is a tribute to Royalty's success as a sire, and as a sire of sires, that in the decade since it was first offered, only two winners of the bowl have not been his direct male-line descendants.

Of Royalty's sixteen champions, *Ch. Lionheart Copper* had the most notable show record and also established a strong clan of his own in this remarkable patriarchy. He was Best of Breed on twenty-nine occasions, three times first in the Group, and had twenty other placings. Copper's dam was Ch. Lionheart Comet III by Int. Ch. Cast Iron Monarch and of course of the famed "Comet" family, which will be mentioned later.

The line from Copper that has become the most influential is that of *Ch. Studio Top Brass,* whose dam was Crosswind of gundog fame. Crosswind was by Ch. Lionheart Cold Steel, and in keeping with the metallic naming system, I had applied for "Battle Axe" as first choice for a name, this seeming beautifully applicable as she was tough and—as a pup—willful, so when that was not allowed by the AKC, the second choice, "Crosswind," was. This name was chosen because I was taking flying lessons at the time and could think of nothing harder to handle than crosswinds. That should explain this rather un-Airedaleish name. Brassy too was an independent individual who loved to hunt, but he was destined for the show ring. He had style to the nth degree and passed this attribute on to most of his get. He won the first Pacific Northwest specialty in 1950 and the next year was BOS to Ch. Raylerock Mica. Two generations later the combination of these lines resulted in the production of Ch. Hilltop's Happy Josh and Ch. Hilltop's Kintla Challenge, as will be noted under their sire's name.

Ch. Studio Liontamer brought Brassy the most fame of his nine champions. Liontamer's first Specialty win was the Pacific Northwest event in 1952, followed the same year by his taking the Southern California Twenty-fifth Anniversary Specialty, in an entry of eighty-seven Airedales—the largest in America in thirty years. Next he won the California Airedale Terrier Club's

Ch. Rockley Roasting Hot.

Ch. Roy El Hot Rock (1945).

Lionheart Enchantress (1948).

Ch. Studio Liontamer (Ch. Studio Top Brass ex Lionheart Enchantress), owned by Gladys Brown Edwards. A Group winner, he was handled by John Edwards. *Bennett*

Ch. Studio Top Brass (1948).

41

Specialty at San Mateo, then, three years after his first win, he again took the Southern California affair. He was never campaigned on circuits and was never away from the West Coast. Shown twenty-one times after he was out of the puppy stage, Liontamer ("Simba") won fifteen Bests of Breed and placed in the Group fourteen times. Six of these were Group firsts, including Golden Gate, Beverly-Riviera and Harbor Cities (Long Beach). The latter Group win was especially impressive, for finishing in back of him were several famous Best in Show winners. The 1952 SCAA Specialty was judged by Percy Roberts, who had also officiated at the Westminster show that year.

Liontamer is a full brother of five other champions. Those of a latter litter almost didn't make it into this world at all, for their dam, Lionheart Enchantress, nearly died as a result of blood poisoning. This was because of her rushing in "where Greyhounds [if not angels] feared to tread," and killing a huge, gone-wild tomcat in the woods. The Greyhounds had caught the cat but had let go when he got too tough. Ellie (Enchantress) had never seen a cat close-up before, but it was damaging her gawky friends so she did something about it, silently finishing him off; but he got his revenge posthumously when the wounds from his claws brought on the infection. This was an astounding affair for Ellie, since she was a mild-mannered bitch who liked nothing better than to carry a toy football around all the time . . . without even puncturing it.

The line from Liontamer was originally carried on mainly through the first of his five champions, *Ch. Hilltop's Rocky Top Notch,* but another branch, which has proven to be even more productive, started from an untitled dog, *Coppercrest Brandy.* Since this was a later development taking two generations more to break into the limelight, it is detailed in the next chapter. Rocky's exploits as a gundog are worthy of note in themselves, but it is his career as a show dog and as a sire that gave him a place in Airedale history. He too won the Pacific Northwest Specialty and at the same show won the Group. He won several other such firsts and, like his sire, once he was mature he placed in the Group every time he was Best of Breed, except one. His dam was Lionheart Impact, who was by Ch. Lionheart Banner ex Ch. Lionheart Comet III. Two of Rocky's sons have carried on for him, one by show successes, including the Southern California Specialty, but no branch line descends from him. This was Ch. Hilltop's Happy Josh. The other was Ch. Hilltop's Kintla Challenge, the first Airedale bred on the West Coast to win Best of Breed at Westminster, which he did twice. This feat was repeated around two decades later by another dog of the Top Notch dynasty, and all but one of whose ancestors in tail-male lineage had won the PNW (Pacific Northwest) specialty. This one exception was not a champion (he may have been used only for hunting, but memory fails me on this), but it is through him, *Hilltop's Blitzkrieg,* that the line has descended—a similar situation to that from Coppercrest Brandy. But then when you think of it, all the descendants of Walnut King Nobbler trace back to an uncrowned king, Nobbler himself.

The dam of Challenge and Josh is Cowboy's Cowgirl of Foxglove, a bitch

Ch. Hilltop's Rocky Top Notch (Ch. Studio Liontamer ex Lionheart Impact).

of Replica and intense First Mate breeding, and they were bred by Mr. and Mrs. Frank Slama of Corvallis, Oregon.

The second main branch from Top Brass is that of *Can. & Am. Ch. Lionheart Skyway,* full brother of Liontamer and sire of Ch. Saltash Royal Guardian (Winners Dog at the 1957 Southern California Specialty) and Ch. Sundown Forty-five (Reserve to Guardian at that show). Skyway himself was best of winners at the 1955 Specialty, which was won by his older brother, Liontamer. Skyway's litter sister, Ch. Lionheart Starlight, was Winners Bitch—making a family clean sweep of the top spots. Skyway subsequently became owned by Mary Curran in Canada.

Going back to Copper, we come to the second of his leading sons, *Ch. The Sheik of Ran-Aire.* The Sheik was another outstanding show dog, although he was never campaigned nor widely advertised by his owners and breeders, Mr. and Mrs. George Rankin of North Hollywood. Winner of the Southern California Specialty in 1951, Sheik won several Groups, climaxed by a Best in Show at San Mateo. Ch. Boulder Gulch Son of the Sheik, bred and owned by Florence Fisk Fried, was the Sheik's most successful son, and was a Group winner as well as placing in Groups several times. His litter sisters, Ch. Boulder Gulch Little Sheba and Ch. Boulder Gulch Show Girl, won the California specialty in consecutive years. Sonny's dam brings in a variety of bloodlines. She is Patshee Patricia, tracing to Walnut King Nobbler in tail-male, and her dam was Trucote Dazzle, by Ch. Tiger of Deswood (a son of Merry Sovereign). Son of the Sheik sired Ch. Gooch's Prince Charming, Winners Dog at the 1956 Southern California Specialty.

Ch. Hot Shot of Ran-Aire, founder of the secondary branch of the Royalty dynasty, was out of a full sister of the Sheik. Hot Shot was Winners at the 1949 Southern California Specialty and Best Opposite to Ch. Roy el Tiger Lily in 1951. He sired the Champions Sundown Annie Oakley and Sundown Trigger, the latter winner of the 1954 Southern California Specialty and known as "the Giant Killer" for his success in bowling over the currently successful winners from time to time. The "Sundowns" are bred and owned by Mr. and Mrs. Adrian Eichorn of Malibu, and Trigger and Annie's dam was Marbeth Surprise (by Copper out of a bitch by Ch. Lionheart Cold Steel); hence, their breeding is very similar to that of the "Liontamers." A son of Trigger was Winners Dog at the 1954 Specialty but unfortunately was lost soon afterward.

Going back to Roasting Hot we find the two other main branches of this line. Of these, the line of *Ch. Eleanore's Brigand* is still going strong while that of Ch. Roy el Hot Rock seems to be dying out. Brigand was a full brother of Royalty, and although his name has a piratical ring, he proved his royal lineage by being second only to his brother in the number of champions sired by sons of Roasting Hot. In the "spice litter" sired by Brigand, there were three champions: Eleanore's Allspice, Eleanore's Marjoram, and Eleanore's Ginger. But it was Ch. Aireline Bombsight that gave Eleanore's Brigand his high score. Bombsight's dam was Ch. Fiesolana, who was by Ch. Towyn Speculation ex Stockfield Melody. Speculation was by Warland Michael ex Warland Maple (a full sister of Warland Protector of Shelterock). Michael also was out of Warland Sprite, dam of Protector and Maple. Bombsight was bred by Charles Ryan and sold to the Milroy Kennels in Canada, where he had a successful career. Repurchased by Mr. Ryan, Bombsight was first shown in this country at the 1947 Specialty, when just under four years of age, and so impressed Percy Roberts that he bought a half interest in him. At this show Bombsight went on from the classes to Best of Breed, downing seven champions en route. He was Best of Winners at Westminster but had to bow to the four-and-a-half-year-old Ch. Maralec First Mate for Best of Breed. Two of Bombsight's best-known sons are Ch. Tedhurst Pilot and Ch. Breezewood Ballyhoo.

Ch. Tedhurst Pilot was bred by Ted Becker, and his dam was Ch. Tedhurst Aviatrix, who was by Roasting Hot ex Tedhurst Bruna of the Rampart, a daughter of Ch. Warland Warboy. Ch. Tedhurst Cadet is a son of Pilot ex Tedhurst Belle, the phenomenal producer of champions.

Ch. Breezewood Ballyhoo, owned, trained and exhibited by Jane Ruth, is out of Breezewood Bonfire, who was by a son of Ch. Squire of Siccawei ex Bourbon-Ayr Manhattan (by First Mate). Whelped in 1952, Ballyhoo has won three specialties and one Group, and has already sired two champions.

The third of the main Roasting Hot lines, that of *Ch. Roy el Hot Rock,* was very much in the forefront for a while; but due to the main representatives of later years being bitches, the tail-male inheritance stopped abruptly. Hot Rock was bred and owned by Roy Latham and whelped in 1945. His dam was Ch. Eleanore's Glittering Girl, who was by Ch. Eleanore's Knight ex Roasting Hot's sister, Ch. Eleanore's Hidden Treasure. Hot Rock, known as "Jeep," was shown nineteen times, going Best of Breed fourteen times, placing in the Group eleven times, and was Best Terrier six times.

Ch. Roy el Red was Jeep's most prominent son, winning the *Dog World* Award by acquiring his title in three straight shows. The story of this line concerns its daughters more than its sons, for two of the former made Airedale history on the West Coast. The first was Ric Chashoudian's Ch. Roy el Tiger Lily, twice winner of the Southern California Specialty (1948 and 1950) and Best of Opposite Sex to Copper in 1949. Lil was by Hot Rock out of Hot Rock's own dam, Glittering Girl, and though this breeding may be considered close, it was nowhere near so close as that of Ch. Hazelin's Red Hot Mamacita. 'Cita was sired by Ch. Hazelin's Red Hot, who was by Roy el Red out of Red's dam and granddam, Glittering Girl. 'Cita's dam was Ch. Annjiehills Bloomer Girl, by Hot Rock, which also brought in the name of Glittering Girl, and gave her a large percentage of the pedigree. Like Ric Chashoudian, Mamacita's owner, Daisy Edwards Austad got started as a professional handler with a good Airedale. 'Cita won the Texas Specialty, was Best of Opposite Sex to Liontamer in the Silver Anniversary Specialty—an honor she had had the previous year to the Sheik and that she repeated at the age of seven and a half years to Liontamer's grandson Josh at the 1957 Southern California Specialty. She won several Groups and placed in many others.

Ch. Highmoor Rival is another son of Roasting Hot who started a line that produced champions. This traces down from Rival through Dalehaven Chief Rival, and his son Dalehaven Debonair, who sired Ch. Comrade Speed King. The latter is a Group winner and also a sire of champions. Chief Rival is the maternal grandsire of Only Girl of Ran-Aire, dam of the Sheik.

Going back now to Cotteridge Brigand, the most successful branch after that of Roasting Hot is the branch of Eng. Ch. Monarch of Tullochard, a great-grandsire of *Ch. Squire of Siccawei,* to whom this line owes its fame in America. The line traces down from Monarch to Rural Defiance, then His Lordship of Tullochard to Esquire of Tullochard, sire of the imported Squire. Squire traces to Walnut King Nobbler in many lines, with nearly all the rest of Matador Supreme of Mandarin blood. Many of the names that appear unfamiliar are full brothers or sisters of those we know very well in America. For instance, Fierentina, granddam of Esquire, is a full sister of Ch. Fiesolana, and their dam, Stockfield Melody, is a sister of Ch. Aislaby Joceline of Shelterock. This breeding has already been mentioned under that of Bombsight. Melody's sire, Ch. Aislaby Aethling, a full brother of Cotteridge Brigand, won thirteen CCs by the time he was two years of age, seven of them in succession. Aethling was Best in Show at the National Airedale show for two years in a row, BB at the Midland Airedale show and Best Terrier at Cruft's in 1934. Squire's dam, Siccawei Pica, was by Leader Writer, a son of Newsboy Call and a full brother of Ch. Ridgemoor Sweetberry. The latter was a bitch who founded a strong family in this country, as will be noted later. Many of Squire's antecedents were war babies and were in their prime during the period when no championship shows were held in England. Squire, with his dozen champion sons and daughters, is high on the sire list, with Ch. Tedhurst Equity at the moment supplying the main sub-branch. Owned at one time by Charles Ryan and Percy Roberts, Squire later became the property of the Whitehouse Kennels of Harry Reinhart. A son of Ch. Tedhurst Equity who has done exceptionally well is Can. and Am. Ch. Tedhurst Major, a Best in Show winner in Canada and winner of a couple of Groups, as well as several placements, in this country.

The Canadian-bred *Ch. Fallcrest Harry* was another son of Cotteridge Brigand to found a line in this country. Harry's line is carried on down through Ch. Croftlyn's My Own Mickey, a good winner. Mickey's son Airelore Perfection, in turn, has sons siring champions, thus carrying on this branch. The other line from Harry is through Ch. Croftlyn's Sir Galahad, also a sire of champions.

Ch. Rockley Robin Hood, a Canadian dog as his prefix indicates, founded a line in this country that might not be noted for many branches, but it did feature a few big winners. Ch. Greenburn Infractious is the dog that started this line on its way to fame, and was by a son of Robin Hood—Greenburn Sir Michael. Mike's dam was Rockley Bess, who was by Ch. Warland Warboy. Robin Hood's dam was Ch. Warland Wondrous, a daughter of Walnut King Nobbler. Infractious was out of Greenburn Gingersnapper, a full sister of Sir Michael, Infractious's sire. She was also full sister to Greenburn Inquisition, dam of Ch. Acres Sal of Harham. When Infractious was owned by the Ker-

Wel-Aire Kennels, he was described on the stud card as having a "long, clean, perfectly balanced" head, but Infractious had offspring on the "pony-headed" order, rather round-skulled and broad, during the years he was owned by the Copperdale Kennels in San Francisco. However, this complemented the cobby conformation of the Copperdale dogs. And with the clean-skulled Replica stock of the same kennels, the result was very good and the combination produced several champions. Infractious was more widely advertised than any dog of his time and was well patronized at stud. Although he did not himself sire many champions, his grandson. Ch. Orlaine's Roustabout, had the record number of Group wins by an Airedale—twenty-seven—until the advent of Eng. Ch. Westhay Fiona, imported by the Florsheims.

WALNUT KING NOBBLER LINE—CH. WALNUT CLIPPER OF FREEDOM BRANCH

The second longest Walnut King Nobbler line in this country is that of *Ch. Walnut Clipper of Freedom,* owned by A. L. Zeckendorf's Freedom Kennels. Clipper's dam was Walnut Happy Maid, by Ch. Tavern Leatherface, who was by Ch. Stockfield Aristocrat. So far as extending the line is concerned, Clipper's most noted son is Ch. Freedom Free Lance. Clipper was also a good brood matron sire, one of his daughters, Ch. Walnut Amethyst of Freedom, being dam of three champions, while another, Freedom Forget Me Not, topped this number by one. Forget Me Not's son, Ch. Freedom Full Force (by Free Lance), is the leading sire of the Free Lance line. Ch. Freedom Fireworks, another son of Clipper ex Amethyst, was ten times Best of Breed and also won a Group. Ch. Lance of O'Samequin, Best of Winners at the 1943 Specialty, is another son of Free Lance. Lady Filigree, a full sister of Full Force, was dam of Ch. Aireline Supreme (by Bombsight). Supreme had an enviable record of Group placements and wins, as well as a Best in Show, but died in his prime. He had acquired his title without a defeat.

WALNUT KING NOBBLER LINE—INT. CH. CAST IRON MONARCH BRANCH

Although the sire line founded by *Int. Ch. Cast Iron Monarch* is not a long one, he has been influential through the success of some of his daughters as brood matrons. One of these was Ch. Lionheart Comet III and another was the Best in Show winner Ch. Tesque Muldavin—though the latter was more noted for her show wins than as a producer. Some puppies of this line (as is also the case with the line from Infractious and several others) have a blaze on the chest, and occasionally white toes, this latter marking disappearing when the puppy gets its new coat. Color Bracer of Merzhill, a son of Monarch, has also sired champions.

CH. CLEE COURTIER LINE (FROM WHATNOT)—CH. MATADOR MANDARIN BRANCH

Going back now to the Clee Courtier main line, we come to a branch with more offshoots and taproots than a banyan tree. This is the branch from *Ch. Matador Mandarin,* which has a record second only to that of the Walnut King Nobbler line in this country, with eighty-one American champions tracing to Mandarin in tail-male in the last decade. Mandarin sired only one male champion, Ch. Stockfield Aristocrat, but this dog was a sire of sires, as the whole line seems to be. Mandarin won five CCs in succession, going from novice to Best in Show at Birmingham and also winning this high honor at the National Terrier show and at Bath.

Ch. Stockfield Aristocrat was the winner of nineteen CCs in four years, and sired nine champions. He was sold to Japan along with several other good Airedales, but during his career in England he won many Bests in Show as well as other high honors. Aristocrat's dam was Gleeful Wendy, by Ch. Ileene Brigand, who was by Ch. Mespot Tinker.

Carrying on this line was *Ch. Waycon Aristocrat,* sire of only two champions, but they "made" him, for they were the great sire *Ch. Wolstanton Bostock* and the good winner and producer Ch. Warland Wedding Gift. Waycon Aristocrat's dam was Ch. Sweet Damsel's Legacy by Warland Protector, and this was one of the many instances where Protector aided in giving producing ability to a line. Bostock sired five English and one Continental champion. Among his best sons was Ch. Broadcaster of Harham, while his daughter Ch. Ridgemoor Sweetberry founded a very strong family of her own. Chathall News was a prominent progenitor in the English branches of this line. Berrycroft Atoppa, unable to compete in championship shows due to World War II, was another son of Bostock who founded an enduring line, as did Waycon Designer, an uncrowned son of Waycon Aristocrat.

Carrying on the *Broadcaster* dynasty, *Ch. Harham's Expert Explorer* had the most sensational show career and sired the most champions, but his line at present is shorter than that of Ch. Harham's Rocket. Broadcaster's dam, Lady Conjuror, was also the dam of Cast Iron Monarch, who was by Stockfield Aristocrat. Expert Explorer, bred and owned by Harold Florsheim's Harham Kennels, was Best of Breed thirty-five times from 1949 to 1953, including twice at Westminster (1950 and 1953), and won the Terrier Group eight times.

Ch. Harham's Rocket won thirteen Bests of Breed and one Best in Show. His dam, Adoration of Aldon, was by Cotteridge Brigand, who was by Warland Protector ex Eng. Ch. Warland Wishbone. Ch. Ardendale Repeat Performance was an especially well-named dog so far as siring champions was concerned, dittoing down the line with seven title holders. Of these, Ch. Ardendale Mr. Trouble sired three more, and his line is carried on by Ch. Gingerbred Number One Boy, a California-bred dog that had the distinction of winning his title in the East, taking Best of Winners at Morris and Essex, Best of Breed at Plainfield, Middlesex and the New England Specialty. On his Eastern tour he was accompanied by his litter sister, Ch. Annjiehill's Show Off II, making the trip unique in that she took all her points at these shows, including the New England Specialty. A full brother of Mr. Trouble, Ch. Ardendale Trouble's Double, is also the sire of champions.

The third of the Broadcaster lines is that of *Ch. Oakhaven's Flaming Rocket* and includes Ch. Buckthorn Blackjack, grandsire of Pixie of Alii, Hawaii's first champion bitch. Blackjack was sired by Cinnibar Rags ex Ch. Buckthorn Sal, a Best in Show winner sired by Flaming Rocket. Sal was out of Vasona's Liberty Bell, who was Lionheart-bred throughout and sired by Ch. Lionheart Cold Steel.

Returning now to Bostock, we find the excellent sire line of Berrycroft Atoppa. Unable to compete in championship shows himself, due to wartime cancellation of such events, Atoppa sired a number of champions and sires of champions. Among them was *Ch. Holmbury Bandit,* the breed's first postwar champion in England, and sire of seven champions, of which three were in one litter: Weycroft Wondrous, Weycroft Wishful and Weycroft Wyldboy. Both Wondrous and Wyldboy were imported to America. In England, Wyldboy had a remarkable show career, but gained his American title after a rather slow start. He proved to a laster, however, and at the age of eight years polished off the younger dogs for a Best Opposite placement to Fiona at the 1957 Morris and Essex Show. His death a few months after his Morris and Essex showing was a great blow to his owner, Mrs. Claire Dixon, and his handler, Sheila Lyster.

Eng. & Am. Ch. Murose Replica was undoubtedly the most famous of the *Bandit* sons and was older than Wyldboy. He won seventeen CCs in fourteen months, and in this country, though well along in years, he won the Specialty, was Best of Breed at Westminster and Morris and Essex and won six Groups as well as a Best in Show.

Although Replica sired four champion sons, three non-champions have done more in carrying on the line in this country, with another untitled son carrying the load in England. Replica was whelped April 15, 1948, and was five years of age when imported.

As to the bloodlines behind Replica, Atoppa's sire and dam were both by Ch. Waycon Aristocrat; Bandit's dam brings in Briggus Bonnie Boy (by Junemore Bonnie Boy ex a daughter of Mandarin) and again Bostock as the maternal grandsire. Replica's dam, Murose Lassie, has Shelterock Merry Sovereign as her paternal grandsire, and this dog was also the grandsire of her dam. Here the influence of Merry Sovereign on the distaff side begins to show up. Replica was widely advertised in America. Wyldboy was not—nor was he shown often. After the dispersal of the Buttsark Kennels, which had imported him, Replica was sold to Mrs. Griffin's Copperdale Kennels in California. There he was bred to bitches of all bloodlines and shapes, with the resultant variance of type in the first generation. Greenburn Infractious was also owned

Ch. Harham's Expert Explorer (1948).

Ch. Bengal Bahadur of Harham (1950).

Ch. Aireline Star Monarch (1951).

Ch. Roy el Tiger Lily (1946).

Ch. Sierradale Chica, UDT (1939).

English C. Son of Merrijak (Holmbury Murraysgate Merrijak ex Nelson Lassie).

by these kennels at this time, and second- and third-generation crosses of the two lines have produced some fine Airedales.

As has already been seen, many a strong line is founded by a dog that never became a champion, and that is the case of *Waycon Designer,* son of Ch. Waycon Aristocrat. Designer's dam was Ch. Flower of Fashion, by Ch. Aislaby Aethling. Designer not only sent the Merrijak line on its way to glory but he also figures prominently "through the middle of the pedigree" in the background of many winners and producers. Designer's son *Can. Ch. Murraysgate Monty* carried on the line, siring Holmbury Murraysgate Merrijack. Monty was sold to Canada after winning eight Bests in Show at open and member shows, Dan Hargreaves of British Columbia importing him. Monty's career was mainly during the championless war period, but he did win his classes at the first London postwar show shortly before exportation. The "Merri" of this line comes from Murraysgate Merry Mascot, a daughter of Merry Sovereign. She belongs to a well-known producing family, as will be shown later. Mascot, bred to Ch. Warland Warboy, produced Murraysgate Merriment, dam of Monty. Monty's son, Merrijack, unfortunately died young after the start of a promising career, with one CC to his credit, but he had sired Ch. Son of Merrijak and thereby won his place in Airedale history. Son of Merrijak's dam was Nelson Lassie, by Cashton Herald. Son of Merrijak was hard to condition—a trait that some of his inherit—and this caused him to be retired without gaining his title in this country although he lacked only a few points. He turned out to be a sensational sire and outstripped Replica as a sire even though he was never advertised.

In England, Son of Merrijak had sired Ch. Bengal Bengali, winner at Crufts, and *Bengal Bahadour,* who, after his importation by Mr. Florsheim, was known as Bengal Bahadur (without the "o") of Harham. These dogs were litter brothers, but Bahadur started more slowly than Bengali and it took him some time to get under way in this country, but once in condition he was almost impossible to stop. Among his thirty Bests of Breed were those of Westminster in 1954 and 1955, and in addition to winning a Best in Show and two Groups, he had several Group placements. He also won the New King Bowl four times and the Illinois Specialty once.

King of the Merrijak line is *Can. & Am. Ch. Aireline Star Monarch,* owned by Charles Marck of El Cajon, California. As his prefix indicates, he was bred by Charles Ryan, then in partnership with Percy Roberts. This great campaigner has eighty-two Best of Breed wins to his credit and sixty-six Group placements, topped off by five Best in Show wins. Star Monarch's dam, Aireline Classic, is by First Mate out of Aireline Queen. The latter is by Ch. Eleanore's Brigand. The fact that Star Monarch sired three champions in one litter, the dam being Ch. River Aire Rock-C, UDT, would indicate that he nicks well with the Roasting Hot lines of Lionheart bitches, Rock-C being of that breeding.

Another line from Merrijak is that of *Ch. Ardendale Revenger,* whose dam is Ardendale Top Me. His son Ch. Westbank Etaoin Shrdlu proved himself by winning the Northern Ohio Specialty on his first venture into the show ring, then going on to a Group third. He has placed in several other Groups. This dog's young son, Ch. Westbank Main Event, also owned and bred by Jane Merrill, finished his championship at ten months of age, in seven consecutive shows, winding up with points to spare in four- and five-point entries.

CH. CLEE COURTIER LINE—MATADOR SUPREME BRANCH

Matador Supreme was a full brother of the sensational Mandarin. His son *Ravenslea Red Pepper* was purchased by J. P. Hall especially to mate with Warland bitches. One of these, Ch. Warland Watto of Oxenhill, by Briggus Bonny Boy (who was by Ch. Junemore Bonnie Boy), produced Ch. Warland Wattotstuff, sire of the famous *Ch. Warland Warboy.* (Wattotstuff is usually misspelled—leaving out the second "t.") Watto was herself exported to America, where she won the points at both the Specialty and Westminster in 1938. Blue Flash, dam of Warboy, was a granddaughter of Red Pepper and purchased especially as a brood bitch for the Warland Kennel.

Ch. Warland Warboy was imported to Canada by Sid Perkins of Rockley fame and was shortly thereafter sold to Mrs. Joseph Urmston. Warboy was Best of Breed at the 1945 Westminster show but no Specialty was held that year, nor was the Airedale Bowl offered during the war years. However, Warboy won the New King Bowl three times, was Best in Show on several occasions, with numerous Group placements and wins. Although he is credited with only nine champions in this country, he is named in the background of many of today's winners. The line of Can. Ch. Shining Rip Rap, founded by Rockley Man o' War, is the longest Warboy line at present, although many of the Pepperidge Airedales are strongly linebred to him.

CH. CLEE COURTIER LINE—CH. WARBRECK ECLIPSE BRANCH

The fourth of the Courtier branches is that of *Ch. Warbreck Eclipse,* a dog that had been practically unshown in England and so had none of the usual fanfare when he was imported by James Manning. He was entered at Westminister, but Col. Guggenheim's Wolstanton Superb was Best of Breed, placing over Flornell Tavern Maid, who was also owned by James Manning. Eclipse, by Ch. Clee Courtier out of Flornell Brentwood Lady, was whelped September 3, 1928, and his only appearance in English shows had been at Leeds, where he was awarded four first prizes. All the contenders for top honors at the 1930 Specialty—Tavern Maid, Eclipse, Superb and Eng. Ch. Belfort Supreme of Shelterock—were by Clee Courtier, which is in itself a tribute to Courtier's success as a sire.

Digressing from the Eclipse line for a moment, it is of interest to note the influence two of the other foregoing imports had on the breed. Belfort Supreme, a big winner and an English champion, died after he had been here about a year. But he sired three champions, including Shelterock Madame Supreme, the dam of Shelterock My Superex, who was the maternal grandsire of Rockley Roasting Hot. Madame Supreme is the founder of the amazing family of Tedhurst brood matrons that includes Tedhurst Belle, leading Airedale matron as to number of American champions produced. This blood is doubled in Belle's pedigree, for she is by Eleanore's Brigand, by Rockley Roasting Hot, and also brings in lines from Roasting Hot's sister, Hidden Treasure.

Warbreck Eclipse founded a tail-male line that is being carried on by the well-known Sierradale line of obedience-trained champions, of which *Ch. Rusty Dusty, UDT,* is probably the most noted, for he holds the bench title and all obedience degrees, as well as being the sire of several champions. May Pridham, owner of the Sierradales, is an obedience teacher, which explains her interest in having Airedales accomplished in this art. Her most famous Airedale, however, Ch. Sierradale Squaw, did not have time for obedience work but acquired seventy-five Bests of Breed, a Specialty win, and numerous Group placings in her career as a showgirl. The Eclipse line comes down through his son *Ch. Rascal of Bri* to Bighorn Duke, full brother of Lou Holliday's Ch. Lionheart Comet, founder of the "Comet" line of famed brood matrons. Rascal's dam was by Int. Ch. Flornell Mixer out of Rose Bri, who was a Group winner by Ch. Ruler's Double. Foundation bitch of this strain was Ch. Sierradale Chica, UDT, by Ch. Shelterock Monmouth Squire, a full brother of Merry Sovereign and winner of the Airedale Bowl at the 1936 Eastern Dog Club show. Chica's dam was Lionheart Jill, a daughter of Comet and sired by Eng. Ch. Walnut Gamecock of Brandwood, who was by Walnut King Nobbler. The branch from Rusty Dusty that is longest at present is from *Sierradale Sitting Bull,* whose dam was Chica. His most noted son is *Ch. Sierradale Sitting Bull II,* out of Ch. Sierradale Firefly, CD, who was a full sister to the senior Bull. Sitting Bull II was the sire of the famous Squaw. A full brother to Sitting Bull was Sierradale Lone Indian, and two of the three champions sired by this dog were out of Squaw, which makes this very close inbreeding to Rusty Dusty and Chica. Ch. Sierradale War Drum, UDT, by Rusty Dusty out of Ch. Sierradale War Bonnet, is among the champions of this line who acquired the UDT.

CH. CLEE COURTIER LINE—INT. CH. JUNEMORE BONNIE BOY BRANCH

The last of the Courtier tail-male lines in this country is that of *Int. Ch. Junemore Bonnie Boy.* He sired two English champions, and one line in this country is brought down through *Authority's Replica,* whose son *Ch. Elmer's First Mate* is the sire of two champions, one of which, Pool Forge Flapper, is the dam of three champions. Another line comes down through Croftlyn's Sir Galahad. Bonnie Boy is more noted for his daughters than his sons, and consequently his line does not show his actual influence. One of his daughters was Cumbrian Chrysoberyl, dam of Ch. Newsgirl Charming, whose family will be delineated later; another is Crosslye Brunette, dam of Tri. Int. Ch. Cotteridge Brigand, star of the Walnut King Nobbler line. Both the sire and dam of Ch. Junemore Bonnie Boy were international champions, and his dam, Int. Ch. Clonmel Cuddle Up, was by another international champion—Warland Ditto. Cuddle Up was purchased from Holland Buckley by Mrs. Marriott and spent seven years in India, where she produced three champions. Apparently she was about ten years of age when she produced the litter of which Bonnie Boy was a member, for he was whelped after her return from India.

FOUNDATION TAIL-FEMALE FAMILIES

The foregoing has been entirely from the tail-male point of view, touching on the feminine side of the ledger only to give the names of dams of outstanding sires. The following line of descent is through the dams—those matrons that seem to pass on their producing qualities to their daughters generation after generation. These families, as a rule, form the foundations of strains, rather than do sires. Through most of these are found the old "American" lines, tracing back in extended pedigrees to early importations.

There are seven major families—those founded by Ch. Fiesolana, Hekla Cleopatra, Ch. Lionheart Comet, Ch. Ridgemoor Sweetberry, Rockley Glitter, Ch. Walnut Review of Shelterock and Warland Sprite. Of these only Cleopatra and Comet were American-bred, but their later lines bring in some older American strains. The lines that follow are dealt with alphabetically.

THE CH. FIESOLANA FAMILY

Ch. Fiesolana won the challenge certificate at Cruft's in 1938 and was owned in America by the Aireline Kennels of Charles Ryan. Her breeding has already been given under that of her sister, Fierentina, in the pedigree of Ch. Squire of Siccawei. Fiesolana's daughter *Ch. Warland Warbride,* bred in England, was the dam of four champions, but it is to the untitled *Aireline Queen* that most of this family now trace. Queen, by Ch. Eleanore's Brigand, founded six families, of which that of *Aireline Classic* is possibly the most notable. Classic, by Ch. Maralec First Mate, was herself dam of four champions: Aireline Star Monarch, Aireline Merryboy, Aireline Storm Queen (all by Eng. Ch. Son of Merrijack) and Wyndhill Lillabet, by Ch. Bengal Bahadur of Harham. *Storm Queen* was the dam of the Best in Show bitch *Ch. Benaire Crown Jewel,* Ch. Benaire Miss Chiff and Benaire Tennessee Storm, all producers of winners. Another daughter of Classic is *Aireline Symbol,* by Squire.

Symbol produced six champions, but her daughter *Aireline Peerless Pearl* brought added distinction to the family by producing the magnificent Ch. Axel's Columbus, a dog that won the summer Specialty in 1956, the New England Specialty in 1957, Best of Breed at Morris and Essex in 1956 and Best Opposite to Eng. and Am. Ch. Westhay Fiona at the 1957 summer Specialty. Columbus was sired by the German-bred Ch. Axel v.d. Limpurger Residenz, who also sired Ch. Axel's Duplicate. The sire of Peerless Pearl is Star Monarch.

Another line from Queen is that of *Aireline Atalanta,* whose daughter Ch. Wyndhill Wasp was the dam of Ch. Birchrun Scorpio and Ch. Buckeye Sweet Talk. The third line from Queen is that of *Craigston Happy Birthday,* by First Mate; this line is carried on by the Champions Craigston Hot Rocks (by Lightning Coslea) and Craigston Monopoly (by Bahadur). The fourth line from Queen is that of *Ch. Aireline Passing Review,* a sister of Happy Birthday and producer of two champions, of which one is Rancho Valle Baronessa, by Ch. Lionheart Barrister. Baronessa produced two champions, including the daughter Lawrence's N.K. Only One, who in turn produced Ch. Lawrence's M.C. Shirley's Kim. The fifth line from Queen is that of *Wee Jezebel,* by Roasting Hot; Wee Jezebel has already been mentioned as the dam of Ch. Jezebel's Infractious Son, but here is of more note as to family because she produced the champion bitch Lady Elgin. Queen's sixth producing daughter is *Ch. Aireline Lovely Lady* (sister of Wee Jezebel), whose line comes down through Cotswold Dowager Duchess (dam of one champion) through Blackheath Coca to Ch. Blackheath Geisha Girl, by Son of Merrijak.

THE HEKLA CLEOPATRA FAMILY

The Hekla Cleopatra family traces down mostly through *Eleanore's Princess,* dam of four champions. Cleopatra was by the American-bred Ch. Willinez Defiance. Her daughter Hekla's Queen of the East was by Ch. Warbreck Eclipse. Queen was also the dam of Eleanore's Princess, who was sired by Ch. Aislaby Jocelyn of Shelterock, who was in turn by Ch. Aislaby Aethling. Princess' daughter *Ch. Maralec Super Sis,* by Maralec Bingo Boy, was the dam of Bourbon-Ayr Manhattan, by First Mate. Manhattan's daughter *Breezewood Bonfire,* by Aireline Monarch, produced two champions, one of which, Breezewood Ballyhoo, has already been mentioned (Bombsight sire line). Another line to Princess is that of *Maralec Surprise,* by Roasting Hot, and one of the champion offspring of Surprise is Super Sis of Renidrag. Ch. Maralec Jocelinette, another daughter of Princess, was sired by Roasting Hot. *Maralec First Lady,* a sister of Maralec Super Sis, is the dam of Ch. Quarryhill Princess, sired by Lionheart Local Boy. Quarryhill Princess is the dam of Quarryhill Home Ruler, sire of Ch. Raylerock Mica, a good producing bitch of the Rockley Glitter family.

56

THE CH. LIONHEART COMET FAMILY

The Lionheart Comet family is really the family of her dam, *Lou's Cross,* as this brings in two other producing lines of identical breeding to that of Comet. Cross was by Ch. Lou's J. M. and her dam was Criterion Cute Girl, whose sire had two close crosses to Ch. Soudan Swiveller and whose dam was by the imported Warland By Product. It is through J. M. that the Lionheart line is brought down to Cross, who is by Pepper Tree Don, a son of Ditto and out of Lou's Electress; the latter's dam, Lou's Suffragette, was also by Ditto. Suffragette's dam was Lionheart Cross (by Lionheart Politician ex Lionheart Queen), the foundation bitch of the Lionheart strain.

Comet was the dam of four champions (by three different dogs), and her sisters Carry On and Away were dams of one each and founded families producing several others. These bitches were by Ch. Rascal of Bri, a son of Ch. Warbreck Eclipse. The line second to Comet's is that of Carry On, which produced, among others, *Ch. Buckthorn Sal*—a Best in Show winner and dam of three champions.

Sal was a great-granddaughter of Carry On, and was by Ch. Lionheart Cold Steel ex Vasona's Liberty Bell. Bell also founded another branch through Cinnibar Imp. It is the Comets, however, who brought fame to Lou's Cross. Although five daughters carry on from Comet, three carry most of the fame. *Ch. Lionheart Comet II,* by Rockley Roasting Hot, won two Groups and was second in the Group five times. She was the dam of six champions, the main producer again being a Comet—*Ch. Lionheart Comet III.* The latter was dam of three champions and founded quite a champion-filled and many-branched family of her own. She was the dam of *Lionheart Enchantress,* who was retired to the matron ranks with twelve points toward her title, but who made up for the lack of the final points by producing six champions, including one with a Canadian title as well. Of these, the daughters are Ch. Lionheart Starlight and Ch. Lionheart Clee, the rest being dogs.

Studio Miniature, full sister to the foregoing champions, is also the dam of a champion. Another daughter of Comet III is *Lionheart Irene, UD,* by Ch. Lionheart Banner. She is the dam of two champion daughters—*River-Aire Rock-C, UDT,* and *River-Aire Revel, UD,* both by Royalty. Rock-C is the dam of two champions by Star Monarch, River-Aire Bonniroxie and River-Aire Brisance. *Muncie of Lionheart* is a litter sister of Revel and Rock-C and is the dam of two champions by Ch. Studio Liontamer, one of which is a bitch— Lionheart Abigail.

Going back to Comet III, Irene's little sister *Lionheart Impact* is the dam of Ch. Hilltop's Rocky Top Notch, a dog by Liontamer that is very influential in the Pacific Northwest. *Lionheart Comet IV* is, of course, out of Comet III and sired by Royalty.

Backtracking to *Comet II,* we come to another of her daughters, *Ch. Lionheart Baroness* (by Royalty), who produced three champion bitches. A full sister to Comet III (by Int. Ch. Cast Iron Monarch) was the Best in Show

Ch. Lionheart Comet I (1933).

Ch. Lionheart Comet II (1940).

Ch. Lionheart Comet III (1942).

winner Ch. Tesuque Muldavin. And a daughter of Comet II by Royalty was Ch. Lionheart Betsey, producer of a line for the Phelaire Kennels in Texas. Again going back—this time to the original Comet—we come to the untitled *Lionheart Jill,* who was by Ch. Walnut Gamecock of Brandwood ex Comet. Jill's daughter *Crosswind* was more noted as a hunting dog than as a producer, and the bitch line stops with her, for she carries on only through a sire line, that of Ch. Studio Top Brass, whose career has already been outlined. Jill's daughter *Ch. Sierradale Chica, UDT,* was more obliging in the family-continuing line, however, producing *Ch. Sierradale Firefly, CD,* dam of three champions, and *Ch. Sierradale Osalita, CD,* both by Ch. Rusty Dusty, UDT. Osalita is the dam of Sierradale Sundance, who is the dam of Ch. Thunderbird Indian Feather.

Again going back to *Comet I,* we come to the final family to be outlined—that of *Lionheart Star,* sister of Comet II. She was the dam of Miss Victory (by Eleanore's Knight), dam of Happy Polly (who was by Cold Steel). Polly was the dam of *Marbeth Surprise,* who was by Copper, and Surprise was the dam of three champions, her daughters being Ch. Sundown Serenade (by Harham's Beaming Boy) and Ch. Sundown Annie Oakley (by Ch. Hot Shot of Ran-Aire).

The Comet line nicked exceptionally well with Ch. Eleanore's Royalty of Lionheart, and the majority of the West Coast winners have at least one cross to Comet, or the blend of the various Comet families with Royalty. At the Twenty-fifth Anniversary Specialty of the Southern California Airedale Association, fifty-three of the eighty-seven Airedales entered traced to Comet in one or more lines, with eleven of the fourteen champions in competition tracing to this bitch, either through the sire or dam, or both. The winner of the Specialty, Liontamer, traced to Comet four times, three of these lines through the sire. Ch. The Sheik of Ran-Aire (winner of the previous Specialty) had one cross to Comet through his sire, Copper (winner of the 1949 Specialty). Ch. Sundown Trigger, whose pedigree shows three Comet lines, won the 1953 event. And Liontamer and Trigger won the 1953 and 1954 renewals of the California club's Specialty in San Mateo, with the litter sisters Ch. Boulder Gulch Sheba and Ch. Boulder Gulch Show Girl winning in 1955 and 1956 respectively. Little Sheba and Show Girl are by the Sheik.

Although Royalty takes credit for siring the largest number of champions of any Airedale on the West Coast, the majority were from Lionheart bitches, or those tracing in some line to Comet. The leading sires on the coast are of the Royalty-Comet combination to some degree, diffusing this blood still further throughout the West. Royalty-Comet dogs have won in the country's largest Specialties, on occasion have topped all breeds for Best in Show and very often have won the Terrier Groups in strongest competition against Eastern and English-bred Terriers. Comet herself was winner of the 1935 Southern California Specialty and was Best Opposite in 1936 to Ch. Shelterock Monmouth Squire, the brother of Int. Ch. Shelterock Merry Sovereign. Comet was defeated only once in her sex, and in memory of this great foundation bitch, Mr. and Mrs. Holliday donated "The Lionheart Comet Bowl," a perpetual trophy won by the Best of Breed Airedale at the Southern California Specialty. Winners of the trophy have already been listed under the "Royalty" section of the foregoing sire lines.

THE CH. RIDGEMOOR SWEETBERRY FAMILY

Bred in England, *Ch. Ridgemoor Sweetberry* was by Wolstanton Bostock ex Newsgirl Charming. She was bred by William Burrows and was owned in America by Mrs. Loree. *Newsgirl Charming* founded other families in England, but it is the American-bred lines of the imported Sweetberry with which we are concerned here. Through Eleanore's Margolow and Ch. Warlaine Belle Canto, there are two short lines, with a third and longer line coming down through *Ch. Eleanore's Sweetberry,* dam of three champions including the bitch Ch. Seaward's Hobby. Margolow was sired by Roasting Hot, Belle by Ch. Eleanore's Corporal Jack and Sweetberry by Ch. Eleanore's Allspice. A sister of Eleanore's Sweetberry, Dillie of Beverwyk, produced Vicky of Beverwyk when bred to Ch. Warland Warboy. Vicky was the dam of *Trucote Dazzle,* who was by Ch. Tiger of Deswood. Dazzle was the dam of Patshee Patricia, by Patshee Captain Courageous, and Patricia was the dam of four champions, all by Ch. The Sheik of Ran-Aire. Two of these, Boulder Gulch Little Sheba and Boulder Gulch Showgirl, have already been mentioned.

Another daughter of Dazzle is Patshee Dutchess, CDX, dam of Ch. Elroy's Top Kick, CD. Dutchess is unusual in that as the result of a severe illness, she nearly lost her hearing, and in fact was totally deaf while being trained for the first degree in obedience, learning all her cues by hand signal. She regained enough of her hearing to qualify for the trials, but even so her performance is unique. She and Top Kick are owned and trained by Mr. and Mrs. E. T. McElroy. Dutchess is by Trucote War King, by Warboy, while Top Kick brings in the lines of the Canadian dog Lamorna Prince Nobbler, a son of Walnut King Nobbler. Top Kick, like Columbus, is not of a sire line that produced enough champions to be included in the foregoing section.

Founder of the longest line and producer of the most champions in the Ridgemoor Sweetberry family was Sweetberry's daughter *Ch. Eleanore's Blackeyed Susan,* also by Allspice. One of her daughters was Milroy's Ariel, by Bombsight, and she produced Ch. Shining Dulcie, sired by Ch. Shining Rip Rap. The strongest Susan line is that of *Milroy's Aireline Susan,* sister of Ariel. Three of her daughters, all by Squire, produced champions, with *Ch. Ardendale Annabell* taking top credit with six, all by Ch. Ardendale Repeat Performance. One of her daughters, Ch. Ardendale Our Best, proved the aptness of her name by going Best in Show on one occasion. However, as often proves the case, it was Ardendale Top Me, one of Annabell's untitled daughters, who has so far been the best producer, with five champions as her score, all by Son of Merrijak.

When the influence of the sires tracing directly to Sweetberry is also considered, such as Ch. Eleanore's Royalty of Lionheart, Ch. Eleanore's Brigand and the latter's son Bombsight, as well as the remarkable records of others of these lines, it is not hard to realize Sweetberry's contribution to modern Airedales.

THE ROCKLEY GLITTER FAMILY

Rockley Glitter is another whose heritage is carried on by a son, namely Ch. Rockley Roasting Hot, sire of twenty American champions, including the two "Eleanores" mentioned above. However, her daughters were also outstanding both as winners and as producers. Foremost, of course, was the sensational *Ch. Rockley Riot Act,* litter sister of Roasting Hot and Ch. Rockley Hidden Treasure. Riot Act won thirty-seven Bests of Breed, with three Groups and Bests in Show to her credit, as well as many Group placements. Riot Act was the dam of the "spice" litter, which was sired by her nephew, Eleanore's Brigand. Of these, the bitches that carried on the line were Ch. Eleanore's Marjoram and Ch. Eleanore's Ginger. Marjoram is the dam of Ch. Trucote Invasion Belle, by Warboy, but it is her sister *Tedhurst Bruna of the Rampart* who proved to be the producer. Her daughter by Roasting Hot, Ch. Tedhurst Aviatrix, is the dam of a pair of champions, but another daughter, by First Mate, was not only an outstanding winner and producer of four champions, but she founded her own branch of this family. This was *Can. & Am. Ch. Tedhurst Pin Up Girl.* Pin Up Girl's daughter *Ch. Raylerock Mica,* by Quarryhill Home Ruler, was most outstanding, winning one Group and placing in several. Mica's daughter *Cowboy's Cowgirl of Foxglove,* by Replica's Cowboy of Buttsark (Ch. Murose Replica ex Ch. Tedhurst Boots), produced three champions by Ch. Hilltop's Rocky Top Notch and described in the "Roasting Hot" dynasty. One of the three was a daughter, Ch. Hilltop's Rockette. The other daughter of Mica is a litter sister of Cowgirl, this being Foxglove Saucy Sal, dam of Ch. Foxglove Studio Joye, by Ch. Studio Top Brass. Joye has already produced daughters that seem destined to carry on as befits the line.

The second of the "spice" litter, *Ginger,* is the dam of *Ch. Annjiehill's Show Off,* by Ch. Roy el Hot Rock. In a single litter by Ch. Ardendale Mr Trouble, Show Off produced Ch. Gingerbred Number One Boy, Ch. Gingerbred Show Off's Own and Ch. Annjiehill's Show Off II. The "Gingerbreds" are owned by Mr. and Mrs. Chester Perry of Temecula, California, and have the distinction of having an all-champion tail-female family for five generations back to Riot Act. Ch. Gingerbred the Boy Friend is the fourteenth champion in tail-male. On paper, the line breeding of the Gingerbreds is most interesting.

Going back to Glitter's other daughter *Hidden Treasure* we find that although she had three daughters among her six champion produce, the main line comes down through *Ch. Eleanore's Glittering Girl,* by Eleanore's Knight. She was the dam of four champions, her daughter *Ch. Roy el Tiger Lily* (by

Hot Rock) was the dam of three and *Ch. Steelcote Reflection* (Lil's daughter sired by Ch. Lionheart Copper) was the dam of Ch. Steelcote Misty Morn, who was by Ch. Roy el Red of Hazelin. Another daughter of Reflection is Steelcote's Sweetheart, sired by Ch. The Sheik of Ran-Aire, and the dam of Ch. Steelcote's Shooting Star. The intense inbreeding of the "Roy els" and the "Hazelins" has been given under the "Roasting Hot" sire line.

THE INT. CH. WALNUT REVIEW OF SHELTEROCK FAMILY

The family of *Int. Ch. Walnut Review of Shelterock* is mainly that of Tedhurst Belle. The line traces down from Review through Shelterock Madame Supreme (by Ch. Belfort Supreme), Hekla Protectress (by Ch. Warland Protector) and Ch. Wykagyl War Bonnet (by Ch. Shelterock Marvelous Style), directly to the sisters Croftlyn's Princess Royal and Wykagyl Fashionette. Princess Royal's daughter Croftlyn's Toby (by Ch. Freedom Free Lance) was the dam of Tedhurst Lady Joyce, dam of *Tedhurst Belle,* whose sire was Eleanore's Brigand. Belle, with nine champions, is at the top of the "leading brood matron" list. One daughter, by Squire, is the dam of two champions. Her sons Ch. Tedhurst Equity and Ch. Tedhurst Cadet have both sired four champions.

THE WARLAND SPRITE FAMILY

The last of the major families is that of *Warland Sprite,* a daughter of Clee Brigand, and previously hailed as the dam of Warland Protector. One Sprite branch was founded by Warland Maple (by Wrose Cargo), sister of Warland Protector. She was the dam of Ch. Warland Wishbone (by Warland Michael), whose daughter Adoration of Aldon produced two champions: Harham's Rocket (mentioned under sire lines) and his sister Adorer. These were by Broadcaster. Adorer produced Harham's Authentic, dam of Harham's Beaming Boy, sire of the Junoesque Ch. Sundown Serenade. The other Sprite branch was Warland Maisie's (by Wrose Anchor); her daughter Warland Gaiety produced *Eng. and Am. Ch. Warland Wedding Gift* (by Waycon Aristocrat). This line then develops two branches, of which the shorter is that of *Warland Merry Wedding.* This bitch, by Merry Sovereign, was the dam of Ch. Warland Wargift of Harham, producer of two champions, including the great Explorer. The other branch is English for a couple more generations, and is from a sister of Merry Wedding, *Murraysgate Merry Mascot.* Her daughter Chathall Miranda (by Warboy) is the dam of two champions, including the imported Thelwyn Yenolam Merry Mascot, by Thelwyn Command. Another daughter was *Murraysgate Winniedale,* already mentioned under the "Merrijak" sire line, and her sire was Waitland's Warlock, also by Merry Sovereign. A daughter of Winniedale's, imported to Canada by Mr. Hargreaves, is Murraysgate Marlyn, dam of Ch. Gooch's Fraserholm Lass, by Murraysgate Monty.

THE TRIDWR MILADY FAMILY

Although this is still primarily an English family, its leading representative in this country, *Eng. & Am. Ch. Westhay Fiona of Harham,* makes its inclusion necessary in order to give the background of this phenomenal bitch that in one year accumulated more Group and Best in Show wins in America than any other Airedale in the history of the breed. The complete background of the family is given in the chapter on English dogs, so we will only touch on it here.

Sired by Eng. Ch. Westhay Jamus, Fiona is out of *Eng. Ch. Riverina Westhay Flayre,* subsequently owned in Sweden. Fiona made her debut in a show in the fall of 1956, shortly after importation, the object being to secure a blue ribbon that would qualify her for entry at Westminster. Not stopping with merely the "points" or the blue, she went on to Best of Breed and then first in the Group. In 1957 she collected twenty-seven Group firsts, with a scattered few lower placements—but rarely "lower" than second—and seven Bests in Show. Fiona's sire, Jamus, is by Raimon Nobbler of Noremarsh ex Westhay Souvenir. Nobbler is by Bengal Bash 'em, by Bengal Lancer, while Souvenir brings in a line to Replica through her sire, Westhay Solo King.

OTHER FAMILIES

At first glance it would seem that certain great Airedales of the past left no outstanding descendants, if, in fact, any offspring at all. One of these was Int. Ch. Glenmavis Solitaire of Freedom, a sensational show bitch. However, though not shown in any family mentioned herein, the bloodlines of Solitaire are perpetuated through most of the Freedom strain, with line breeding to her further intensifying this inheritance. Another marvel of the 1930s was Tri. In. Ch. Briggus Princess, and both Princess and Solitaire were by Walnut King Nobbler. Princess is the dam of Ch. La Condesa, and oddly enough, this line is carried on down through a so-called "hunting" strain rather than modern show Airedales.

The Airedales of Hawaii deserve mention, due to an upsurge of interest in the breed to the extent that an Airedale club was formed in 1957. Not too many years ago Airedales were among the "rare" breeds on the Islands, and the formidable quarantine, paralleling England's, discouraged importation of dogs. However, many service men, transferred to the Islands, took along their Airedales, as did other new residents, and the breed flourished in its new home. Entries in shows have been good, averaging higher than in many mainland shows having fair Airedale representation, and the Airedale population has

Canadian Ch. Murraysgate Monty.

Ch. Westhay Fiona of Harham (Ch. Westhay Jamus ex Ch. Riverina West-hay Flayre), owned by Harham Kennels, was one of the standout winners of all time. At her first show in America she qualified for Westminster by winning the Terrier Group and repeated that performance at Westminster itself.

Ch. Riverina Siccawei Phoebus.

been increasing by virtue of the many new litters being produced. The year 1957 saw two champions crowned, the first Airedales ever to gain the title in Hawaii.

Both the 1957 champions had previously placed in Groups, and the day Thora Sands' Ch. Just Plain Brick gained his title, he also placed second in the Group. Brick, bred in Washington, is by Ch. Studio Top Brass ex Just Plain Dinahmite, by Ch. Studio Liontamer. The bitch champion is Pixie of Alii, bred and owned by Thelma Emanual in Hawaii. Pixie's sire is Surfrider's Poi Boy (by Ch. Buckthorn Black Jack ex Ch. Buckthorn Sal). And her dam is Saltysan's Alii (by Alii O Na Ilio out of Ch. Saltysan's Empress of Royalty) and is predominately "Lionheart" in breeding. Others bring in "Roy el," "Lyon," and "Ouachita."

This chapter has been devoted mainly to bloodlines that have produced the majority of Airedale champions in America prior to 1960. The prospective buyer of a "pet" puppy might wonder why so much emphasis is placed on championships, and Group and Best in Show wins, when all that he himself is interested in is having a typical Airedale of good temperament, not a show specimen. Dog shows are the only place where dogs can be compared with one another as to adherence to the breed Standard, and the more individuals of his breed a dog can defeat in the show ring, the greater is the chance that he is a superior dog himself, especially if those he defeats are of high quality. The title of champion means that the dog is a little better than the average, for he has had to compete with a certain number of dogs of his own breed under several judges. Quality is as important in dogs as in anything else, and "blood will tell," even if the dog is desired only as a family pet and will never see the show ring.

Naturally in this summary we are restricted to the lines producing the majority of modern champions, so there are some of the lesser-known lines not represented. However, nearly every quality-bred Airedale of today traces to one and usually several of these lines, and in this way nearly everyone can trace his Airedale's family tree.

To avoid repetition of the title "Ch." where individuals already have been mentioned by title, the prefix has occasionally been omitted on subsequent mention of the dogs.

"HUNTING" STRAINS

There are some Airedales in America that, though registered, would not have any relatives whatsoever on any of the foregoing lines since the days of Ch. King Oorang and his contemporaries. These are Airedales of the "Oorang" strain, and since they are almost never exhibited, they naturally would have no show records with the AKC from which to compile statistics. The Oorang strain was founded well before 1920 by Walter Lingo in Ohio, who was interested in the hunting potentialities of the breed. Mr. Lingo decided on the Ch. Oorang line as best suited for his purpose, and so enthusiastic was he about the Oorang line that he used the old dog's name as a trademark. The most noted stud dog of the Oorang Kennels was King Oorang II, who was, as the catalog stated, from "a long line of champions." He was indeed of the most fashionable bloodlines of his time, being by Ch. Rockley Oorang out of a daughter of Ch. Prince of York. Other stud dogs in use during the early 1920s were of intense Crompton Oorang lines with Ch. Abbey King Nobbler or his sire, Ch. Soudan Swiveller, giving added champion-bred background. King Oorang had quite a record as a gundog, big-game dog, dogfighter and even as a sheepherder!

The Oorang Kennels did things on a big scale in the boom days of the Airedale. They advertised that they could supply any type or size, from thirty-five to one hundred pounds, and the dogs were priced according to show qualities or training. Some of the older stock was sold fully trained as to hunting experience on the type of game specified by the buyer. The brood matrons were kept by local farmers, the litters being brought to the kennels for sale, and apparently the breeding is still handled in this way.

During the boom days, the Oorang Kennels had an extensive publicity campaign, both in the press and by athletic exhibitions. The trainers were American Indians, headed by the famous Olympic star Jim Thorpe of the Sac and Fox Tribe. They had a professional football team, and the Airedales, of course, went along as mascots, putting on acts of their own, especially as "war dogs" in sham battles staged by the teams during the war years. All of this publicity put the Oorang Airedales right on the map. Even after the boom, they were advertised in sports magazines, but always as "Oorang AIREDALES," never as "Airedale TERRIERS," which brought about the confusion in the public mind as to an imaginary difference between Oorang Airedales and Airedale Terriers, a befuddlement that confounds the uninitiated to this day.

Considering the vast numbers bred, it can be seen that all thought of show qualities, except in the very upper tier, was sidetracked. Today the Oorangs are still as varied as in the old days with the thirty-five to one-hundred-pound weight classifications. There is no such thing as an "Oorang type," for they can be tall, short, lathy or cobby, sheep-coated or pin-wire, gray-tan or mahogany, grizzle or black-saddled. So can dogs of any other strains that have been bred without consideration of type for several generations. On the other hand, a reasonably typical Airedale of the Oorang strain can produce show-quality Airedales when bred to prepotent, sound and typical individuals of show strains, and several champions have been of such breeding. However, it should be again emphasized that neither Oorang nor any other strain has the corner on the Airedale's hunting potential. The Lionhearts are proof that show-quality Airedales can hunt, train well for obedience or do anything an Airedale ever could do, and so can other strains. In fact, it is harder to keep an Airedale *from* hunting than it is to find one reluctant to hunt. The foregoing should answer the question so often asked—"What is the difference between Oorangs and Airedales?"

There are several other breeders who also advertise "sporting Airedales" in hunting magazines. Prominent among them are the Lyons, Scarborough and Ouachita. All are located in rural or mountainous areas where the young stock gets hunting experience, starting out with the puppies following their dams on excursions after small game. Many are then used on larger game when the opportunity is afforded. These are truly "hunting" strains, in that they get some experience as such. But all of the foregoing are based largely on modern show strains and some Oorang blood. Familiar names in the Lyons strain are Ch. Warland Warbride (Warboy-Fiesolana) and Ch. Maralec First Mate. The Scarboroughs show such champions as Warland Protector, Fallcrest Harry, Rockley Roasting Hot, Fiesolana, Ridgemoor Sweetberry and Aireline Apollo II in their background. Similarly, the Ouachita Airedales have the Champions Broadcaster, Bombsight, Cast Iron Monarch, Fallcrest Harry and Roasting Hot. It is interesting to note that in this, a hunting strain, is found the name of Int. Ch. Briggus Princess. She was the dam of Ch. La Condesa, who was in turn the dam of Ch. Royal Commando. He was the sire of McCoy's Ozark Rambler, close up in the pedigree of the early Ouachitas.

Ch. Finlair Tiger of Stone Ridge, "Gator" handled by Bob Larouech.

5

Outstanding Sires
Since the 1960s

THIS CHAPTER UPDATES the reader from the 1960s, naming the top winning show dogs and the top sires. As well you know, many good dogs are never shown, but all the available information comes from the American Kennel Club show records. By examining your new puppy's pedigree and referring to the direct male line of descent appearing in the Appendix, it may be possible to trace your dog's lineage back to the original Airedale Jerry.

CH. ERNIE'S JACK FLASH

In the beginning Ch. Ernie's Jack Flash (known to his friends as "Josh") was owned and campaigned by Denise and Mike Tobey of the Pacific Northwest and Jan Framke of Stone Ridge Kennel fame, and later by Carol and Lewis Scott of the Scottshire prefix. Josh won the ATCA Airedale Bowl, the top memorial trophy for Airedales, under Terrier Specialist Mr. John Marvin, in New York in 1977. From there he took New Orleans by storm and won the Bowl again under the Scotts' ownership. On his way, he won and retired the Steve Woods Memorial trophy of the Pacific Northwest, went Best in Show four times and was top Airedale in 1979. Some of his better-known sons are Champions Loc Aire's Maestro and Virtuoso, who in turn sired Ch. Fresh Aire Meistersinger Loc and Ch. Cedarcrest Star Contender. Another son was Ch.

Ch. Ernie's Jack Flash. *Missy*

Ch. Kinetic Jack Be Quick (Jack Flash son).
Lindemaier

Ch. Fresh Aire Miestersinger Loc (Jack Flash grandson), a champion in three shows. Handled by Susan DePew. *Olson*

Ch. Love's Stoney Burke. *Ludwig*

Ch. Geoffrey Earl of Stratford.   *Ludwig*

Ch. Jerilee's Jumping Jericho, a Geoff son, won the ATCA Airedale Bowl under judge Thelma Brown, handler Ric Chashoudian.
Shafer

Ch. Sunnydale Doc Holiday, another Geoff son who has proven to be an outstanding sire in his own right.
Missy

Stone Ridge Union Jack owned by Dick and Jan Framke of Stone Ridge Kennels. Still another son was Ch. Kinetic Jack Be Quick for the Kinetic Kennel of Doctors Suzanne and John Hampton. The Hamptons, along with the Tobeys and the then Janet Johnson (now Framke), watched him win the Airedale Bowl at the Chain-O-Lakes Specialty in Illinois in June 1980. Another son to be recognized was Ch. Kiryat Sampson's Tartan, who in turn kept the line going by siring Forbes Gordon's Ch. Tartan's Mr. Sage and Steve and Bonnie Gilbert's Ch. Tartan Bannochburn Drummond, one of the first modern Airedales to go from the breed ring to excel in hunting and working trials.

CH. LOVE'S STONEY BURKE

Stoney came down the line from Gladys Brown Edwards' beloved "Simba," Ch. Studio Liontamer, through Coppercrest Brandy, owned and bred by the Dutchers but not shown, as a veterinarian docked his tail too short. Brandy sired Siouxaire's Chief Duff, bred and owned by Dorothy Tizbir, herself part American Indian, thus her dogs bore Indian names. Stoney won the first Mila Brodie Award for the futurity winner for the Southern California Airedale Association, went on to finish his championship and was specialed by Johnny Coglan. Stoney had the questionable distinction to be asked by judge Percy Roberts to leave the ring at the Westminster Show for being a naughty Airedale who would not stop barking at the judge. His show career cut short by being noisy, he returned home to stand at stud. His son Love's Gabriel of Coppercrest was purchased by Carl Silver for his Indianaire Kennel of Phoenix, Arizona. Another son, Ch. Despot of Dominaire, was owned by Jean and Lyndol Wilson and founded the Dominaire Airedales, with sons Ch. Coppercrest Ruddy Rogueaire and Ch. Quincy Christopher Murase being shown. Ch. Coppercrest Jonathan Swift, handled by Bob Jordan, sired several champions, including Ch. Coppercrest Mr. McTavish, Sweepstakes winner at Montgomery County in 1978. His half-brother, Ch. Coppercrest Little John, repeated the Sweepstakes win at Montgomery County in 1980. Stoney's son Ch. Geoffrey Earl of Stratford, owned and exhibited by Elinor and Walter Hellmann and handled by Johnny Coglan, in addition to making a name for himself in the show ring, is best remembered for putting his stamp on two illustrious sons.

CH. JERILEE'S JUMPING JERICHO

Jericho, sired by Geoff out of Flintkote River Princess, was purchased by Leslie and Jerry Rosenstock, and was handled by Ric Chashoudian and Clay Coady to many great wins. He was three times Best of Breed at the Beverly Hills Kennel Club shows and Best of Breed at Westminster in 1974 and again in 1975, this time adding a Group IV. Jericho was a Specialty winner at the Great Lakes, Southern California Airedale Association and the California Airedale Terrier Club. By 1977 Jericho had one hundred Bests of Breed and twenty Group placements, and had won the ATCA Airedale Bowl at the Montgomery County Specialty with an entry of 130 Airedales in 1976 under English Judge Mr. W. N. Robinson, C.B.E. Jericho sired Ch. Brown's Jigsaw John, who in turn sired many champions, including the Kingsmen champions for Karen Schaffner of Michigan. They include Ch. Kingsmen Lord of the Rings, who produced Ch. Cripple Creek Frodo Baggins and Ch. Cripple Creek Bilbo Baggins, Ch. Kingsmen Baron Nickolaus, who sired Ch. Kingsmen Dexter Darcy, Ch. Kingsmen Maxwell Arthur and Ch. Gingerbred's Britain. Another Kingsmen champion was Ch. Kingmen's Sergeant Saxon, sire of eight champions. Handled by Alison Korn, Saxon won the ATCA Airedale Bowl in Minnesota at the Floating Specialty in June 1985. In a repeat of Jericho's breeding, Geoff sired another son, Ch. Coppercrest Contender, owned jointly by Leslie Rosenstock and Gini Dreyfus of "Ringtrue" Airedales. Contender was another Specialty winner, with Metropolitan Washington and New England wins. He won Best of Breed sixteen times and had Group placements.

CH. SUNNYDALE DOC HOLIDAY

Another of Geoff's sons to have far-reaching influence on the modern-day Airedale world was Ch. Sunnydale's Doc Holiday for Jack and Mary Sanderson's Sunnydale Kennels, located in Santa Rosa, California. The Sandersons bred their Ch. Sunnydale Holiday, a small but very typy bitch, to Geoff to produce Doc Holiday and Dame Holiday. Doc won the Sweepstakes at the California Airedale Terrier Club and finished his championship in 1977. Doc did not enjoy the shows, much preferring to stay home and guard his girls. Doc has sired at least sixty-four champions, and often it has been said and demonstrated that whatever bitch was serviced by him would produce something good. One of his well-known sons was Ch. Rudigan Robear.

CH. RUDIGAN ROBEAR

Robear was sired by Doc out of Ch. Lionheart Little Lulu for the Cudigans. Robear was handled by Wood Wornall for Rod and Ruth Cudigan to win the Champion Briarcroft Perfection Memorial trophy awarded to Winners Dog at the New York Specialty in 1980. He had his name inscribed on the William Barclay Memorial trophy for Best of Opposite Sex at the Pacific Northwest Floating ATCA Specialty to his half-sister Am. & Can. Ch. Sunnydale Ginny Robin, who went Best of Breed to win the ATCA Airedale Bowl under breeder Judge Charles Foley of Anfeald Airedales in 1980, Best Opposite again at the New England Regional Specialty in 1981, each time being defeated for Best of Breed by a different Doc daughter, this time Ch. Coppercrest Centerfold. From Robear came Ch. Dandyaire Dixie Jazzman, bred and shown by Wilma and Reg Carter of Northern California. Jazzman sired five champions, including Ch. Taryn Indiana Jones of Karyn and Tom Reilly of Kansas City, Missouri.

Other Doc sons are John and Jill Fanning's Ch. Waggery's High Country, and Maggie Hochstetler's Ch. Good Medicine Golliwog Jake; Ch. Sunnydale Holmes, another Doc son, was out of Ch. Sunnydale Bouncing Billie. Holmes was sold to Barbara Casso of Mexico. After becoming both an American and Canadian Champion, he went on to get his Mexican Championship.

Another Doc son is Ch. Sunnydale Wichita Lineman, who in turn sired Ch. Sunnydale Tanglewood Ted. Ted, owned and exhibited by Kathy and Walt Zimmerman, is litter brother to Ch. Sunnydale Triton; another Lineman son is Sunnydale Pendragon, who at present is the Sandersons' house couch potato. "Gunner," as his family calls him, is the sire of Ch. Coppercrest Un Poco Loco, handled by Connie Clark. He in turn sired recent winner Ch. Coppercrest Sunnydale Pico and litter sister Ch. Coppercrest Sunnydale CiCi, winner of the Northern California Sweepstakes under breeder-judge Jill Fanning.

Doc produced the famous litter for Georgia and Russ McRae containing Ch. Brisline's London Fog, Ch. Brisline's Lady's Man, Ch. Brisline's Lavender Mist and Ch. Brisline's Live It Up from their well-known Ch. Brisline's Inspiration, a daughter of Ch. Sunnydale Ho-Ray for Brisline, a litter sister to Holmes. Ch. Brisline's Lady's Man, "Rudy," as he is known at home, is the sire of six champions including the present-day Best in Show winner, Ch. Harringtons Kantankras Kyna, who came south from Alaska to conquer shows on the east coast. Still another Doc son is Ch. Sunnydale Quartermaster out of Ch. Sunnydale Woodhue Amy, a Doc daughter bred back to her father. Cheryl Black bought Quartermaster, who sired three Blackdale champions for Cheryl and two White Rose Champions for Bobbie Brennan. Ch. White Rose Doc Watson currently is being shown by Chris Nance for Bobbie. Not to be forgotten is his Texas son, Ch. Woodhue Joint Venture, owned and shown by Isabel Strempek. But Doc's greatest fame comes from his many champion daughters, discussed in the ladies' chapter.

SANBROOK SENATOR

The Anfeald breeding of Regina and Charlie Foley marks a line of male descent from Sanbrook Senator through Ch. Seabrook Senturian, whose son Anfeald Royal Grundy's Britt sired the winning Ch. Anfeald Brandywine. From Brandywine came son Anfeald Hot Spur to sire Ch. Anfeald Moses, winner of the ATCA Airedale Bowl at the New England Specialty in 1981. Moses got his name after he was found lying under a bush when daylight came. His dam neglected to inform the Foleys that she had dropped him, but all ended well and he became special.

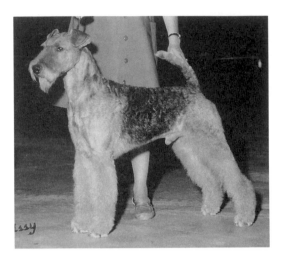

Ch. Brisline's Lady's Man, breeder/owner Georgia McRae. *Missy*

Am. & Can. Ch. Anfeald Moses, won the Veteran Class at Montgomery County; judge Ed Bivin, handler Chris Nance. *Ashbey*

Three young brothers—Bravo True Grit, Bravo Comet's Streak, and Bravo Starbuck.

Ch. Bengal Sabu, owned by Barbara Strebeigh, Tuck Dell and Harold Florsheim and bred by Molly Harmsworth, was one of the most influential sires of modern times. He came to the United States in 1959 as an unshown yearling. By the time he was retired he was a multiple BIS and Specialty winner with a record that included seven Airedale Bowl wins. He sired dozens of champions and was the beginning of an Airedale dynasty that still shines today.

CH. BENGAL BAHADUR OF HARHAM

The Ch. Matador Mandarin line continues to the present time down through Eng. Ch. Son of Merrijack. Their influence through Ch. Bengal Bahadur of Harham and his son Ch. Danhow Farouk was known in Jim McLynn's Ch. Talyn's Tom Tom, sire of Ch. Talyn's Man About Town. Himself a sire of four champions, he joined with Ch. Talyn's Yohorum, Ch. Talyn's River Rogue and Ch. Talyn's Ironclad Leave to win the ATCA Airedale Bowl eleven times, establishing a record for an American kennel.

Also descending from Ch. Bengal Bahadur of Harham was Aireline Hallmark, sire of Marion Simmonsen's Ch. Wraggletaggle Checkmate, who, when bred to Ch. Dandyaire for Cinnabar, a daughter of Ch. Aireline Star Monarch out of Ch. Burnwell Bessie, produced Ch. Dandyaire Cinnabar Gremlin for Wilma and Reg Carter. Gremlin sired Ch. Caper, and Ch. Barbate Excalibur, who sired Ch. Anfeald Sam I Am of Britham, whose son is Ch. Britham Bourguignon. Another Gremlin son was Ch. Jumping Jack Flash.

Another Checkmate son was Ch. Lay Dee Ayr Nicodemus, owned and shown by Dee and Dave Leahy of the Lay Dee Ayr Kennel in Western Pennsylvania. Nicodemus sired five champions.

Another noted son of Bahadur of Harham was Ch. Benaire Queen's Ransom. Benaire, located in the Great Lakes area, was the kennel prefix of Virginia Bensman. From Ch. Queen's Ransom came Ch. Erowah Command Performance and Ch. Benaire Erowah Crown Prince. In turn, Ch. Crown Prince produced Ch. Benaire King's Counsel, and he sired Ch. Cyndale Smiling Sam. Another son, Ch. Benaire Courtney's Duet, sired Ch. Benaire Argus Blackjack and Ch. Argus Checkmate, who sired Ch. Argus Mr. C J, the sire of Ch. Clintwood Busby and Ch. Wagtail Me N My Arrow. "Argus" is the prefix of Alma and Mike Dooley. Another son, Ch. Benaire Argus Atlas, sired three champions, including Ch. Rivendell Oakenshield. Also from Ch. Bengal Bahadur of Harham came Ch. Querencia's Bengal Diplomat, sire of Ch. Querencia's King Little of the Querencia kennel of Countess Ercilia LeNye.

ENG. CH. SON OF MERRIJACK

Blackheath Exchequer, another son of Eng. Ch. Son of Merrijack, sired Ch. Toprock's Blackwood. Among his four-champion get was Ch. Glenaire Alistar; from him came the first of the Pequods for Jan and Al Stevens of New England. Coming down their line is Ch. Pequod Sea Bird, sire of Ch. Pequod T'Gallant Royal, who sired Ch. Pequod Salt Horse, and from him came the well-known Ch. Pequod Blackbeard the Pirate, shown to many wins by Roberta (Krohne) Campbell and Ron Krohne. "Blackie" was number one Airedale in 1975, 1976 and 1977, with four Bests in Show and many group placements. He sired six champions.

Another son of Ch. Son of Merrijack was Can. & Am. Ch. Aireline Star

78

Monarch, who won the ATCA Airedale Bowl at the winter Specialty in 1952, owned by Charles Ryan. Charley and Ann Marck purchased and brought "Colonel" home to California, where Roland Muller handled him to many wins, including the ATCA Airedale Bowl at the Southern California Airedale Specialty in 1956. Colonel sired the foundation bitch of Coppercrest Kennels, Ch. Scatterfoot Tim Tam, bred by Georgiana Wooldridge from her Scatterfoot Lady, descended from Ch. Walnut King Nobbler. More about Tim Tam in the chapter reserved for the ladies. While in Northern California, Wilma Carter bred her Ch. Burnweel Bessie, a Ch. Murose Replica daughter, to Colonel, and produced Ch. Dandyaire Cottage Commando, Ch. Dandyaire Friend Freddy and Ch. Dandyaire Flint Fire.

CH. BENGAL SABU

Ch. Bengal Sabu, imported and owned by Barbara Strebeigh, Tuck Dell and Harold Florsheim, and bred by Molly Harmsworth, was one of the most influential sires of modern times. He came to the United States in 1959 as an unshown yearling. By the time he was retired, he was a multiple BIS and Specialty winner, with a record that included seven ATCA Airedale Bowl wins. He sired dozens of champions, and was the founder of an Airedale dynasty that still shines today.

Jim McLynn's Ch. Talyn's River Rogue (multiple bowl winner—three times in 1968, two times in 1969, two times in 1970) was sired by Ch. Bengal Sabu and produced a bowl-winning (1971 and 1972) son, Ch. Talyn's Ironclad Leave, as well as several winning Dandyaire dogs for Wilma Carter.

Champions Birchrun Bartender, Bash 'em and Prizefighter, all sons of the great Sabu, produced nicely for the Blackburns and the Buccaneer Kennels, and of course for Barbara Strebeigh and Adele Abe of Birchrun fame.

Another dog to leave his mark was Bengal Turith Comet. Imported by Ric Chashoudian, Comet was bred the next day to Ch. Bravo Bonanza Belle de AAA, owned by Hub Zempke. This was to be his one and only breeding, as several days later he suddenly died.

CH. BRAVO TRUE GRIT

Fortunately for the breed, Ch. Bravo Bonanza Belle whelped an outstanding litter. Ric, who raised the pups, was especially taken with two males. Although they were different types, they were both outstanding. At six months, Bravo True Grit was the more mature of the two pups, while Bravo Star Buck was the more lean and elegant one, that just needed time to body out.

Ric began showing True Grit. Realizing he had all the makings of a "great one," except financial backing, Ric asked Janet Framke to find inter-

Ch. Finlair Lyon of Stone Ridge (litter brother to "Gator"), owned by Paul Gyori, handled by Bob Larouech. *Booth*

Ch. Argus Stone Ridge Hunky Dory (Supermaster son) won the ATCA Airedale Bowl in 1975 with handler Ric Chashoudian. *Shafer*

Ch. Optimist of Mynair, imported by Stone Ridge Kennels, twice won the ATCA Airedale Bowl in 1973; handler George Ward. *Booth*

80

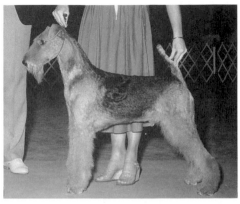

Ch. Stone Ridge Strongbow (Ch. Bravo True Grit ex Ch. Clarkedale Joy D'Evalynn). *Ashbey*

Ch. Jolee Aire's William Tell (Strongbow son, True Grit grandson). *Booth*

Ch. Bravo True Grit was Best in Show at the Montgomery County Specialty handled by fourteen-year-old Philip Fitzpatrick III. *Ashbey*

ested backers. Janet got together a group of True Grit admirers consisting of Trudy and Trevor Evans (Bryn-Hafod), Gary and Joanne Vohs (Jolee Aire), Evalynn Wolf (Evalynn) and herself (Stone Ridge). The group, sometimes referred to as "The Syndicate," was reminiscent of the days when Barbara Strebeigh, Tuck Dell and Harold Florsheim pooled resources to campaign Ch. Bengal Sabu.

Ch. Bravo True Grit won the ATCA Bowl in Minnesota in 1981. He won not only the bowl under Arthur Lodge (Mynair Kennels) at Montgomery County (largest Terrier show in the world) but, handled by fourteen-year-old Philip Fitzpatrick III, went on to Best in Show under Barbara Keenan. Needless to say, the crowd gathered at ringside for Best in Show went wild! To see this sweet, polite, fourteen-year-old with black horn-rimmed glasses and braces beat the top Terriers and their seasoned handlers from all over the country was the thrill of a lifetime!

From there, "Toby" went on to win the Bowl in Illinois and Houston, Texas, and Montgomery County again in 1982. While he was a great show dog, True Grit's greatest legacy is in the top-winning get he sired and the mark he left on the breed. True Grit's most famous son to date has to be Ch. Finlair Tiger of Stone Ridge, known to all as "Gator."

From True Grit came other sons to be reckoned with. Ch. Stone Ridge Strongbow and his brother Ch. Stone Ridge Bucko Bravo were out of Ch. Clarkedale Joy D'Evalynn. Strongbow was BOW at Montgomery County in 1983, owned and handled by Gary Vohs of Jolee Aire Kennels in Wisconsin. In 1989 he won the Veterans' Class at Montgomery County owner-handled by Lotus Tutton of Fairewood Kennels in Canada.

Strongbow produced Ch. Jolee Aire William Tell, who won the ATCI Sweepstakes in 1985, following in his sire's paw prints. "Bo" won the ATCI sweeps in 1983. William Tell sired Ch. Nipmuc Lord Philip, CD, for Ed and Bonnie Peterson of Montpelier, Vermont, and his littermate, Ch. Nimuc Lord Theodore, for the Augs in Illinois.

A great-grandson of Sabu was Brulyn's Baha-Dur. He was the sire of two of Arthur and Mavis Lodge's top-winning Airedales, Ch. Optimist of Mynair and his brother Int. Ch. Oscar of Mynair. Optimist was top Airedale in England in 1970. He was imported by Stone Ridge Kennels to win the Airedale Bowl twice in 1971, and in 1973 to go Best of Breed at Westminster. Oscar is behind June Dutcher's Australian import Ch. Strongfort Saturn, who, in turn, produced Ch. Sunnydale's Satellite, Ch. Sunnydale's Schweppes and Ch. Coppercrest Queen's Counsel. Optimist also sired Am. & Can. Ch. Jolee Aire Stone Ridge Stomp, number one Airedale in Canada. Stomp sired two more number one Airedales in Canada for the MacLarens and Carole and Al Preece.

Ch. Bengal Flyer (brother to Figaro) was another English Best in Show dog behind some of our best lines. A Flyer son, Ch. Aristocrat of White House, produced Carl and Sarah Macklin's champions Harbour Hills Iroquoi, Indian Ink and Millhouse. Flyer also sired Jim McLynn's Ch. Talyn's Yohorum, a top winner for several years.

Ch. Strongfort Saturn (Australian import by Copper-crest Kennels), judge Neoma Eberhardt, handler Robert Milano. *Lindemaier*

Am. & Can. Ch. Coppercrest Queen's Counsel (Saturn son), owned by Alncaire Kennels of Al and Carole Preece of Canada. *Missy*

Ch. Sunnydale Satellite (Saturn son), bred and owned by Sunnydale Kennels. *Bergman*

Ch. Sunnydale's Viva Zipata (Satellite son), bred and owned by Sunnydale Kennels.

Int. Ch. Stone Ridge Bengal Bravo (Sahib son).

Int. Ch. Bengal Sahib—top Terrier in England, 1980, imported by Stone Ridge Kennels.

Ch. M.J.'s Stone Ridge Chosen One (Bengal Bravo son), bred by Janet Framke, owned by Steve and Bonnie Gilbert, handled by Philip Fitzpatrick, won the ATCA Airedale Bowl under Judge Jane Forsyth. *Ashbey*

Ch. Bengal Gunga Din was the sire of Bengal Buldeo, who was imported by Virginia Bensman, the top midwest breeder and exhibitor for many years. Buldeo produced Ch. Bengal Flamboyant while still in England. Flamboyant is in the pedigree of many of our top dogs today.

Ch. Bengal Saladin (a Flamboyant son) is the sire of Int. Ch. Bengal Sahib, England's top terrier in 1980. Sahib was imported by Janet Framke, co-owned with Mrs. R. F. Clark, Jr. With Peter Green handling, Sahib was Winners Dog all three days at the Montgomery County weekend. Owner-handled, he won the Canadian National Specialty under Richard Hensel. Eventually he became number one Airedale in Argentina, imported there by the Fairyland Kennels of Julio De Christofaro.

Before leaving the United States, Sahib produced Mex. & Am. Ch. Stone Ridge Bengal Bravo, the Specialty winning sire of Ch. M.J.'s Stone Ridge Chosen One, owned by Bonnie and Steve Gilbert, and his littermate, Ch. Stone Ridge Shannon O'Regent, co-owned by Brian and Lotus Tutton of Canada and Martha Graham of Iowa.

Another lovely son of Bravo is Ch. Anfeald's Supernatural, owned and bred by Charles and Regina Foley, conceived during a snowstorm in Ohio in a Holiday Inn! (Ch. Anfeald's Moses was found under a bush in the Foleys' back yard during a rainstorm!) Raising Airedales is not always this difficult; Moses went on to win an Airedale Bowl while "Magic" is just starting his show career.

True Grit also sired Ch. Jolee Aire Stitch 'n Tyme and Ch. Jolee Aire Just 'n Tyme for the Vohs. The Salzbachs of Forepaughs Kennel in Minnesota bred to Strongbow, and got Ch. Forepaugh Pinball Wizard and Ch. Forepaugh's Prudential.

Another True Grit son came from the famous Eden Kennels of Memphis, Tennessee, owned by Betty and Beck Hoisington. Eden's Brass Bamboo was sold to the Vohs and finished by them.

For Texas, True Grit produced Ch. Briggsdale Bear Claw and Ch. Briggsdale Boss of Stone Ridge for Dick and Glenna Briggs, and for the Tartan Kennel and Forbes Gordon, Ch. Tartan's Oil Patch Poppa, Texas Ranger, Black Gold and Liquid Gold. Other top-winning True Grit sons are: Ch. Stone Ridge Jigsaw G-Man (a repeat breeding of Strongbow), Winners Dog at his first show, Montgomery County, from the Bred by Exhibitor class at nine months of age; and Doug and Aletta Moore's Ch. Epoch's Nineteen Eighty-four. Handled by Wood Wornall, "Orwell" was a Specialty winner and multiple Group placer.

True Grit also was the grandsire of Ch. Waggin-Aire's Jonah for Scott and Dottie Boeving of Wingate, North Carolina, and Terrydale's Admiral Drummer for Stephen and Mary Clark of Atherton, California. Drummer produced Ch. Terrydale's Avenging Angel and Ch. Terrydale Heaven Kan Wait.

Ch. Stone Ridge Fame of Fireside, CD, owned by Dick Framke, sired Ch. Stone Ridge American Storm, CD, Ch. Royalcrest New Generation and Ch. Royalcrest Oldham's Aquila.

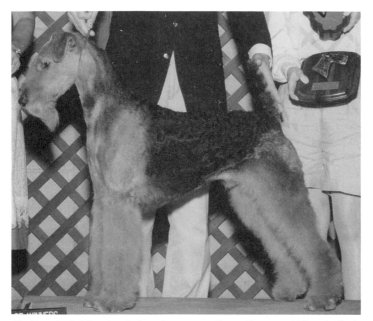

Ch. Bryn Hafod Sparhawk, breeders-owners Trevor Evans and Rhonda Davis.
Booth

Ch. Safari's Jack Armstrong, owners Don Ritter, Pat Patterson and Diana Dozier. *Rinehart*

CH. FINLAIR TIGER OF STONE RIDGE

"Gator's" dam was Kathy and Bob Finley's Ch. Finlair Bodacious. Thanks to the outstanding conditioning and handling of Bob La Rouech and the love and financial support of Bruck and Glenna Holmberg (Edgemont) of Park Ridge, Illinois, Gator became the top-winning Airedale of all time. He was number one Airedale 1983–1984 with twenty-five all-breed Bests in Show, including Best of Breed at the Westminster show in New York going on to Group IV, one of the few modern Airedales to win a Group placement at this prestigious show. He was Best of Breed at thirteen Specialties, winning the ATCA Bowl three times including his last show, where Gator came out of retirement for the one-hundred-year anniversary show to win the Bowl from the Veterans Class at Montgomery County. Gator has sired sixty-seven champions and recently celebrated his tenth birthday by receiving the news that he had just become a father again to nine bouncing puppies, which will probably add to his list of champion get.

CH. BRAVO STAR BUCK

Ch. Bravo Star Buck bodied out to a beautiful young dog and was purchased by Diana Dozier. Star Buck had a super show career, and proved his value by siring over sixty champions. In 1988 he won the Veterans Class at Montgomery County over several well-known senior citizens, and in 1989 he won the Stud Dog class at the Twin Cities Airedale Specialty in Minnesota. Star Buck lives in semi-retirement with Dick and Dianne Leslie in Minnesota and spends his time being the household gentleman-in-residence, playing with his puppies and teaching them to dig holes and share his delightful Airedale sense of humor.

One of his top sons was Ch. Blackjack's Mighty Samson, who won the ATCA Bowl at Montgomery County in 1984, shown by Peter Green for owners Tom and Sandy Pesota. He repeated his bowl win in Florida in 1985. Samson sired Ch. Blackjack's Nostradamus, who became an English champion and a Swedish champion, and was the top sire in England in 1988.

Another handsome son of Samson is Ch. Blackheath's Sam's Son, owned by Teresa Beyerle. Ch. Blackheath's Sizzling, also a Samson son, just finished his championship in 1989.

A repeat of Nostradamus's breeding produced Ch. Blackjack Ringo Starr, who became a champion in Argentina before being returned to the States to be shown to his championship by Connie Clark.

Ch. Bravo Comet's Streak is owned by Phyllis Madaus of Sanford, Florida. Streak is the sire of Ch. Hayrob's Jolly Jeremy.

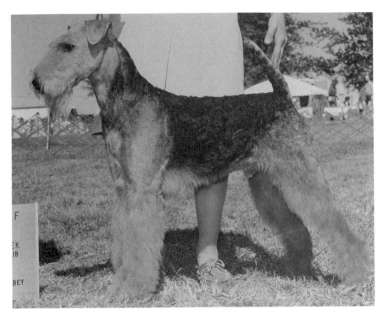

Am. & Can. Ch. Jokyl Fair Play, imported by Cyril and Bonnie Moyher (Semper Fi Kennels), handler Margery Good. *Ashbey*

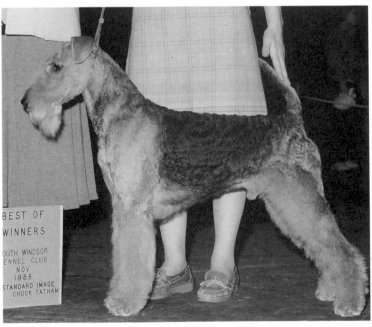

Ch. Stirling Jazz Dancer, bred by Dr. Shirley Good and Susan Rodgers, owned by David Goldman and Jacques Abbotto, handled by Margarey Good. *Tatham*

CH. TURITH COUNTRY COUSIN

Turith Country Cousin, the same breeding as Bengal Turith Comet, was imported by Roberta "Bobbie" Brennan. He produced Ch. White Rose Rocka My Soul and Ch. Allegro Vivace for Bobbie, as well as Ch. Maximus of Meadow Creek for the Griffin girls; Ch. Tartan's Chief of the Clan and Ch. Tartan's Country Bumpkin for Forbes Gordon; and Ch. Stirling's Great Legacy for Susan Rogers and Shirley Good. Other champion sons are Ch. Birchrun Six Boys Amos, Ch. Jolabar's Andy of Talyn and Ch. Seneca Country Sport.

CH. JOKYL BENGAL FIGARO

English, American, Canadian, German, Dutch Ch. Jokyl Bengal Figaro had an outstanding show career even before he was imported to the United States. Figaro also starred in the Walt Disney film *The Ballad of Hector*. Unfortunately he was not widely used at stud here because of rumors about his temperament. I would like to report that I had the good fortune of seeing him running freely through the home and estate of George and Olive Jackson (Jokyl) when he was nine years old. One could not have asked for a more wonderful, sweet and stable disposition in a dog!

While still in England, Figaro sired Eng. Ch. Jokyl Space Leader, who in turn sired Ch. Jokyl Prince Regent, a multiple bowl winner, and Figaro's most famous son, Eng. & Am. Ch. Jokyl Superman.

Superman was imported by Mr. and Mrs. Gilbert Morcroft and shown by Bill Thompson. In 1969 and 1970 Superman led the breed in all systems. Superman was bred by J. E. Derrick and was the greatest sire of that decade, succeeding Sabu for that title.

He sired Ch. Lay Dee Ayr's Wakanda for Dave and Dee Leahy, Ch. Suzark Open Sesame for Park Peters and Ch. Harbour Hill's Klark Kent for Carl and Sarah Macklin. Wilma Carter's Superman son, Ch. Dandyaire's Quickfire, won the New England Bowl.

One of Superman's most outstanding sons was Ch. Jokyl Supermaster, bred by Olive Jackson and imported by Dr. and Mrs. F. Neal Johnson (Stone Ridge). Supermaster was a Best in Show and Airedale bowl winner, and produced Ch. Argus Stone Ridge Hunky Dory (a multiple Bowl winner, who in turn produced Ch. Stone Ridge Seventy-six, also a Best in Show and multiple Specialty winner).

Bred to Bob and Betty Hoisington's Ch. Bengal Springtime, Supermaster sired Ch. Eden's Spring Hepatica. This promising dog swallowed a baby pacifier and tragically died at a young age, but not before producing one of the loveliest Airedales ever, Ch. Eden's Sal Sorbus. You will find this great dog in the pedigree of many of today's top-winning Airedales.

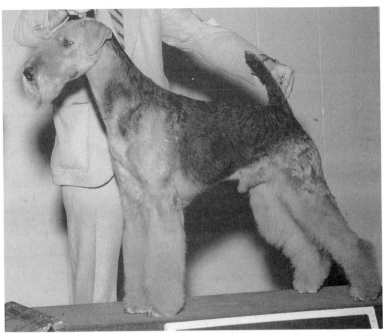

Ch. Turith Forrester of Junaken, imported and owned by Carol Scott and Rose Richards. *Cott/Francis*

Ch. Jokyl Supercopy, imported and owned by Pam and John Rorke.
Booth

91

Ch. Jokyl Superman, imported and owned by Gilbert Morcroft.   *Tauske*

Ch. Jokyl Supermaster, top Airedale in England in 1970.

Ch. Eden's Sal Sorbus (Ch. Eden's Hepatica ex Ch. Bengal Springtime (Super-master grandson), owned by Betty and Beck Hoisington of Eden Kennels.

Ludwig

ENG. CH. SICCAWEI GALLIARD

Eng. Ch. Siccawei Galliard was a top producer in England in the 1970s and sired Ch. Jokyl Cinerama, imported by Joan Bolton of Tropic-Aire Kennels in Florida.

Ch. Turith Brigand (a Galliard son) produced Ch. Glentop's Krackerjack, another of England's top winners. Krackerjack is the grandsire of Ch. Glentop's Yentl, CD, imported and co-owned by Mike and Denise Tobey and Janet Framke. Yentl produced Ch. Stone Ridge Traveler (Winners Dog at Montgomery County) for Judith Ball of Washington. Traveler is out of Ch. Clarkedale Joy D'Evalynn, and was bred to Ch. Coppercrest Dinah's Krystal, producing some lovely pups soon to be seen in the ring.

Another Galliard top-winning son was Ch. Turith Adonis, owned by Walter Troutman. Adonis won the Airedale Bowl nine times, Best of Breed at Westminster three consecutive years and sired the record holding CC winner in England, Perincourt Playful, England's 1979 Dog of the Year.

Galliard also produced Eng. Ch. Jokyl Gallipants, who sired Ch. Jokyl Hillcross Hot Rod, imported by John and Pam Rorke of Michigan, and Ch. Shadli Fantom, imported by Rose Richards of California.

The Eden Kennel (Betty Hoisington) imported two Galliard sons, Eng. & Am. Ch. Jokyl Spic N' Span and, later, Jokyl Speedy Bairn of Eden. Spic produced Ch. Piccadilly's Patent Pending, Ch. Eden's Leucojum, Ch. Flintkote Galahad and Ch. Stone Ridge Simonize and his litter mate Ch. Stone Ridge Phase III, owned by Nancy and Del Whitney of Long Grove, Illinois.

Simonize, co-owned by Mary Curran and Janet Framke, won the Montgomery County Sweepstake and later won an Airedale Bowl in Atlanta in 1976. He sired Ch. Stone Ridge Inspector Clouseau, CDX.

Another son of Spic was Briardale Shshown Indian, who in turn sired Int. Ch. Shshown Que Forte, CD, who had many champion sons but is best known for siring the Best in Show bitch Ch. Briardale's Luv's Elegant Lady, out of Ch. Wafer's April Luv of Briardale. Another Spic son, Ch. Schaire's Ajax, sired Ch. Schaire's Doctor Jakyl, CDX, for breeder Joey Finneran in Pennsylvania and owner-handler Nancy Sutphen. Ch. Jokyl Fair Play, imported by Cyril and Bonnie Moyer of Virginia, is a great-great-grandson of Spic N' Span.

Ch. Jokyl Supercopy (a Spic grandson) was imported by Pam and John Rorke of Michigan, and produced Ch. Rorke's Prime Rib and Ch. Rorke's Canned Heat.

Another Galliard son to be noted was Ch. Saredon Military Man, sire of Eng. & Am. Ch. Turith Echelon of Saredon, imported by Lewis and Carol Scott for their Scottshire dogs. "Reggie," as he was fondly called, sired Ch. Santana's Wild Bill, Ch. Scottshire's Ambassador Toby, Ch. Bravo Echelon of Santeric (sire of Ch. Scottshire's Black Bart, whose painting became famous) and Ch. Meadow Creeks Kinetic Comet for breeders John and Suzanne Hampton, who sold him to Joan and Carol Griffin. For Dick and Diane Schlicht of

Ch. Glentop's Yentl, CD, owners Mike and Denise Tobey and Janet Framke.

Ross

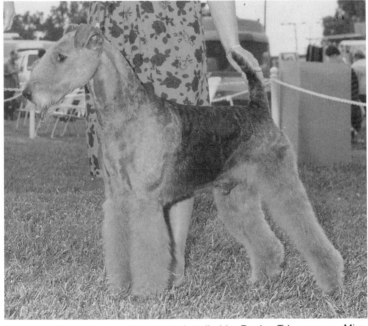

Ch. Stone Ridge Traveler (Yentl son), handled by Denise Tobey. *Missy*

Ch. Turith Echelon of Saredon, imported and owned by Lew and Carol Scott of Scott-shire Airedales.

Ch. Bravo Ironman of Santeric, owned by Carol Scott.

Am. & Can. Ch. Fonaire Iron Ancistrodon (Ironman son), bred by the Fontaines of Canada, owned by Carol Scott and Rose Richards. *Ashbey*

Ch. D'Aire Whistlin' Dixie (Ch. D'Aire Upper Echelon ex Ch. D'Aire Windsong, True Grit grandson), bred and owned by D'Aire Kennels.

the D'Aire Kennels in Minnesota, he produced Ch. D'Aire's Upper Echelon, sire of Ch. D'Aire's Whistlin' Dixie, a Group winner. Another son was Ch. Bravo Ironman of Santeric, sire of Am. & Can. Ch. Fonaire Iron Ancistrodon, bred by the Fontaines of Quebec, Canada, but owned and campaigned by Rose Richards of Blazoncrest and Carol Scott of Scottshire.

ENG. CH. LANEWOOD LYSANDER—THE LINE OF DESCENT

Coming down the line of male descent from Eng. Ch. Riverina Siccawei Phoebus is Eng. Ch. Lanewood Lysander. From him came So. Afr. Ch. Bengal Skipper of Limebell. Next down the line is Ch. Bengal Leprechaun, who emigrated to the United States. From Leprechaun, bred to Ch. Bengal Bibi, came Ch. Bilmar Bengal Fere of Barbate, the first to carry the kennel prefix of Sybil and Sherwin Kevy. From him came Barbate Chiparoo, sire of Ch. Rivendell Angus, Winners Dog at Montgomery County in 1973. From Angus came Ch. Anfeald Irish Whisky. Another Chiparoo son is Ch. Britham Lord of the Rings, the sire of Ch. Britham Croissants.

To return to Ch. Bilmar Bengal Fere of Barbate, another son, Barbate Chorister, sired Barbate Dante. Dante was the sire of Ch. Barbate Henchman. Henchman came to the west coast and sired ten champions.

For the Birchrun kennel of Barbara Strebeigh, Leprechaun sired Ch. Birchrun's Most Happy Fella. He sired Ch. Jackson's Conquistador and Ch. Sir Terry of Indianaire for Carl Silver in Arizona. Ch. Jackson's Conquistador kept the line going by siring Ch. Jackson's Lord Lashbrook, Ch. Jackson's John Paul Jones (the sire of Ch. Meadowlark's Aristotle) and Ch. Jackson's Calculator (sire of Ch. Jackson's Sir John Falstaff).

Before leaving England, Bengal Skipper of Limebell sired Bengal Leander, who sired Ch. Bengal Havildar, who was imported to the United States and owned by Betty Hoisington. For her he sired four champions, Ch. Eden's Jon-Quil, Ch. Eden's Dandilion, Ch. Eden's Zwart Narcis and Ch. Eden's Dutchman of Senoj. For Coppercrest he sired Ch. Coppercrest Cosmopolitan.

Another son that emigrated to the United States was Eng. & Am. Ch. Jokyl Bengal Lionheart, co-owned by Charley Marck and Miss Sarah Coleman Brock, handled by Ric Chashoudian. "Skipper" was used at stud extensively; among his get are Ch. Cyrano Apollo (winner of the Ch. Lionheart Comet Memorial Bowl from the classes), Ch. Cyrano Admiral's Alert and Ch. Lion Hill MacDuff.

For Kitty and Wally Nesbitt, Skipper sired Ch. Tibsen's Skipper's Hercules and Ch. Tibsen's Diamond Jim. For the Lionheart Kennel of Miss Brock, he sired Ch. Lionheart Gladwyn. For Georgiana Wooldridge's Scatterfoot Kennel, he sired Ch. Scatterfoot My Boy Sam. And for Karl Nelson of the Flintkote prefix came Ch. Flintkote Jokyl Krackerjack, who won the Mila Brodie gold medal award for Sweepstakes winner of the SCAA in 1970. Krackerjack kept the line going by producing Ch. Flintkote Jack's Red Alert and Ch. Flintkote Jack's Lord Byron.

Ch. Coppercrest Rifleman (Winstony Exceptional son), owned by Lynn Donaldson. *Ludwig*

Ch. Coppercrest Tempest (Rifleman son), owner Virginia Latham. *Missy*

Another son from the Lionheart Kennels was Lionheart Ute, who sired Ch. Lionheart Factor, winner of the regional SCAA Specialty and the Ch. Lionheart Comet Memorial Bowl in 1970 and again in 1971. Factor sired the Pekarskys' Ch. Ironsides Pek's Bad Boy; from Pek's Bad Boy came Ch. Ironsides Pacific Station, who won the ATCA Airedale Bowl at Montgomery County in 1975. Pacific Station sired Ch. Ironsides Skipper and Ch. Ironsides Skuttlebutt, the sire of Ironside's Battle Station.

For the Golliwog prefix of Maggie Hochstettler, Pek's Bad Boy sired Ch. Golliwog's Ichabod Crane and Ch. Golliwog's Infidel.

To get back to Factor, son Ch. Blazon Lionheart Victor, owned by Pat McDonough, was handled by Bob Jordan to impressive wins, and another son was Ch. Blazon Lionheart Fax Favour.

Lionheart Ute continued the line by siring Ch. Briardale Charlie Brown, sire of Ch. Briardale Kung Fu, for Carole Bullwinkle. Kung Fu had the honor of winning the Lionheart Comet Memorial Bowl in June 1977 at the SCAA Regional Specialty on Saturday, then repeating his Best of Breed win on Sunday to take the ATCA Airedale Bowl under Australian judge Ernest Schache. Kung Fu continued the legacy by siring four champions, including Ch. Finlair Banquo, who in turn sired Ch. Briardale's Prodigal Son, Ch. Corgaire's Foxfire and Ch. Hubbard's Corgaire's Gator, the sire of Ch. Hubbard's Garnet Ray.

To return to Eng. Ch. Lanewood Lysander, another son who came to the United States was Ch. Winstony Exceptional, owned and exhibited by May Pridham of the Sierradale Kennels. Coppercrest Kennels took advantage of breeding their Ch. Coppercrest Red Marvel to this import; together they produced four champions, Ch. Coppercrest Ramrod, Ch. Coppercrest Rifleman, Ch. Coppercrest Redstone Rufus and Ch. Coppercrest Irish Lady.

Ch. Coppercrest Ramrod, known as "Gringo," produced son Ch. Coppercrest Courier, and from a Stoney Burke daughter, produced Ch. Coppercrest Santana; when she was bred back to her father, she produced Saltisan, who when bred to Ch. Sunnydale's Doc Holiday, produced the ATCA Airedale Bowl–winning Ch. Sunnydale Coppercrest Dinah, thus repeating the bowl-winning tradition of her great-great grandmother Tim Tam in 1962, and her grandfather Ramrod in 1972. Ch. Coppercrest Rifleman ("Poncho") sired Best in Show son Ch. Terragate Adobe Red out of Ch. Sunnydale's Gold Digger, a Ch. Sunnydale Bouncin' Billie daughter and sister to Am. & Can. Ch. Sunnydale's Ginny Robin, winner of seven Bests in Show.

Rifleman sired three male champions: Ch. Coppercrest Tempest, Ch. Brigand of Coppercrest and Ch. Terragate's Adobe Red, who sired Ch. Cymbeline Richmond Rascal, Ch. Adobe Brick O'Sullivan and Ch. Devonshire's Red Alert.

Another Winstony son was Ch. Roy-Al Coppercrest, who was exported to Japan and is showing up in Japanese pedigrees. For owner May Pridham, Winstony sired Ch. Sierradale Warbow, the father of Ch. Sierradale El Jefe.

6

Leading Ladies—Past, Present and Future

T HE DISTAFF SIDE of the Airedale world took women's lib literally and have come into their own, rivaling their male counterparts for the top wins. In this chapter we review many of the foundation bitches of several kennels and their progeny.

AM. & ENG. CH. BENGAL SPRINGTIME

Am. & Eng. Ch. Bengal Springtime was imported to the United States by Betty Hoisington; however, before leaving England, "Spring" produced Eng. Ch. Bengal Flamboyant, who sired Ch. Bengal Donna, dam of thirteen champions, including Ch. Bengal Veda by Ch. Bengal Mogul and Ch. Blackburn's Angelita Grande by Can. Ch. Bengal Badrudin. Also from Spring's son Flamboyant came Eng. Ch. Bengal Biscuit, whose son Eng. & Arg. Ch. Bengal Tarquin sired the well-known Ch. Turith Country Cousin and Bengal Turith Comet when bred to Prelude of Turith. From Flamboyant, when bred to Eng. Ch. Siccawei Impudent Miss, came Eng. Ch. Siccawei Galliard, who with Prelude of Turith produced Ch. Turith Adonis and Ch. Turith Forrester of Junaken. Galliard, bred to Ch. Jokyl Cinderella, produced Ch. Jokyl Cinerama, sire of Tropic-Aire Alter Ego for the Boltons of Florida. Another offspring of the Galliard ex Cinderella match was Aust. Ch. Jokyl Cinella, dam of Ch. Strongfort Saturn.

Eng. & Am. Ch. Bengal Springtime, imported and loved by Betty Hoisington and daughter Bec.

Jokyl Baby Bewitched of Eden (daughter of Eng. Ch. Siccawei Galliard), dam of four champions sired by Ch. Eden's Sal Sorbus.

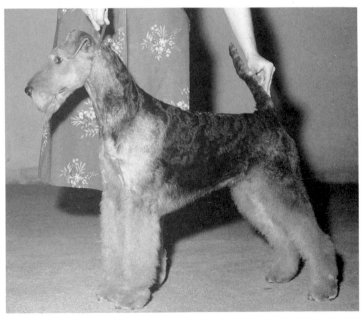

Ch. American Dream, owned by Mike and Denise Tobey. *Lindemaier*

Ch. Stone Ridge Patty O'Rorke, owners Pam and John Rorke.
Booth

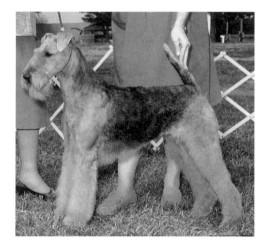

Ch. Rorke's Queen of Hearts (by Ch. Jokyl Supercopy ex Pattie O'Rorke), breeders-owners Pam and John Rorke.
Booth

Ch. Lancelot Wendy's Samantha (Ch. Black Jack's Mighty Samson ex Ch. Lancelot Lady Gwendolyn) won BOB at the New England Specialty; Judge Stig Ahlberg, handler Peter Green, owner Lucia Carballo.
Ashbey

104

When Galliard was bred to Jokyl Baby Bunting, they produced Ch. Westmoor's Warlock, the sire of Ch. Clarkedale Joy D'Evalynn. Galliard's son, Ch. Saredon Military Man, bred to Prelude of Turith produced Am. & Eng. Ch. Turith Echelon of Saredon. Daughter Jenirox Cora, bred to Loudwell Krisp, produced Eng. Ch. Jenirox Katie Krunch who, bred to Adonis, produced Ch. Blackjack Rambling Rose and Ch. Blackjack Tom Terrorific; bred to Ch. Bravo Star Buck, she produced Ch. Blackjack Chemin-de-Fer and litter brother Ch. Blackjack Mighty Samson.

Bred to Ch. Jokyl Supermaster, Spring produced Ch. Eden's Spring Hepatica, sire of Eden's great Ch. Eden's Sal Sorbus. Spring's descending line has gone on and on until she has a listing of over four hundred progeny carrying her genes.

CH. BURNWEEL BESSIE

Another great bitch and the originator of a long line of descendants is Ch. Burnweel Bessie, owned by Wilma Carter. "Coffee" was a daughter of Eng. & Am. Ch. Murose Replica ex Cinnabar Almaden. Bred to Ch. Aireline Star Monarch, Coffee produced Ch. Chancrest Topper, Ch. Dandyaire Carmichael Cowboy and Ch. Dandyaire Cottage Commando, CD, who, bred to Ch. Foxglove Joy, produced Dandyaire Enjoyment, who, with Ch. Talyn's Yohorum, produced Chahoudis Boom Boom La Rue, dam of Ch. Ironsides Pek's Bad Boy, the start of the Ironsides Kennel of the Pekarskys. He sired Ch. Ironsides Pacific Station, ATCA Airedale Bowl winner in 1975. A sister to Pek's Bad Boy was Ch. Briardale's Big Bertha. Bertha, daughter of Ch. Lionheart Factor, was bred to Lionheart Ute to produce Ch. Briardale's Charlie Brown; he in turn, when bred to Briardale Duchess of Windsor, produced Ch. Briardale Kung Fu (ATCA Airedale Bowl winner in 1977). Kung Fu, bred to Kathy and Bob Finley's Ch. Finlair Kitty of Red En Nad, produced Ch. Finlair Banquo, Ch. Finlair Bodacious and Ch. Finlair Briardale Barnstorm. Ch. Finlair Bodacious, bred to Best in Show Ch. Bravo True Grit, produced Best in Show Ch. Finlair Tiger of Stone Ridge and Best in Show Ch. Finlair Isis in a repeat breeding. Kung Fu, when bred to Ch. Dandyaire Venus, produced Ch. Wafer April Luv of Briardale, dam of Best in Show Ch. Briardale Luv's Elegant Lady, dam of Best in Show Ch. Terrydale's Adorable Lady.

Ch. Aireline Star Monarch's daughter Ch. Dandyaire For Cinnabar bred to Ch. Wraggletaggle Checkmate produced Ch. Dandyaire Cinnabar Gadabout and Ch. Dandyaire Cinnabar Gremlin, who sired Ch. Carryall of Dandyaire, the dam of Dandyaire Kaniksu (by Ch. Bengal Flyer). Kaniksu, bred to Ch. Talyn's River Rogue, produced Ch. Dandyaire Monarch, Ch. Dandyaire Matthew and Ch. Dandyaire Mephisto, the sire of Ch. Golliwog's Obeah, who was owned and campaigned by John and Jill Fanning; from her came many of the Waggery champions, including Ch. Waggery's Circe of Tarawood and Ch. Waggery's California Comet.

Ch. Dandyaire Kaniksu, dam of 12 champions (Ch. Bengal Flyer ex Am. & Can. Ch. Carryall of Dandyaire), breeder-owner Wilma Carter.

Ch. Dandyaire Quite Contrary (Ch. Jokyl Superman ex Ch. Dandyaire Kaniksu), dam of seven champions; breeder-owner Wilma Carter.

Ch. Dandyaire Brass Band, dam of 5 champions (Ch. Sunnydale's Holmes ex Dandyaire Xpresso Lady), breeder-owner Wilma Carter. *Missy*

Ch. Dandyaire Easy Street (Brass Band daughter), breeder-owner Wilma Carter. *Missy*

Ch. Coppercrest Irish Lady (Ch. Winstony Exceptional ex Ch. Coppercrest Red Marvel), owned by Bruce and Thalia Hart. *Ludwig*

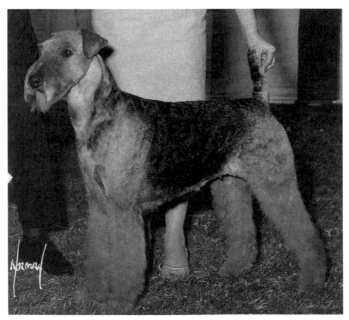

Ch. Scatterfoot Tim Tam (Am. & Can. Ch. Aireline Star Monarch ex Scatterfoot Lady), was Best of Breed from the classes at the SCAA Specialty under breeder-judge Cecil Schoeneck (Hatdale Kennels) winning the ATCA Airedale Bowl, Lionheart Comet Memorial Bowl and Lou Holiday Memorial Silver Tray. Daisy Austad handled her for owners June and Robin Dutcher. *Norman*

Kaniksu, bred to Ch. Talyn's River Rogue, produced Ch. Dandyaire Miss Bristol, foundation bitch of Georgia and Russ McRae's Brisline's Airedales.

CH. SCATTERFOOT TIM TAM

Ch. Scatterfoot Tim Tam (Am. & Can. Ch. Aireline Star Monarch ex Scatterfoot Lady) was the foundation bitch for the Dutchers' Coppercrest Kennels. She won the SCAA Specialty and the ATCA Airedale Bowl in 1962. When Tim Tam was bred to Gladys Brown Edwards's Ch. Studio Liontamer, she produced daughter Ch. Scatterfoot Sheba and son Scatterfoot Mr. Magoo. Unfortunately the veterinarian docked the tails too short to be shown on the rest of the litter; still, son Coppercrest Brandy became a forceful stud dog. Tim Tam bred to Ch. Town Girl's Challenge produced her famous "Red" litter: Ch. Coppercrest Red Blaze, Ch. Coppercrest Red Flame, Ch. Coppercrest Red Rocket, Ch. Coppercrest Red Marvel, Ch. Coppercrest Red Flare and Coppercrest Red Queen. Rocket and Queen each produced a champion when bred to Ch. Dandyaire Cinnabar Gremlin. Ch. Coppercrest Red Flare, bred to Brandy's son Siouxaire's Chief Duff, produced Ch. Love's Stoney Burke, who, when bred back to his dam's little sister, Red Marvel, produced Ch. Coppercrest Royal Rendition (winner of the New England Specialty and the New King Bowl and the Wm. L. Barclay trophy for BOS in 1970 at Westminster), Ch. Coppercrest Royal Request and Ch. Coppercrest Royal Regalia. Red Marvel, or "Margay" as she was called, bred to Ch. Winstony Exceptional (imported son of Eng. Ch. Lanewood Lysander) produced four champions: Ch. Coppercrest Ramrod (ATCA Airedale Bowl winner in 1972), Ch. Coppercrest Rifleman, Ch. Coppercrest Redstone Rufus and Ch. Coppercrest Irish Lady (1973 winner of the Wm. L. Barclay trophy for BOS at Montgomery County). Ch. Coppercrest Red Flare was inbred to her son Ch. Love's Stoney Burke, producing Ch. Geoffrey Earl of Stratford, who sired Ch. Jerilee's Jumping Jericho (winner of the Montgomery Specialty and the ATCA Airedale Bowl in 1976) and Ch. Sunnydale's Doc Holiday, destined to become one of the breed's leading sires.

To get back to Margay's son Ch. Coppercrest Ramrod, when inbred to his daughter Ch. Coppercrest Santana, produced Coppercrest Saltisan, bred to Ch. Sunnydale's Doc Holiday to produce Ch. Coppercrest Kiesta Fiesta, Ch. Anfeald Charlie's Angel (Winners Bitch Montgomery County 1982), Ch. Morgan Earl of Stratford (BIS in Canada) and Ch. Sunnydale Coppercrest Dinah (who won the ATCA Airedale Bowl twice in three weeks in 1983, first on the west coast and second at Montgomery County [east coast], being the first bitch to win the breed at Montgomery County in twenty-five years).

CH. SUNNYDALE'S HOLIDAY

Ch. Sunnydale's Holiday, foundation bitch at the Sunnydale Kennels of Jack and Mary Sanderson, was sired by Eng. & Am. Ch. Jokyl Superior ex River-aire Proud Piper. "Holly" bred to Ch. Geoffey Earl of Stratford produced Ch. Sunnydale Doc Holiday and Ch. Sunnydale Dame Holiday. Doc bred to Ch. Sunnydale's Bouncing Billie (Dandyaire Quebec Ike ex Ch. Dandyaire Lots O'Happiness) produced Ch. Sunnydale's Ginny Robin and Ch. Sunnydale's Gold Digger. Am. & Can. Ch. Sunnydale's Ginny Robin blazed a streak of seven Bests in Show, starting as a youngster by winning the Northern California Sweepstakes and the Southern California Sweepstakes handled by Suzanne Sanderson, daughter of Jack and Mary. Ginny Robin went BOS to win the Wm. L. Barclay Memorial for 1977 at Montgomery County handled by Clay Coady. When she grew up, she went on the show road with handler Paul Booher, which culminated in winning the ATCA Airedale Bowl at the Floating Specialty in Washington on Saturday under breeder-judge Charles Foley; and then on Sunday went Best of Breed, Group I, and Best in Show.

Ch. Sunnydale's Gold Digger bred to Ch. Coppercrest Rifleman produced the Best in Show Ch. Terragate Adobe Red.

CH. SUNNYDALE COPPERCREST DINAH

Dinah was co-owned by the Sandersons and breeder June Dutcher. She started her rise to fame by going Winners Bitch and Best Opposite Sex at the Floating Specialty at Atlanta in 1983, and went on to win the ATCA Airedale Terrier Bowl at the Floating Specialty at San Raphael, California, under Judge Annemarie Moore. Three weeks later she again won the ATCA Airedale Bowl by going Best of Breed at Montgomery County under breeder-judge Charles Foley. Dinah was the first bitch to win Best of Breed at Montgomery County since Fiona, twenty-seven years before. On that day she had her name placed on the Willinez Defiance Memorial Trophy (offered if the BOB is American-bred and the owner is an ATCA member) and also the Harold Florsheim Memorial Trophy (offered to the BOB winner if American-bred) at Montgomery County.

In October 1983 Dinah's show career came to an untimely end when she was lost by the airline while en route home from a show. When found, it was determined she had sustained some brain damage. Dinah was bred to Ch. Stone Ridge Strongbow and produced a litter of five, including Ch. Coppercrest Dinah's Krystal, who made her championship within three weeks by going Winners Bitch at two Colorado shows, one of them being a Floating Specialty judged by Annemarie Moore, and winning the Sweepstakes under breeder-judge Marion Simmonson. Litter sister Ch. Coppercrest Dinah's Alexis finished, but litter brother Coppercrest Dinah's Blake was not shown

Ch. Sunnydale Coppercrest Dinah (Ch. Sunnydale's Doc Holiday ex Coppercrest Saltisan, Santana granddaughter) won Best of Breed at Montgomery County All-Terrier show. Judge was Charles Foley, handler Robert Milano, breeders-owners June and Robin Dutcher. Dinah was the first bitch to win Best of Breed at Montgomery County in twenty-five years.

Ashbey

Ch. Coppercrest Dinah's Krystal (Ch. Stone Ridge Strongbow ex Ch. Sunnydale Coppercrest Dinah), breeder-owner Coppercrest Kennels. She finished in four shows. *Ludwig*

Ch. Anfeald Charlie's Angel (Ch. Sunnydale Doc Holiday ex Coppercrest Saltisan, litter sister to Dinah), owned by Charles and Regina Foley.

Ashbey

Ch. Anfeald Lo and Behold (Ch. Anfeald Moses ex Ch. Anfeald Charlie's Angel), breeders-owners Charles and Regina Foley. *Tatham*

because his sisters bit his tail, causing severe damage. Although the tail recovered after several surgeries, the dog was extremely sensitive about anyone touching it. Bred to Ch. Sunnydale's Satellite (Ch. Strongfort Saturn ex Ch. Sunnydale's Oriole's Song, daughter of Sunnydale Ginny Robin), she produced Ch. Coppercrest Dinah's Jason.

CH. TALYN'S BLACKEYED SUSAN

Ch. Talyn's Blackeyed Susan (Ch. Tedhurst Major ex Ch. Lavender Hills Heather), when bred to Ch. Danrow of Farouk, produced Ch. Talyn's Tom Tom and Ch. Talyn's Tuppence, who produced eleven champions including Ch. Talyn's Yohorum, Ch. Talyn's Yankee Clipper and Ch. Talyn's You Betcha, who with Ch. Bengal Sabu produced Ch. Talyn's River Rogue. Tuppence bred to Ch. Bengal Leprechaun produced Ch. Talyn's Ironclad Leave; when bred to Ch. Jokyl Bengal Figaro, she produced Ch. Talyn's Man About Town. Among Yohorum, River Rogue, Man About Town and Ironclad Leave (all descending from "Susie"), they have won the ATCA Airedale Bowl eleven times, a record for an American kennel.

CH. REFFAL QUALITY QUEEN

Ch. Reffal Quality Queen (Int. Ch. Jokyl Bengal Figaro ex Ch. Reffal Humdinger, CDX) was bred to Am. & Eng. Ch. Jokyl Superman, producing Ch. Lay Dee Ayr's Wakanda, who produced six champions. Queen was bred twice to Ch. Lay Dee Ayr's Nicodemus, twice to Ch. Jokyl Superman and once to her son by Nicodemus, Ch. Lay Dee Ayre's Hi-Jacker, whose daughter Ch. Lay Dee Ayre's Captivator produced three champions by Ch. Sunnydale's Doc Holiday, while another daughter, Ch. Westmoor's Lady Serina, produced five champions.

BUCCANEER'S BABETTE'S CLARION

Buccaneer's Babette's Clarion ("Candy") was the foundation bitch at Moraine Kennels. Candy bred to Ch. Jokyl Superman produced Ch. Moraine Bright Promise who, when bred to Eng. & Am. Ch. Optimist of Mynair, produced five champions—among them, Ch. Moraine Bold Ruler and Ch. Moraine Promises, Promises. Promises, Promises bred to Ch. Jokyl Supermaster produced Ch. Moraine Promise Her Anything, who in turn bred to Ch. Turith Adonis produced Ch. Promises to Keep, herself the dam of five champions. The sister of Promises, Promises, Ch. Tempestuous Corus, produced seven champions. Bright Promise bred to Jokyl Prince Regent produced Ch. Moraine Bold Ruler, the sire of eight champions, including Ch. Moraine

Ch. Sunnydale's Ginny Robin (Ch. Sunnydale's Doc Holiday ex Ch. Sunnydale's Bouncing Billie) won Best in Show, handled by Paul Booher for breeders-owners Jack and Mary Sanderson. *Callea*

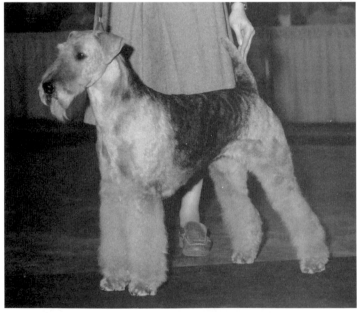

Ch. Moraine Promises to Keep (Ch. Turith Adonis ex Ch. Moraine Promise Her Anything), breeder-owner Mareth Kipp. *Shater*

Ch. Dandyaire Miss Bristol (Ch. Talyn's River Rogue ex Ch. Dandyaire Kaniksu), foundation bitch for Brisline Airedales.

Ch. Sunnydale's Ho-Ray for Brisline (Ch. Sunnydale's Doc Holiday ex Ch. Sunnydale's Bouncing Billie).   *Ashbey*

Ch. Brisline's Inspiration (Ch. Brisline's Ragtime Cowboy ex Ch. Sunnydale Ho-Ray for Brisline), dam of twelve champions. *Cook*

Ch. Brisline's Dazzledale (Ch. Brisline's Blockbuster ex Brisline's Chocolate Chip). *Olson*

D'Aire Naughty Sadie, dam of Ch. D'Aire Unchained Melody. Ch. Moraine Putwyn Promise, sister of Bold Ruler, was dam of four champions, while a brother, Ch. Moraine Blackjack, sired three champions. Bright Promise bred to Ch. Jokyl Superman produced Ch. Moraine Forest Fire, who produced Ch. Revere Sir Lancelot and Ch. Lady Sabrina of Westmoor.

Ch. Moraine Future Promise (Ch. Jokyl Supermaster ex Ch. Moraine Bright Promise) was the dam of Ch. Moraine D'Aire Naughty Sadie (by Ch. Moraine Bold Ruler), who became the foundation bitch for the D'Aire Kennels of Dick and Diane Schlicht of Minnesota.

CH. DANDYAIRE MISS BRISTOL

Ch. Dandyaire Miss Bristol was the foundation bitch of Georgia and Russ McRae's Brisline Airedales, together with Ch. Sunnydale Ho-Ray for Brisline (Ch. Sunnydale Doc Holiday ex Ch. Sunnydale's Bouncing Billie), who when bred to Brisline's Ragtime Cowboy (son of Ch. Waggery's California Comet), produced Ch. Brisline's Inspiration. "Izzy" then bred to Ch. Sunnydale's Doc Holiday produced Ch. Brisline's London Fog, Ch. Brisline's Live It Up, Ch. Brisline's Lavender Mist and Ch. Brisline's Lady's Man, sire of Ch. Harrington's Kantankres Kyna, the Best in Show dog from Alaska, and Ch. Dandyaire Good Cracker. Ch. Sunnydale Ho-Ray for Brisline bred to Ch. Ernie's Jack Flash produced Ch. Brisline Sassenach Tristan and Ch. Brisline's Scaramouche.

CH. CLARKEDALE'S JOY D'EVALYNN

Jackson's Astral Amber bred to Ch. Jokyl Bengal Lionheart produced Dazzling Diana, who was then bred to Ch. Jackson's Conquistador and produced Jackson's Lucy Locket. Lucy bred to Mynair Unique produced Ch. Jackson's Peggy O'Neal; Peggy bred to Ch. Westmoor's Warlock produced Ch. Clarkedale's Joy D'Evalynn. Ch. Joy D'Evalynn bred to Ch. Bravo True Grit produced Ch. Stone Ridge Strongbow, Ch. Stone Ridge Bucko Bravo and Ch. Stone Ridge Jigsaw G-Man. When bred to Ch. Glentop's Yentl, Joy D'Evalynn produced Ch. Stone Ridge Traveler, who was shown by Mike and Denise Tobey.

CH. STONE RIDGE SHANNON O'REGENT

Ch. Stone Ridge Shannon O'Regent is the granddaughter of Ch. Clarkedale's Joy D'Evalynn and the full sister to M.J.'s Stone Ridge Chosen One. Co-owned by Brian and Lotus Tutton and Martha Graham, Shannon won both Wisconsin Airedale Specialties in 1989, was Best of Opposite Sex at

Ch. Clarkedale Joy D'Evalynn (Ch. Westmoor's Warlock ex Ch. Jackson's Peggy O'Neal).

Ch. Finlair Bodacious (Ch. Briardale's Kung Fu ex Finlair Kitty of Rek En Nad), dam of two Best in Show winners, Ch. Finlair Tiger of Stone Ridge and Ch. Finlair Isis. Handled by Mike Kemp for breeders-owners Bob and Kathy Finley. *Van Sickle*

Am. & Can. Ch. Stone Ridge Shannon O'Regent (Ch. Stone Ridge Bengal Bravo ex Stone Ridge Steel Breeze) won Best of Breed at Westminster 1989 under judge Edd Bivin. Handled by Susan De Pew for owners Lotus and Brian Tutton and Martha Graham and breeder Janet Framke.

Tatham

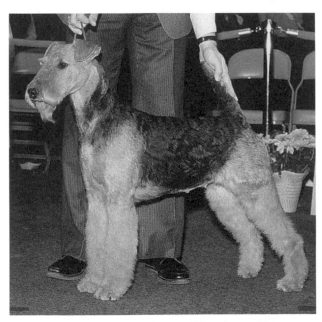

Ch. Bryn Hafod Hey Penny, winner at Westminster 1981.

Ashbey

119

Coppercrest Sunnydale CiCi (Ch. Coppercrest Un Poco Loco ex Ch. Coppercrest Ciara) won the Sweepstakes under breeder-judge Jill Fanning at the CATC show. Handled by Paul Kirkman for breeder June Dutcher and owners Jack and Mary Sanderson. *Missy*

Am. & Can. Ch. Stirling Heart of Gold, a Group placing bitch owner-conditioned and -handled. Breeders-owners Dr. Shirley Good and Susan Rodgers. *Paw Prints*

Grayslake Specialty in Illinois and the Great Western Specialty in California and was Best of Breed at Westminster in 1989; further, she took a Best in Show in Canada. Shannon's dam, Stone Ridge Steel Breeze, is from a repeat breeding of Ch. Stone Ridge Strongbow. She also produced Ch. Stone Ridge Tornado Watch, owned and shown by Becky and Woody Scherer and now owned by Georgi Bruner of Indianapolis, Indiana, and Int. Ch. Stone Ridge Storm Warning and Ch. Stone Ridge Hot N' Humid, who were shown by Mike and Denise Tobey and co-owned with Janet Framke. With Ch. Bravo True Grit as her grandsire on her dam's side, and Int. Ch. Bengal Sahib as her grandsire on the sire's side, Shannon should produce exciting things in the whelping box.

CH. FINLAIR BODACIOUS

Ch. Finlair Bodacious (Ch. Briardale's Kung Fu ex Ch. Finlair Kitty of Red En Nad) was Best of Opposite Sex handled by Michael Kemp at the 1979 ATCA Floating Specialty in New Orleans, winning the Wm. L. Barclay Memorial Trophy. When bred to Ch. Bravo True Grit, she produced Ch. Finlair Tiger of Stone Ridge, who won many Bests in Show, Ch. Finlair Fleur de Lis, Ch. Finlair Fantasy, Ch. Finlair Fyfanella and Ch. Finlair Lyon of Stone Ridge, all from the first litter. From the second breeding came Can. Ch. Graphic Narration. The third time she produced Ch. Finlair Isis (also with many Bests in Show), Ch. Finlair Imperial Trent, Ch. Finlair Infanta and Ch. Finlair Intruder of Ivie. At twelve years of age, she is now the matriarch of the Finley household, in charge of grandchildren and/or puppies.

CH. FINLAIR ISIS

Ch. Finlair Isis (Ch. Bravo True Grit ex Ch. Finlair Bodacious) was a repeat breeding of Ch. Finlair Tiger of Stone Ridge. Isis started her show career in 1984 at Montgomery County going Best of Winners from the puppy class handled by Bob Larouech to win the Ethel Braxton Memorial Trophy for breeders Bob and Kathy Finley and owners Carol and Lew Scott. Isis went on to collect eleven Bests in Show, fifty-one Group I, thirty-six Group II, twelve Group III and four Group IV, with 137 Bests of Breed and seven Bests of Opposite. She won the ATCA Airedale Bowl in 1985 at Montgomery County under judge Edd Bivin and again in 1986 at the Floating Specialty in Colorado under judge Annemarie Moore. Bowl three was won in 1986 at Chain O'Lakes Floating Specialty in Illinois under judge Jane Forsyth; bowl four in 1976 at Montgomery County under Australian judge Keith Lovell; bowl five in 1987 at the Floating Specialty at the Bronx County Kennel Club in New York under judge James Reynolds. The sixth bowl win was at Montgomery County in 1987 under judge Mareth Kipp. What is left for this great bitch? To retire and have her puppies carry on her winning ways.

TERRY-ALL KC
BEST IN SHOW

Ch. Finlair Isis (Ch. Bravo True Grit ex Ch. Finlair Bodacious) won Best in Show with handler Bob Larouech for owners Lew and Carol Scott and breeders Bob and Kathy Finley. Isis won eleven Bests in Show. *Cott/Daigle/Franc*

Ch. Briardale's Luv's Elegant Lady (Ch. Shshown Que Forte, CD ex Ch. Wafer April Luv of Briardale), handled by Maripi Wooldridge for owners Steve and Terry Clark. *Lindemaier*

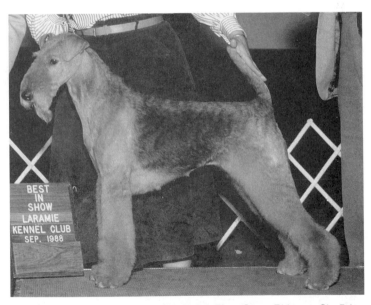

Ch. Terrydale's Adorable Lady (Ch. Finlair Tiger Stone Ridge ex Ch. Briardale's Luv's Elegant Lady) won Best in Show handled by Maripi Wooldridge for breeders-owners Steve and Mary Clark. A Best in Show daughter of a Best in Show sire. *Rhinehart*

Ch. Tartan's Oil Patch Star (Ch. Bravo Starbuck ex Ch. Tartan's Oil Patch Mama) won the ATCA Airedale Bowl and the Wm. L. Barclay Memorial Trophy for Best of Breed at Montgomery County, under German breeder-judge Dr. Crista von Bardeleben. Handled by Michael Kemp for breeder-owner Forbes Gordon.

Ashbey

Ch. Wagtail Woodhue (Ch. Ernie's Jack Flash ex Ch. Wagtail Amber-Light), owner Izzy Strempek of Woodhue Airedales.

Roberts

CH. BRIARDALE'S LUV'S ELEGANT LADY

Ch. Briardale's Luv's Elegant Lady (Ch. Shshown Que Forte ex Ch. Wafer April Luv of Briardale), bred by Jeannine Harrington and Carole Bullwinkle, is owned by Stephen and Mary Clark. "Cassie" was shown by Maripi Wooldridge to several Specialty wins. She was bred to Ch. Finlair Tiger of Stone Ridge to produce her Best in Show daughter Ch. Terrydale's Adorable Lady, also shown by Maripi Wooldridge for the Clarks.

CH. TERRYDALE'S ADORABLE LADY

Adorable Lady was sired by Ch. Finlair Tiger of Stone Ridge out of Ch. Briardale's Luv's Elegant Lady. This lovely daughter went out to conquer and surpassed her dam's record by earning ten Bests in Show and ten Specialty Best of Breed wins, becoming number one Airedale, all-systems, for 1988 and number one Terrier Bitch, all-systems, in 1988.

CH. TARTAN OIL PATCH STAR

Ch. Tartan Oil Patch Star (Ch. Bravo Star Buck ex Ch. Tartan's Oil Patch Mama) won the ATCA Airedale Bowl in 1989 at the Montgomery County Specialty handled by Michael Kemp for owner-breeder Forbes Gordon. Also a multiple Group winner, several times Patches has been Best of Opposite Sex at Montgomery, winning the Wm. L. Barclay Memorial Trophy, but in 1989 she went all the way to Group IV after taking Best of Breed under the renowned German breeder-judge Dr. Christa von Bardeleben. In 1990 Patches won Best of Breed at the prestigious Westminster Kennel Club show under Judge Charles Foley, presented by Michael Kemp. Forbes Gordon now has had the thrill of winning the "big ones" with a bitch that he bred himself!

Ch. Bravo True Grit won the ATCA Airedale Bowl under judge Arthur Lodge, handled by Peter Green.

Ashbey

7

The Airedale Terrier
Club of America

THE AIREDALE TERRIER CLUB of America was founded in 1900 by several ardent supporters of the breed and has grown and expanded to a present membership of more than 724 American and Canadian members, plus members located in eleven foreign countries. The object of this group of fanciers is to promote the breeding of purebred Airedale Terriers, and it does all it can to protect and advance the interests of the breed.

The officers and the directors who represent all portions of the country are a dedicated group who govern and direct the activities of the club. The annual Specialty is held during October in conjunction with the Montgomery County Kennel Club Terrier show on the Temple University grounds. This show has grown until there are usually in excess of 150 top Airedales competing for honors. Spectators come from all parts of the United States, Canada and Mexico, as well as visitors from overseas. In addition, the club usually holds two floating Specialty shows which are moved about the country. The privilege of hosting these shows is sought by the regional clubs.

The Airedale Bowl, a sterling silver perpetual trophy valued at $14,000, has been offered in competition at the Parent Club shows since 1910. The winners' names engraved on the bowl and its pedestals is a history of the breed greats. The William L. Barclay Memorial Trophy, valued at $2,500, is offered for the Best of Opposite Sex to the Best of Breed. In addition, there are many more memorial trophies offered by well-known Airedale fanciers.

The ATCA works through its officers, directors and various committees

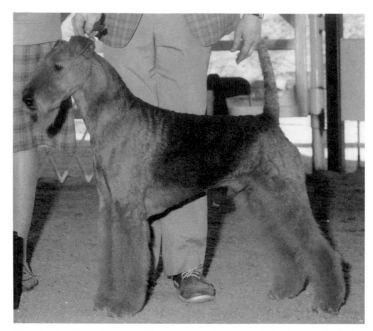

Ch. Finlair Tiger of Stone Ridge won the ATCA Airedale Bowl under judge Anne Clark, handled by Robert Larouech. *Graham*

Ch. Anfeald Moses won the ATCA Airedale Bowl under judge Dorothea Daniell-Jenkins, handled by breeder-owner Charlie Foley. *Gilbert*

to assist the AKC in promoting the standards for the Airedale breed, and to acquaint the general public with the attributes of the Airedale through videotapes, seminars and written breed information. Members are kept in contact with each other through the newsletter, which is published several times each year and contains accounts of the activities and events of the different parts of the country. Every ten years a yearbook is published describing the top dogs of the decade and the club's activities.

Local clubs, now numbering seventeen, are sanctioned or licensed by the AKC with the approval of the ATCA to hold Specialties and sanctioned matches for the exhibition of the Airedale. Regional memorial trophies are offered honoring a region's well-known breed enthusiasts. In addition, clubs work on a local level to educate the public on the qualities of the well-bred Airedale. Persons interested in contacting the Parent Club or a regional club can request the name and address of the secretary from the AKC, 51 Madison Avenue, New York, NY 10001.

Ch. Ginger Xmas Carol won Best in Show at the Manchester Dog Show, handled by Mary Swash.

David Dalton

8

Airedales in England

by Mary Swash, Jokyl Kennels

THE LAST TEN YEARS have been very exciting ones in the United Kingdom for our breed. Many Group and Best in Show winners have been produced, including Best in Show at Crufts, the most famous show in the world.

Following closely on the heels of Ch. Tanworth Merriment, who broke the existing breed record of CCs formerly held by Ch. Riverina Tweedsbairn (Crufts Best in Show Winner in 1961) and Ch. Jokyl Smartie Pants, winner of eighteen CCs (probably the most won by a bitch up to that date), came Ch. Perrancourt Playful. This bitch was Top Dog, all-breeds, 1978 and broke the breed record by winning thirty-four CCs and thirty BOBs. She was a great show lady and completely dominated the ring from June 1978 right through to Crufts 1980, winning ten Groups, two Bests in Show, all-breeds, and three Reserve Bests in Show, all-breeds, plus Best in Show, National Terrier. These wins gave her the title Dog of the Year in 1979.

Playful was by Am. Ch. Turith Adonis and was twice mated to her paternal grandfather Ch. Siccawei Galliard. From these matings she produced two English champions—Perrancourt Play the Game of Jokyl and Perrancourt Pirate. The latter is now at stud in Denmark.

In 1980 Ch. Bengal Sahib was the top Airedale Terrier in England, winning four Groups, one Best in Show, all-breeds, and two Reserve Best in Show, all-breeds. Sadly, he was to be Molly Harmsworth's last champion, as she died on July 29, 1981. Sahib was Best of Breed at Crufts in 1981 and went on to win eleven more CCs that year, although he was bested for the title of Top Airedale by Ch. Glentops Crackerjack, who won two Groups and one Best in Show. This very sound dog sired three English champions and Germany's top-winning dog for 1981 and 1983 before his untimely death in 1983 at the very young age of five years. His sire was Ch. Turith Brigand, a full brother to Adonis. It is unfortunate that Crackerjack's early demise meant that several leading breeders didn't get the chance to use him. I know that Jokyl fully intended to, but who could guess that his life would be so short.

Crufts 1982 started off a great run for Mynair Silver Sunbeam, who won seventeen CCs, ten Bests of Breed, six Terrier Groups and her Best in Show. She was sired by Sw. Ch. Copperstone Hannibal Hayes, the Swedish dog imported by Mavis and Arthur Lodge. Sunbeam ended up second top Terrier in 1982. Other bitches to be made up were Jokyl Buttons N' Bows and Jokyl Hot Gossip of Hillcross. Top male was Saredon Super Trouper with fifteen CCs, eleven BOBs and one Group win.

Crackerjack won two more CCs and Bengal Sahib, one. Other males to be made up were Turith Echelon of Saredon and Jokyl Smart Enough.

The year 1983 was definitely the Year of the Airedale, with Ch. Jokyl Gallipants literally taking all before him, winning twelve Groups, seven Bests in Show, all-breeds, two Reserve Bests in Show and Best in Show at the National Terrier. He was Top Dog, all-breeds, by a huge margin. He also won a hot Pro Dogs competition. Only one other dog acquired his title in 1983— Deerhunter of Sportdon.

On the other hand, Airedale bitches produced six champions. The first, Ginger Veronica, was sent to England from Italy, bred from English parents. Then came Loudwell Nosegay, Jokyl Swanky Pants, Jokyl Hot Lips (owned by Dodo Sandahl and taken to Sweden with her, where she became top Airedale of 1984); Jetstream Summer Morn became the first champion for Jeanne Sargeant, and Glentops Ocean Mist became the first champion sired by Crackerjack.

In 1984 Gallipants was Best of Breed at Crufts and in the last four of the Group. He won the Contest of Champions competition (winning a color TV for his owners) and also the Pedigree Chum Champion Stakes finals. Later in the year, he won the Group at Windsor and again at Bournemouth, where he went on to Reserve Best in Show. He was top Airedale again that year. Gallipants was top Airedale sire in 1985 and 1987 and top Terrier sire in 1986. In 1985 Gallipants was again Best of Breed at Crufts and again in the last four in Group (his last show). His sire was Ch. Siccawei Galliard, a dog who sired more English champions than any other post-war dog. His dam, Ch. Jokyl Smartie Pants, set another record as the dam of seven English champions. Other winners in 1984 were Gallipants's full brother Sunday Best, half brother (ex Playful) Perrancourt Pirate and Cocas Cosmos. Deerhunter won four more CCs.

In bitches, Mrs. Millar's Karudon Kalypso won seven CCs; Shadli

Ch. Bengal Flamboyant at twelve years of age with Mollie Harmsworth.

Ch. Jokyl Gallipants.

133

Classy Charmer, nine CCs; Glentops Raggity Ann and Perrancourt Play the Game of Jokyl were made up.

Another terrific year for Airedales was 1985, with Ch. Ginger Xmas Carol starting the year by winning the CC at Crufts, but being beaten for Best of Breed by Gallipants, this being his last appearance. The next event was Manchester, and Xmas Carol went through to Best in Show, two Reserve Bests in Show and Reserve Best in Show at the National Terrier. One other bitch managed to gain her title that year—Ch. Junaken Valldeb. She has proved a great brood bitch, producing five English champions, all sired by Gallipants.

No male dog managed to win Best of Breed. Ten different dogs won CCs; two emerged as top dogs, Ch. Jimwin Jackpot and Ch. Saredon the Jazzsinger, with six CCs each. Ch. Albana Prairie and Ch. Shadli Fanton also gained their titles.

The 1986 show season started with a great boost for the breed with Ch. Ginger Xmas Carol going through to Best in Show at Crufts, exactly twenty-five years after Tweedsbairn's great win. This was to be her last show, and what a way to retire! The rest of 1986 was divided in dogs by Ch. Saredon the Jazzsinger with fourteen CCs, and Ch. Stargus Sea King with seven CCs. In bitches, Ch. Jokyl Vivacious and Ch. Something Special for Jokyl each won six CCs, with Something Special winning a Group at Southern Counties. Other champions made up were Ch. Junaken Vanity, Ch. Beacytan Gay Paree and Ch. Beacytan Koh-I-Nor.

In 1987, Jazzsinger and Sea King won some more CCs, and the interesting import, Am. Ch. Blackjack's Nostradamus, won five CCs. The biggest winner of the year, however, was Ch. Saredon Handyman with eleven CCs and one Group win. Something Special won two more CCs, and the Junaken bitches, "Valetta," "Veejay" and "Vallotta" of Beacytan, were made up to champions, as was Dendaric Figurehead.

The year 1988 didn't produce a Group winner. Handyman won a further fourteen CCs. Ch. Glentops Trick or Treat won six, and Ch. Shadli Magnum of Robroyd was also made up. Bitches had lots of changes, with Ch. Junaken Veni Vedi Vici and Ch. Saredon September Morn making the third Jazzsinger child to be made up. Ch. Jokyl American Dream and Ch. Beacytan Serendipity were the first of the Nostradamus kids to gain their titles, and Mr. Gould made up his first champion, homebred Broen Eyebury Princess. American Dream was top-winning bitch.

Handyman won six more CCs in 1989, looking set fair to beat Playful's winning record but leaving Britain for Japan before achieving that record. His chief opponent, Ch. Jokyl Hillcross Hotshot (Gallipants's eleventh English champion) won ten CCs, one Group first and two Group seconds. Other champions made up were Florac King of Scotts at Stargus (now in the United States, Ballintober Gold of Saredon and Beacytan Troubador.

A record number of seven bitches won their titles, four of them by Nostradamus—Jokyl Liberty Lady, and Jokyl What a Gem (ex Ch. Jokyl Buttons N' Bows, also American Dream's dam), Beacytan Vanilla and

McKerros Caledonian Girl, George Dale's Codale Margarite and another Broen—Apple of My Eye. The last champion of the year was Jokyl Something Else. Nostradamus was the top Airedale sire in 1988 and 1989.

We are all looking forward to the new decade and the possibility of more imports from the United States.

Bengal Turith Comet with Mollie Harmsworth.

Am. & Can. Ch. Morgan Earl of Stratford (Ch. Sunnydale's Doc Holiday ex Coppercrest Saltisan, litter brother to Ch. Sunnydale Coppercrest Dinah) winning Best in show at Hamilton Kennel Club of Canada under Judge Dr. David Doane. Handled by owner Al Preece. *Smith*

9

Airedales Around
the World

THE AIREDALE PRESENCE is felt strongly in many areas of the world. Airedale activity has been notable even in areas where showing entails a considerable amount of travel. In Australia, for example, the last quarter century has seen a steady increase of exhibitors in several disciplines. In other areas such as Latin America, Japan and on the Continent, the Airedale's all-around ability as a "useful dog" for police and other work has been preserved in conjunction with the breed's popularity as a show dog. As the world gets smaller, bloodlines are intermingled, thereby increasing the quality of the Airedale the world over.

CANADA *by Lotus Tutton*

The Airedale Terrier Club of Canada was formed by a group of Airedale breeders, exhibitors and enthusiasts in the southwestern area of Ontario. The goal of this group is to promote the Airedale Terrier for the betterment of the breed. On March 22, 1970, at the Canadian National Sportsmen's Show, the club constitution and by-laws were approved and the election of officers took place. Many memorial trophies are offered at various shows under various terms of reference. Most of these are offered at the ATCC Specialty show each year.

Lotus and Brian Tutton (Fairewood Kennels) of Barrie began showing

Am. & Can. Ch. Fairewood's Celebration (Ch. Turith Eschelon of Saredon ex Scottshire's Lady Lahring). Bred, owned and handled by Lotus Tutton.

Smith

Ch. Alncaire Mr. Dress-up (Ch. Jolee Aire's Stone Ridge Stomp ex Ch. Alncaire Odds Are Even). Bred, owned and handled by Al Preece.

Stonham

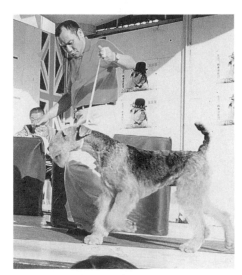

Airedale Dog Exhibition at a department store in the Ginza, Tokyo.

Japan Airedale being shown at the Championship show.

Ch. Stone Ridge Dragon Slayer (Mex. & Am. Ch.), owned by Selso Tuck Schnider, Mexico.

Am. & Jap. Ch. Tartan's Mr. Sage at home in Kansas after his relocation from Japan.

The Tsuji Airedales in the Kansas winter.

their male English import, Ch. Honeybrook Buddha, in 1973. He was the sire of their first Specialty winning bitch, Ch. Fairewood's First Choice; her dam was The Clarion, bred by Mary Curran. They have bred and shown several Best in Show and Group-winning Airedales, and their Ch. Stone Ridge Shannon O'Regent was the number one Airedale in Canada for 1989.

Al and Carole Preece of Alncaire Kennels bred and exhibited their Best in Show Ch. Alncaire Mr. Dress-up (Ch. Jolee Aire Stone Ridge Stomp ex Ch. Alncaire Odds Are Even). Mr. Dress-up was the number one Airedale and number nine Terrier in Canada in 1982. They also owned and exhibited Can. & Am. Ch. Morgan Earl of Stratford to Best in Show. He was the litter brother to Am. Ch. Sunnydale Coppercrest Dinah, Best of Breed winner at Montgomery County in 1983.

Ken and Margaret MacLaren's Best in Show Ch. Montford's Bannockburn Battler (Ch. Jolee Aire Stone Ridge Stomp ex Ch. Montford's Classic Bonaventure) was another Stomp son of note.

Vera Chapman imported and co-owned Can. Ch. Stone Ridge Count Nicolai, one of the top dogs in Canada in 1989.

The Fontaines of Quebec owned and campaigned Can. Ch. Coppercrest Peggy to her championship; when bred to Ch. Bravo Ironman of Santeric, Peggy produced several Canadian champions, including Can. & Am. Ch. Fonaire Iron Ancistrodon.

Marilyn and Everett Mincey of British Columbia (Cymbeline Kennels) successfully campaigned Ch. Cymbeline Avant Garde and Ch. Cymbeline Special Angel, who bred to Ch. Terragate's Adobe Red produced two champions.

JAPAN

This update was provided by the late Yoko Sekido, breeder and owner of the Paulownia Kennels. She was also chief director of the Airedale Terrier Club of the Japan Police Dog Association.

Airedale Terriers first were introduced in Japan by a Colonel Soichi Imada, who wrote a book entitled *An All-round Dog: Airedale Terrier* in 1931, followed in 1937 by *A Review of Airedale Terriers.* In these writings he talked with enthusiasm about the wonderful character of the Airedale Terrier.

When the Imperial Military Dog Association was established in 1932, Airedale Terriers as well as German Shepherds and Dobermans were chosen for their capability for military use. Though Airedale Terriers love peace by nature, it is noteworthy that they were recognized as being clever. The Japan Police Dog Association was set up in 1947. There is no organization corresponding to The Kennel Club or AKC in Japan. Each group, association or club that deals with Airedale Terriers issues a herdbook; thus it is impossible to know the exact number of Airedale Terriers in Japan. The Airedale Terrier Club of the Japan Police Dog Association has the greatest number registered,

Ch. Rangeaire Rolls Royce, winner of four Best Exhibit in Show, has many champion sons and daughters as well as champion grandchildren (Australian).

Ch. Rangeaire Rockin' Robin, sired by Ch. Rangeaire Rolls Royce (Australian), was awarded Group placements and two Best Puppy in Show awards including ATC of Vic 1982. Dam of 3 Australian Champions including Aust. Ch. Rangeaire Raggtime.

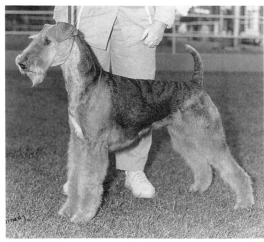

Ch. Rangeaire Raggtime (Ch. Rangeaire Raggs ex Ch. Rangeaire Rockin' Robin), Australian Airedale of the year 1986. 48 CC's 535 Challenge points, 18 Group Placements.   *Robins*

Aust. & NZ. Ch. Loudwell Fife & Drum. *Hutchison*

NZ. Ch. Hillmere Echoist (Aust. & NZ. Ch. Loudwell Fife & Drum ex Ch. Hillmere Zither, CD)—"Jerry" at twelve months, owned by Paul Clarke.

Eng. & Aust. Ch. Loudwell Venue (NZ Ch. Loudwell Krisp ex Eng. Ch. Loudwell Starlight.

and it is estimated that there are 230 to 240 puppies registered a year. About 450 members of the Japan Police Dog Association are Airedale owners.

All dogs accepted as police dogs must take part in a common training competition held by the Police Dog Association. Airedale owners are making efforts to achieve good results, believing in aggressively participating in such competition where each participant is examined on a common basis. A training competition of the Police Dog Association is held on three successive days in autumn, and approximately a thousand dogs are brought from all over Japan to the Kirigamine Plateau to compete.

The Japan Champion Exhibition (show) in the spring is a very interesting event. One male and one female champion are selected from among the adult dogs, one-and-one-half years or older. Most of these dogs have completed a basic training course; the older dogs have completed both basic and advanced training courses. Some of the championship winners have taken part in the training competition as well, aiming to be recognized both for good appearance and for excellent quality. Often top winners in the show ring also achieve good marks in the training competition.

The Japanese have found Airedales to be all-around dogs. This is good because a dog who is a watchdog at a poultry farm may have a show-dog brother or another that is accredited as a part-time police dog. In order to be a part-time police dog, a dog has to pass a qualification test given in each prefecture every year. If it passes the test with good marks, it will help the police in guarding, sorting or following footprints as a volunteer.

We hope generations to come will understand how wonderful Airedales are. We'll do our best to think of good opportunities for Airedales we love.

AUSTRALIA

The two major shows in Australia are the Melbourne Royal and the Airedale Terrier Club of Victoria Specialty but there are many other shows held in the various areas of Australia plus additional shows in New Zealand. These shows draw large entries for worldwide judges with not only English and American judges coming to judge but also representatives from Japan and Europe.

Airedales of the English bloodlines of Siccawei and Loudwell have been imported and have been combined successfully with Australian and New Zealand bloodlines to produce many Australian and New Zealand champions. Lately some Airedales of American lines have braved the long quarantine requirements to be integrated into their breeding plans.

Some of the top winners in the last ten years include Ch. Forsvar Dynamite, Ch. Loudwell Whispers (English import), Ch. Old Iron Highpoint, his half-sister Ch. Old Iron Outrage, Ch. Fastlane Vigilante Man, Ch. Forsvar Gambitt, Aus. and N.Z. Ch. Loudwell Fife & Drum (English import), Aus. and N.Z. Ch. Tarahanga Rocket Man, the top Terrier in Victoria (1984) Ch.

Aust. & NZ. Ch. Old Iron Infra Red (Eng. & Aust. Ch. Loudwell Whispers ex Tjuringa Posh), owned by Bob and Denys Howell-Styles of New Zealand.

Aust. Ch. Tarahanga On Show (Aust. & NZ. Ch. Old Iron Infra Red ex NZ. Ch. Tarahanga La Foudre), Top Terrier in Victoria 1984, owned by King and Prentis.   *Hutchison*

Aust. Ch. Old Iron Liquidator (Ch. Ingot Hot Shot ex Ch. Old Iron Havo), owned by David and Isabell Thompson.

145

Tarahanga On Show, Ch. Ingot Red Letter Day, Ch. Old Iron Ask for Trouble, Ch. Rangeaire Raggtime and Ch. Ingot Tuff Enuff.

Many of the kennel owners that are breeding and exhibiting have visited America and have attended our shows where we have enjoyed comparing notes on breeding tactics and sharing "how to" knowledge, to mention a few Wendy Prentis of "Ingot," Di and David Barclay of "York Park," Keith and Trish Lovell of "Tjuringa," Gisela Lesh of "Strongfort," Anne Soraghan of "Old Iron." Other breeders of note are Jane Harvey of "Rangeaire," the Hattons of "Bushveldt," Sue Matthews of "Forsvar," Pauline Lewis of "Moylarg," the Kaszegs of "Old Faithful," the Campbells of "Belltirna," Lorna Schuster of "Hillmere" and Marie Langdon of "Coppermyn."

In the Obedience ring many of the conformation champions have earned obedience titles which once more illustrates that all over the world Airedales combine beauty with brains. One in particular was Ch. Forsvar Executive, CD, CDX, UD owned and trained by Ivan Zhirawel. This dog qualified for his CD at eight months of age and went on to be the only Airedale in Australia to be awarded a perfect 200/200 score in Open Obedience. Another dog, Ch. Coppermyn Clint, CD, CDX owned and trained by Cor Scholten, combines his show and obedience career with being a part-time security dog, hunting dog, trickster and to cap his activities he stars in a TV commercial where "Basso" worked in snow, jumped a ravine, swam icy rivers, crossed a glacier and flew in a helicopter, proving once more the versatility of our chosen breed.

Australia's top obedience Airedales have been:

1978 Ch. Strongfort Samaya, CD; Ch. Camarna High Flyer, CD
1979 Ch. Brookdale Busybody, CD, CDX; Ch. Windview Sweet Alice, CD
1980 Ch. Rangeaire Raglan Boy, CD, CDX
1981 Ch. Rangeaire Raglan Boy again; Ch. Forsvar Executive, CD, CDX, UD
1982 Ch. Hillmere Unique, CD; Ch. Hillmere Zither, CD; Ch. Forsvar Fresco, CD, CDX, UD
1983 Karringbush Alibarba, CD, CDX
1984 Karringbush Alibarba again; Clesha Court Jester, CD; Strongfort Punkin Pie, CD; Ch. Bushveldt Black Bolero, CD; Ch. Bushveldt Balmoral, CD
1985 Foxwood Fotocopy, CD; Ch. Tangmere Babushka, CD
1986 Ch. Rangeaire Willoughby, CD; Greit Hofer's Shadwa Upstage, CD; Larnook Daredevil, CD; Ch. Forsvar Gambitt, CD, CDX, UD
1987 Moylarg Ming Princess, CD
1988 Old Faithful Crusader, CD
1989 Ming Princess, CDX; Shadwa Upstage, CDX (one score was 194/200); Ch. Rangeaire Ragtime Beau, CD

Aust. Ch. Coppermyn Clint, CDX (Ch. Drakehall Dragoon ex Ch. Mynair Keep In Touch), with owner Cor Scholten.

Northern Daily Legom

Ch. Forsvar Gambitt, UD (Forsvar Fresco, UD, ex Ch. Forsvar Fancy Pants).

Obedience information was supplied by Marie Langton for the Airedale Terrier Club of Victoria.

Also from down under comes the delightful *Wake Up Mr. B!,* the story of imaginative Rosie and her willing, able, tolerant and her extra-special friend, the Airedale. Penny Dale, the author, could only have been a survivor from living closely with an Airedale, in order to take us through the antics of this adorable pair. A book for all persons large or small.

10

Hunting and Working Airedales

by Stephen P. Gilbert, originator of the Hunting/Working Committee

---

THE FRUSTRATION of many Airedales in not having an arena (field trials, hunting tests, etc.) to showcase the breed's characteristics as a versatile gundog led the Airedale Terrier Club of America to address these concerns in the fall of 1985. The committee originally was composed of avid hunters Forbes Gordon of Texas, "Park" Peters of Michigan and Steve Gilbert of Ohio.

Since I had the good fortune to grow up with Airedales on my grandfather's farm and my wife, Bonnie, and I have owned Airedales for over twenty years, I know from firsthand experience what an Airedale is capable of doing in the field when properly started and trained by one person with just the right blend of love, patience and obedience to produce a terrific hunting companion. Even though I have witnessed the feats of the Airedale keeping raccoons out of the sweet corn, becoming the most proficient flusher and retriever of pheasants at the local hunting club or swimming two miles out into a rough Lake Erie to retrieve a goose that turned out to be not so crippled, how do you share this information with other sporting enthusiasts and make it believable, particularly when the majority of them have never hunted with a friend and an Airedale in the field, or read anything about them in a gundog magazine?

The Hunting/Working Committee contacted the better-known registries and organizations currently running hunting performance events and re-

Pat Conover-Lox and Amber, first recipients of the Joan Shea Gordon Memorial Trophy, at hunting and working workshop with H/W Committee David Duffey and Mike Samples.

1988 Winners, Pocket Quail Hunt: First—Ch. Moraine Promises Returned, handler Mareth Kipp; Second—Ch. Tartan Bannochburn Drummond, handler "Fitz" Fitzpatrick; Third—tie between Blackheath's Bond, handler Bill Allen and Ch. Glenshiel's Moonshadow, handler Steve Gilbert.

150

quested that the Airedale be permitted to compete. The Hunting Retriever Clubs, Inc., responded. Since they have a "hunt" (HRC hunting test) within a reasonable distance, I entered M.J.'s Drummer (Ch. Tartan's Banochburn Drummond) in two HRC hunts. He passed the second test in the "Started" (beginning) division. In hunting tests the dogs are judged against a standard, so it's pass or fail, rather than pitting one against another to come up with one winner, as in a field trial setting.

My motive for entering Drummer, a six-year-old bench champion, was twofold. First, I needed to learn more about these hunting tests, and second, I wanted to prove beyond any shadow of a doubt that the average family pet Airedale could, with a minimum amount of work and time, train for and have a high probability of winning in this new hunting test game.

The H/W Committee held its first national workshop in Ohio in 1986 for Airedalers interested in the field abilities of the breed. After reviewing and studying tests available to other sporting-dog breeds—their field trials, working certificates, etc.—the original committee was expanded to include interested and knowledgeable Airedalers from other parts of the country. Through them, regional groups were encouraged to hold "field days" in their respective regions.

In 1989 at the Fourth Annual National Workshop in Ohio, the first ATCA Experimental Hunting Test was held for tracking and hunting fur, upland bird hunting and retrieving. Forbes Gordon summarized the activities of the workshop: "The responsiveness of all Airedales in attendance, while not surprising, was gratifying, and has definitely proved to the satisfaction of not only all the Airedalers in attendance, but also to the various experts, that the versatility originally bred into the Airedale is still alive and well."

Some skeptics had raised the issue as to whether any one Airedale could pass all three hunting tests. It was, therefore, particularly heartening to watch TJ's Elder Amber Gal, UDT, SCH I, owner/handler Pat Conover-Lox of Lubbock, Texas, not only pass all three hunting tests, but also excel with typical Airedale enthusiasm in all three disciplines. Amber became the first recipient of the Joan Shea Gordon Memorial Trophy, which symbolizes the number one versatile hunting Airedale of the year based on the dog's performance in all three hunting tests at the workshop.

Training a Puppy to Be a Working Gun Dog is a good guide for beginning training. Another suggested source for starting to train a young Airedale for hunting is *Dave Duffey Trains Gun Dogs* by David Michael Duffey. This book can be well used as a guide, as Dave has great expertise in training gundogs and the ability to communicate his training methods. This book gives an excellent overview of different types of game on which gundogs are used, and what discipline/training is best suited for that particular type of bird.

When reading the sections on the various types of gundogs, please pay particular attention to the Chesapeake Bay Retriever and the Irish Water Spaniel. Just pretend in your mind that your Airedale is half Chessie and half Irish, and you will be amazed at how quickly you determine which methods

Roxie Supergal of Arelsh, UD & Can. UD, retrieving a pheasant at Rice Creek Hunting club in Minnesota.

Sauber's Old Jack and M.J.'s Missy and Tessa with John Sauber, Steve Gilbert and Wayne Micha after a successful pheasant hunt.

Water training—Ch. Glenshiel's Moonshadow.

En route to action.

are best suitable and adaptable to training your Airedale as a great gundog. I've determined this after having hunted with Airedales for many years.

An Airedale pup should be accustomed to loud noises at a young age, including the noise of different transportation such as cars, trucks and boats, slamming doors, the TV and stereo, banging dishes, etc. After your Airedale has been exposed to noise, the introduction to gunfire should not be a problem. You may wish to purchase a cap pistol and shoot off a few rounds every time you feed. The next step would be shooting a blank pistol when you are outside with your dog and having a great deal of fun, like chasing birds or squirrels.

It has been my experience that the Airedales that become the best companion/gun dogs are those that are well socialized by being included as important members of their families and taught good citizenship.

11

Airedales in Obedience

by Frank Foster

The following obedience information was offered by Frank Foster of Deerfield, Illinois. Frank and his wife, Nancy, were the trainers and owners of Willow Aire Proud Piper, UD. Piper was highest-scoring Airedale in the United States for four years in a row (1973–1976). At the Gaines U.S. Obedience Classic trials in 1977, she was tenth-placed "Super Dog" competing against all breeds.

The following discussion of formal obedience exhibiting under American Kennel Club rules is offered for the information of the reader. However, at the outset it seems appropriate to point out that training a dog to obey is necessary for the dog's well-being as well as for the added enjoyment and companionship such training makes possible. The more exacting arena of obedience exhibiting is, or should be, an extension of this basic training that adds an extra dimension of companionship as dog and handler become partners engaging in obedience as a sport. I can't imagine a more thrilling sight than a well-trained Airedale Terrier pouring its abundant spirit and heart into an obedience routine.

NOVICE

In Novice, this would embrace heel work both on and off leash, a stand-for-examination (no extra points for kissing the judge!), a full-length off-leash recall and the group stay exercises of long-sit and long-down, done

Not This. . .

But This. . .

Frank Foster with a four-month-old puppy beginning "HEELING" training.

Can lead to This.

Seneca Cornerstone, CD, after scoring High in Trial at the Minnesota Specialty.

with the handlers standing across the ring facing their dogs. These last group exercises are so called since no fewer than six, nor more than twelve, dogs perform them at the same time.

A perfect score is 200 points, with the minimum qualifying score being at least 50 percent of the available points for each exercise and not less than 170 points in total. The method of scoring is by taking off points for faults committed. Each exhibitor starts out with 200 points; the trick is to hang on to as many of them as possible. Three successful efforts under three different judges at different obedience trials earn the Companion Dog title, and the letters "CD" are entered by the American Kennel Club after the dog's registered name.

OPEN

While Novice work lays the foundation, Open work is where an Airedale can really shine, because of the requirements for jumping and retrieving. Upon entering an Open ring at a trial, the handler gives up the leash and dumbbell to a steward and proceeds to the starting point for the heel exercise. All work is done off leash and includes heeling, drop-on-recall, retrieve on the flat, retrieve over high jump, broad jump and longer group sit-stays and down-stays with the handlers out of the ring and out of sight for three minutes and five minutes, respectively. A dog may not compete in the Open class until it has earned its CD. Again, three successful efforts in Open work cause the CDX (Companion Dog Excellent) to replace the CD after the dog's registered name. Since the work is cumulative, a CDX title signifies that the dog was successful first in the Novice class and then in the Open class.

UTILITY

The highest level of obedience work recognized by the AKC is the Utility class. For an Airedale, Utility is (or should be) more like dessert than a lot of new work. Let's take a look at the Utility requirements.

Signal Exercise involves a full heeling test and, in addition, halting with the dog remaining in standing position and staying that way while the handler goes to the far end of the ring, then dropping smartly to a down position, sitting, coming quickly in and sitting in front and finally moving to the heel position—all in response to signals only, no verbal command being allowed during the entire routine.

Scent Discrimination entails sending the dog to a cluster of articles, four made of metal and four covered with leather, into which the judge has just placed a ninth article, the only one that has been handled by the handler, which the dog must quickly locate and bring back to the handler. The dog does this exercise twice, working a leather article and a metal article.

Ch. Teelawooket's Rebel Rouser executing the BROAD JUMP.

Lave's Elusive Dream, UD, owned by La Verne Van Der Zee performs the RETRIEVE OVER THE HIGH JUMP.

Lay Dee Ayr's Sunlit Jacki, CDX, owned by Chris and Nancy Nieset.

Directed Retrieve requires the dog to start from the center of the ring and, as directed by the handler, retrieve a glove designated by the judge from among three white cotton work gloves placed at equal intervals across the back end of the ring.

Moving Stand and Examination entails a short heeling routine during which the handler halts the dog in a standing position while the handler continues, turns after proceeding another ten to twelve feet, and halts. After the judge examines the dog, the handler calls the dog to the heel position.

Directed Jumping requires the handler to send the dog down the center from one end of the ring to the other. At the far end, the dog should turn and sit. Upon instruction from the judge the handler will send the dog over one of two jumps placed midway between the ends of the ring. This exercise is done twice to demonstrate that the dog will jump each of two different jumps, one a solid barrier and the other a bar suspended from two upright stands. Qualifying three times in Utility earns the Utility Dog (UD) title, which replaces the CDX already entered after the dog's registered name on the records of the AKC.

It should be apparent that a major distinction between Utility and either of the first two levels is the added degree of independence the dog must exercise in much of the Utility routine. This being true, why should Utility be more like dessert than a lot of new work? The answer lies in the dog's earlier training. In Novice it should have learned to heel very well, to come with speed and purpose and to stay like a statue. Open should have added two major strengths, a solid, enthusiastic retrieve and a genuine love for jumping. For the most part, Utility simply uses these acquired skills of the dog to teach slightly different applications that enable the dog to execute the Utility regimen successfully. Scent discrimination builds on the retrieve, adding the association that the target article is the one with the handler's fresh scent. Directed retrieve involves adding the ability to "mark," or take a sighting from the handler, for the direction to the desired glove. Thus, Utility represents the blending and redirecting of skills already learned to aid the dog in mastering its work.

Any seasoned trainer will readily admit that in starting a new dog, the perspective acquired from already having trained through Utility greatly influences how that new pup will be trained and what the trainer will settle for in execution before leaving a particular piece of work. He or she knows the building process that must occur to help the dog succeed and won't accept weak links that could jeopardize that success. There are a number of ways for the new obedience buff to get help starting out. Local park districts frequently offer dog obedience instruction. There may be an obedience club in the area that offers classes to the public. Perhaps you will learn of a private instructor who gives group classes or individual lessons. Unfortunately, the newcomer is more or less at the mercy of the particular instructor, who may be truly outstanding or may be someone who claims expertise but has neither the experience nor the accomplishments to be qualified to instruct. The best thing to do when starting out is to visit the class or instructor you are considering and observe. Good obedience instruction is fun for both the student and the dog. Whether yours is a family pet or a finished champion, an Airedale started in obedience training deserves the fun and challenge of the advanced levels of work. These great Terriers, when well prepared, can add a special dimension of excitement to the sport of obedience that everyone will enjoy, including the Airedale!

RIBBONS AND TITLE CONFIRMATION

Within a few weeks of completing each title, CD, CDX and UD, the American Kennel Club will mail to the registered owner of the dog a certificate evidencing the level of achievement the dog has attained. Placing in the particular class entered at an obedience trial results in being awarded a ribbon: blue for first, red for second, yellow for third and white for fourth. There is another very special distinction between Novice and the two higher levels of work. Once the Companion Dog title has been earned, the dog may no longer be shown in Novice. But dogs may continue to compete in both Open and Utility after earning those titles. If a dog is entered in Open and Utility at the same trial and posts the highest combined score among all other dogs also showing in Open and Utility, it is awarded a blue and green rosette. The dog with the highest score at a trial receives a blue and gold rosette. A green qualifying ribbon also is awarded to each dog receiving a qualifying score. Most clubs offering obedience trials also will put up special awards for class placings or a variety of other special qualifications, such as highest-scoring dog of a particular breed, in addition to the ribbons required by the AKC.

THE AIREDALE IN OBEDIENCE SINCE 1980
by Anne Reese

The Airedale and obedience—what a long way we have come since the 1980s! We began the decade as a sport that was not really recognized or appreciated at the Parent Club level. Many changes have occurred since the question was asked at Montgomery 1985—"Could the board authorize an Obedience committee?" All we had to do was ask. Then the work started!

Aletta Moore was our first chairman, and her committees were responsible for the ATCA's new trophy offering to High Scoring Airedale in Trial at all floaters where there were obedience classes. Aletta and her crew also created the Top Obedience Airedale award and the Top Novice Airedale award. This was a significant step in recognizing the efforts and hard work that our best Airedales put in over the year. We wanted to encourage and congratulate those great novice dogs; we also wanted—most importantly—to promote and encourage the showing of the Airedale Terrier in obedience. We felt the Shuman system (now Front & Foremost) best met the goals we were striving

Willow Aire Proud Piper, UD, owned, trained and loved by Frank and Nancy Foster.

for—rewarding high scores and, by its nature, encouraging the Airedale to be shown often.

Montgomery County weekend is a showcase for the Airedale. The ATCA board authorized the construction of a permanent trophy for the Top Obedience Airedale winner. As with the Airedale Bowl, the obedience dog's name is engraved on this trophy; it is on display every Montgomery County weekend, along with the other permanent trophies offered by the ATCA.

The Top Obedience Airedale award went to the same dog in 1988 and 1989. Crovenay Bingley Barrister, UD, owned, trained and loved by Linda Coates, not only won the award the first two years it was offered, but has been the top-rated Airedale in the Shuman system four times. "Ramsey" and Linda deserve much praise and credit, because a horrible accident in the show ring nearly curtailed Ramsey and his wonderful talents. Qualifying all the way to the bar jump in Utility, Ramsey sailed over the bar and landed in the "baby gate" fencing surrounding the ring. Everything collapsed, with poor Ramsey in the middle stuck in the fencing. Anyone who has ever trained a dog knows what a confidence blower something like that can be. Thankfully, with Linda's patience and a year's worth of training—without being shown—Ramsey built up his confidence! Where so many of us would have given up, Linda believed in this dog and brought him back in a big way! He's started a new career in Tracking and looks forward to success there too.

There were numerous obedience Airedales that deserve mention: The first two Top Novice Airedales, King Jester, CD, owned by Robert Dwyer, and Lave's Sweet N' Spicy Foxy Lady, CD, owned by LaVerne VanDerZee. They hope to progress to the Open and Utility rings and stay in competition for the big award.

Stars in the 1980s were easy to come by. Lave's Precious Gold Dust, UD, has earned the most OTCH points ever for an Airedale. Thirty-four points were compiled by this bitch, who retired from the ring in 1983. "Sugar" was an avid pupil, earning her CD at ten months with scores of 198.5, 197 and 195. At fifteen months she had her CDX, and at the ripe old age of two years, her UD! She made her last appearance in the ring at eleven years of age.

Elliott's Tuffenuff Jeep, CDX/TDX, is also a special star. He's the only Airedale in history to earn the TDX title. Even though Tracking technically isn't an obedience class, this is a significant achievement. His owner, Dorothy Miner, has contributed a great deal to Airedales and Tracking and is a licensed Tracking judge.

So many other names come to mind. Ch. Wataire's Piccadilly Legacy, UDT, has earned every title available except the TDX! On top of that, she has three offspring who have earned Obedience or Tracking titles. Linda Dart owns this exceptional bitch, and what a lot of hard work must have gone into earning titles and producing quality puppies to boot!

One of the truly "all rounders" of the decade has to be Ch. Seneca Newcomer's Chance, CD, TD, B, Sch III, IPO III, which shows "Myles" not only knows obedience, but has been trained for protection work as well. Myles

162

is owned by Maugh Vail and exemplifies the qualities that make the Airedale a dog for all reasons. Maugh writes that Myles is working on his TDX and rescue dog exercises. It seems there isn't anything he can't do!

It was found that for every forty-one Airedales registered, one of them becomes a breed champion. For every eighty-five Airedales registered, only one earns a CD! Out of every six CD Airedales, only one goes on to get his CDX, and out of every three CDX Airedales, just one gets that UD. That's one UD for every 1,494 Airedales registered!

Our Airedales in obedience are well bred. Champion sires accounted for over half of the obedience titleists in the 1980s. One hundred forty-three of our titleists also had champion dams. Eighty sires produced two or more obedience titleists, and forty-nine dams accounted for two or more title earners. The top sires and dams of obedience titleists are:

Sire's Name	*Number of Obedience-titled Offspring*
Ch. Finlair Tiger of Stone Ridge	9
Ch. Sunnydale's Doc Holiday	9
Ch. Stone Ridge Seventy-six	8
Ch. Bravo True Grit	7
Ch. Turith Country Cousin	6
Ch. Blackjack Mighty Samson	5
Ch. Eden's Sal Sorbus	5
Ch. Ernie's Jack Flash	5
Ch. Shshown's Que Forte, CD	5
Ch. Stone Ridge Union Jack	5
Ch. Bravo Star Buck	4
Ch. Briardale Kung Fu	4
Ch. Brown's Jigsaw John	4
Ch. Rudigan Robear	4
Ch. Turith Adonis	4
Ch. White Rose Rocka My Soul	4
Lewis's Cero Von Veto, CD	4

Dam's Name	*Number of Obedience-titled Offspring*
Stone Ridge Amanda	4
Ch. Arelsh Roman Candle, CD	3
Ch. Louline Air O' Tique	3
Ch. Stone Ridge Red Riding Hood	3
Ch. Watair's Piccadilly Legacy, UDT	3
Fairyland Forever Good Florence	3
Lady Ginger Blackstone	3
Reffal Brookwood Blossom, UD	3
Shannon's Reigning Terror	3
Wilhemenia of Cedar Rock	3

As you can see, our top obedience producers are familiar names in the breed ring as well. It is so good to see versatile Airedales producing all-around offspring—not only good-looking Airedales, but those that can work, too. Eighty-three of our obedience dogs were also conformation champions.

Scent discrimination? (Cartoon by Paul Clarke in "Dopey Dale")

12

Dog Agility Training

by Frank Foster

T HE DOG AGILITY Regulations put forth by the National Committee for Dog Agility state, under definition and purpose:

> Agility is similar to an obstacle course run against time. The handler runs with the dog, which is off lead, directing the dog through the course. There are two types of obstacles: various hurdles that the dog must jump, and nonhurdle obstacles, such as the Dog Walk, Teeter-totter, Closed and Open Tunnels, Ladder, Sway Bridge, Weave Hoops and Weave Poles. The course may run from 120 to 150 yards in length, but no specified pattern to the course is required. Although some constraints are imposed on the selection of obstacles to necessitate the use of approximately equal numbers of hurdle and nonhurdle obstacles, these obstacles may be arranged in any sequence. The intent is to insure a balance between standardization and variation in course designs. A certain degree of standardization is believed necessary for the awarding of an Agility degree.
>
> Agility is provided as an additional outlet for those interested in training and exhibiting their dogs. Agility should be recognized primarily as a fun event for dog, handler and spectator alike.

While Agility training is intended as an additional dimension of fun training for dogs, which it certainly is, it also affords some very real therapeutic benefits. Shy dogs learn confidence, indifferent dogs develop a keener working attitude and intense or tentative trainers learn to approach their training with more fun and certainty. Airedales that have been schooled too long in formal obedience work sometimes seem to lose interest. Whether due to the high

"Fitz" Fitzpatrick and Best in Show winner Ch. M.J.'s Stone Ridge Chosen One ("Abe") working on the teeter-totter in an Agility test.

Seneca Newcomers Chance, SCH III, B, CD shown retrieving over a scaling wall as part of a Schutzhund exercise. Dog owned and trained by L. M. Vail. Some of the Agility exercises are related to a few of the Schutzhund I exercises.

intelligence of the breed or to the method of training, try some agility work and watch that attitude bounce back! Although agility training is still in its infancy, interest in this area has already taken on an international scope. To obtain more information or a copy of the Dog Agility Regulations, you may write to The National Committee for Dog Agility, in care of C. L. Kramer, 401 Bluemont Circle, Manhattan, Kansas 66502, or USDAA United States Dog Agility Association, P.O. Box 850955, Richardson, TX 75085. The latter organization also has a complete list of reading materials as well as audio and visual aids available upon request.

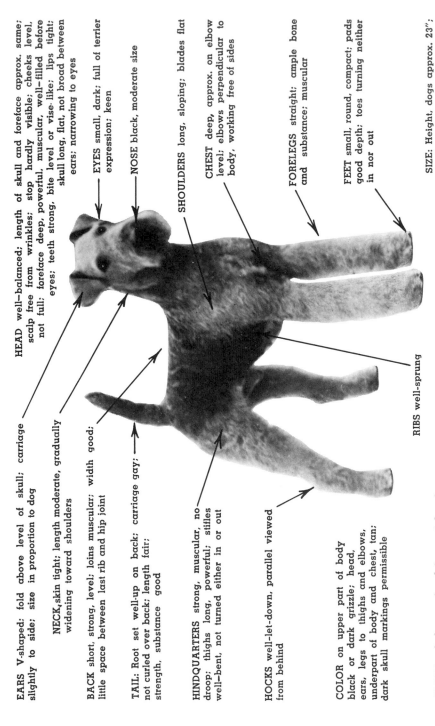

EARS V-shaped; fold above level of skull; carriage slightly to side; size in proportion to dog

HEAD well-balanced; length of skull and foreface approx. same; scalp free from wrinkles; stop hardly visible; cheeks level, not full; foreface deep, powerful, muscular, well-filled before eyes; teeth strong, bite level or vise-like; lips tight; skull long, flat, not broad between ears; narrowing toward shoulders

NECK, skin tight; length moderate, gradually widening toward shoulders

EYES small, dark; full of terrier expression; keen

NOSE black, moderate size

SHOULDERS long, sloping; blades flat

CHEST deep, approx. on elbow level; elbows perpendicular to body, working free of sides

BACK short, strong, level; loins muscular; width good; little space between last rib and hip joint

FORELEGS straight; ample bone and substance; muscular

FEET small, round, compact; pads good depth; toes turning neither in nor out

TAIL: Root set well-up on back; carriage gay; not curled over back; length fair; strength, substance good

SIZE: Height, dogs approx. 23"; bitches slightly less

HINDQUARTERS strong, muscular, no droop; thighs long, powerful; stifles well-bent, not turned either in or out

RIBS well-sprung

HOCKS well-let-down, parallel viewed from behind

COLOR on upper part of body black or dark grizzle; head, ears, legs to thighs and elbows, underpart of body and chest, tan; dark skull markings permissible

COAT hard, dense, wiry; lying straight, close; slight wave permitted; undercoat short, soft

Visualization of the Airedale Terrier Standard, reprinted with permission from Dog Standards Illustrated © 1975, Howell Book House. Note: Descriptions here only approximate wording in the Standard.

168

13

Official Standard and Blueprint of the Airedale Terrier

IF ONLY WE HAD the power to see our dogs as others—judges, for instance—see them! The nearest approach to such a faculty is that rare gift, "an eye for a dog"—the ability to appraise the qualities of a dog at a glance, so far as such can be ascertained by outward appearance. Most of us were born without that power, and consequently we have to learn through experience and constant study how to evaluate the points of a dog.

POINTS TO CONSIDER

There are two pitfalls that trap the newcomer to the dog game, slowing his progress, one being that self-satisfied rosy glow known as "kennel blindness," the other a superficial and usually short-lived egotism that brings on a pernicious affliction known as "fault-judging." The misted vision of kennel blindness glorifies one's own dogs and at the same time makes the dogs owned by others, like Gil Blas's mule, "all faults." Fault-judging affects the owner's dogs as well as his competitors, and in his own dogs he can become so conscious of a fault he is striving to eradicate that he cannot see good points even though they may completely outweigh the fault in question. This attitude, applied to others' dogs, can make them seem worthless because of one obvious

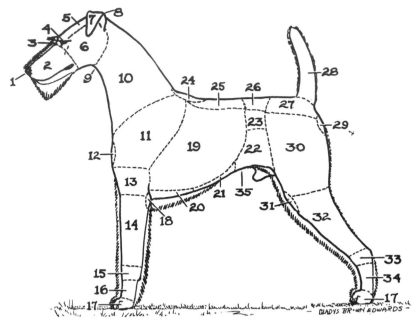

**Points of the Dog
as shown on the Airedale Terrier**

1—Nose
2—Muzzle; foreface
3—Stop
4—Eye
5—Skull; forehead
6—Cheek
7—Ear
8—Occiput (hidden by ear in this view)
9—Throat
10—Neck
11—Shoulder
12—Point of shoulder
13—Upper arm; arm
14—Forearm
15—Knee
16—Front pastern
17—Foot; paw

18—Elbow
19—Ribs
20—Brisket
21—Abdomen, belly
22—Flank
23—Coupling
24—Withers
25—Back
26—Loin
27—Croup; rump
28—Tail; stern
29—Point of buttock
30—Thigh
31—Stifle
32—Gaskin; second thigh
33—Hock
34—Back pastern
35—Tuck-up

Length is measured from point of shoulder to point of buttock (12 to 29)
Height is measured from withers (24) to ground. Length should approximate height on the Airedale.
The QUARTERS are the thighs; the HINDQUARTERS include the croup and hind legs.
The FOREHAND is that point in front of the center of gravity.
The BACKLINE includes the withers, back, loin and croup.

Main Points of the Skeleton

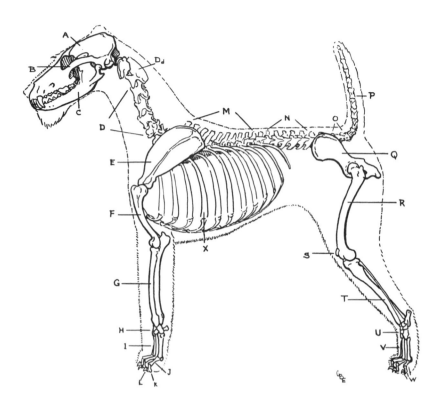

A— Cranium	L— Distal phalanges
B— Malar bone (Zygomatic process of,)	M— Thoracic vertebrae
C— Mandible	N— Lumbar vertebrae
Dd—Atlas (1st cervical vertebra)	O— Sacrum
E— Scapula	P— Caudal vertebrae
F— Humerus	Q— Pelvis
G— Radius and Ulna	R— Femur
H— Carpus	S— Patella
I— Metacarpus	T— Tibia and Fibula
J— 1st phalanges	U— Tarsus
K— 2nd phalanges	V— Metatarsus
	W—Phalanges
	X— Ribs

fault, such "pet hate" possibly being the only fault the fault-judger knows on sight.

The Airedale is a dog of normal conformation, square in proportion of length to height, and in basic points the Airedale Standard is similar to that of other normally conformed dogs. That is, there are no gross exaggerations of any points.

The current official Standard of the breed follows. The balance of this chapter is a point-by-point analysis of the word picture of Airedale perfection. Careful study of the Standard and the analysis, or blueprint, herein will give the reader an excellent basis for understanding what makes an Airedale an Airedale. If the reader will also objectively observe as many specimens in the flesh as possible, he will be well on the way toward really developing an in-depth knowledge of the "King of Terriers."

OFFICIAL STANDARD
OF THE AIREDALE TERRIER

HEAD

Should be well balanced with little apparent difference between the length of skull and foreface. *Skull* should be long and flat, not too broad between the ears and narrowing very slightly to the eyes. Scalp should be free from wrinkles, stop hardly visible and cheeks level and free from fullness. *Ears* should be V-shaped with carriage rather to the side of the head, not pointing to the eyes, small but not out of proportion to the size of the dog. The topline of the folded ear should be above the level of the skull. *Foreface* should be deep, powerful, strong and muscular. Should be well filled up before the eyes. *Eyes* should be dark, small, not prominent, full of terrier expression, keenness and intelligence. *Lips* should be tight. *Nose* should be black and not too small. *Teeth* should be strong and white, free from discoloration or defect. Bite either level or vise-like. A slightly overlapping or scissors bite is permissible without preference.

NECK

Should be of moderate length and thickness gradually widening towards the shoulders. Skin tight, not loose.

The Skull

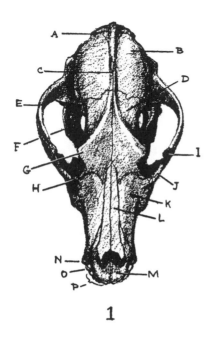

1

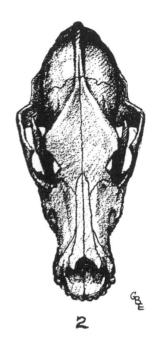

2

"1" Skull of a dog of Samoyed type. "2" Skull of an Airedale. Note that the much wider appearance of the former is due to the wide spacing of the malar bones and that the size of the cranium—the "brainroom"—is the same in both.

A—Interparietal bone
B—Parietal bone of the cranium
C—Parietal crest
D—Frontal bone
E—Zygomatic process of the temporal bone
F—Coronoid process of the mandible
G—Supraorbital process
H—Lacrimal bone

I—Zygomatic process of the malar bone
J—Malar bone
K—Maxilla
L—Nasal bone
M—Body of premaxilla
N—Canine tooth
O—Canine tooth (lower)
P—Incisors

173

The Skull and Dentition

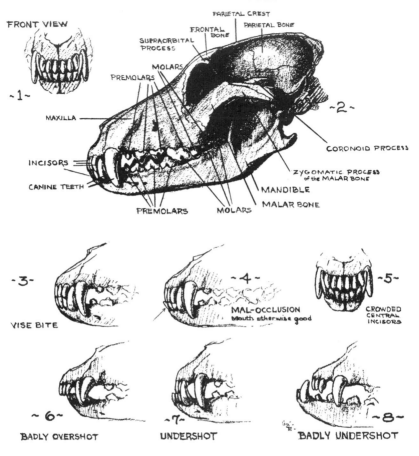

Nos. "1" and "2" show the perfect scissors bit, with No. 3, a vise or pincer bite, considered equally good. On the live dog the teeth of course are partially covered by the gums, and in the front view the lower lip fits in between the canine tooth (fang) and the jaw. The smaller premolars are almost buried in the gums in some cases, but ideally are of fair size. Occasionally a premolar is missing, but is usually compensated by larger size of the others. The mal-occlusion of the incisors, shown in No. "4" is due to the centrals growing forward in too flat an angle. The mouth shown is otherwise excellent. No. "5" is a common fault, with central incisors too small and crowded by unusually large corners and intermediates. Aside from "looks" this is not a serious fault, except that it might be inherited, while a mal-occlusion may be due to late shedding of milk teeth; "6" is a "pig jaw," badly overshot, and an abomination in a Terrier, accompanying a weak lower jaw. "7" Undershot jaw. Note the obvious difference between this and the mal-occlusion, especially the position of the fangs, and the face-to-face position of the premolars, rather than interlocking. "8" should never be seen in a Terrier, and is the deliberately-bred undershot jaw of a Boxer.

Heads and Expression

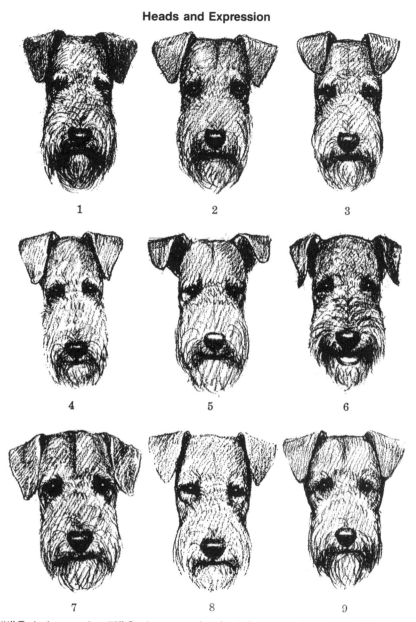

"1" Typical expression. "2" Staring expression due to large, round, light eyes. "3" High, Fox Terrier ears, pointing to the eye. "4" Very narrow head, with little space between eyes or ears. "5" Flying ears. "6" Same head as No. 1, but in a less stern mood, and ears relaxed. "7" Broad head, large eyes, Houndy ears. "8" Same type head as No. 1, but trimmed too close in front of eyes at corners of mouth, making the head appear cheeky. "9" Broad, coarse skull.

175

SHOULDERS AND CHEST

Shoulders long and sloping well into the back. Shoulder blades flat. From the front, chest deep but not broad. The depth of the chest should be approximately on a level with the elbows.

BODY

Back should be short, strong and level. Ribs well sprung. Loins muscular and of good width. There should be but little space between the last rib and the hip joint.

HINDQUARTERS

Should be strong and muscular with no droop.

TAIL

The root of the tail should be set well up on the back. It should be carried gaily but not curled over the back. It should be of good strength and substance and of fair length.

LEGS

Forelegs should be perfectly straight, with plenty of muscle and bone. *Elbows* should be perpendicular to the body, working free of sides. *Thighs* should be long and powerful with muscular second thigh, stifles well bent, not turned either in or out, hocks well let down parallel with each other when viewed from behind. *Feet* should be small, round and compact with a good depth of pad, well cushioned; the toes moderately arched, not turned either in or out.

COAT

Should be hard, dense and wiry, lying straight and close, covering the dog well over the body and legs. Some of the hardest are crinkling or just slightly waved. At the base of the hard very stiff hair should be a shorter growth of softer hair termed the undercoat.

COLOR

The head and ears should be tan, the ears being of a darker shade than the rest. Dark markings on either side of the skull are permissible. The legs up to the thighs and elbows and the under-part of the body and chest are also tan and the tan frequently runs into the shoulder. The sides and upper parts of the body should be black or dark grizzle. A red mixture is often found in the black and is not to be considered objectionable. A small white blaze on the chest is a characteristic of certain strains of the breed.

SIZE

Dogs should measure approximately 23 inches in height at the shoulder; bitches, slightly less. Both sexes should be sturdy, well muscled and boned.

MOVEMENT

Movement or action is the crucial test of conformation. Movement should be free. As seen from the front the forelegs should swing perpendicular from the body free from the sides, the feet the same distance apart as the elbows. As seen from the rear the hind legs should be parallel with each other, neither too close nor too far apart, but so placed as to give a strong well-balanced stance and movement. The toes should not be turned either in or out.

FAULTS

Yellow eyes, hound ears, white feet, soft coat, being much over or under the size limit, being undershot or overshot, having poor movement, are faults which should be severely penalized.

SCALE OF POINTS

Head	10	Color	5
Neck, shoulders and chest	10	Size	10
Body	10	Movement	10
Hindquarters and tail	10	General characteristics and	
Legs and feet	10	expression	15
Coat	10	TOTAL	100

Approved July 14, 1959

Shoulder Angulation

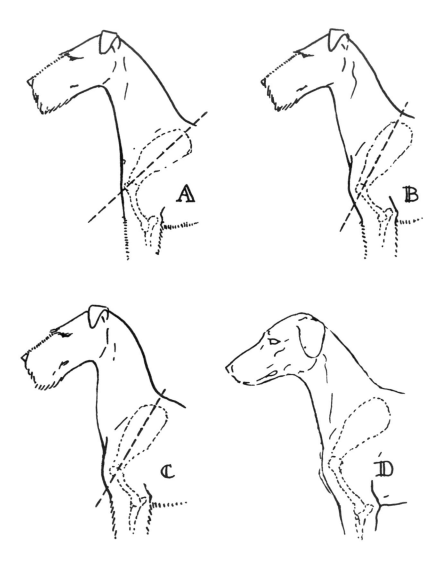

"A"—good Terrier front. "B" and "C" show straight shoulders and the undesirable "ewe" neck and "swan" neck, respectively. "D," the sort of front common to most breeds of dogs, different from the Terrier front in the length and angle of the upper arm (humerus). The greater length of the humerus places the leg farther under the dog.

Hindquarters Angulation

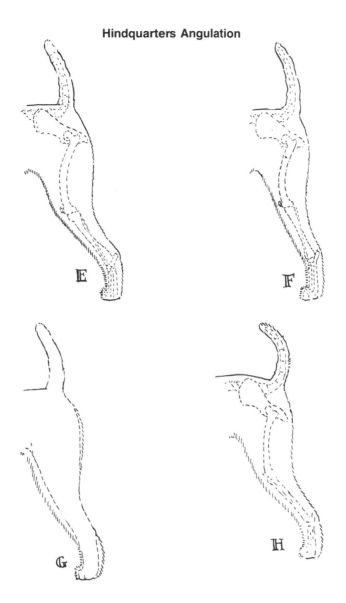

"E," correct angulation and tailset. "F," straight stifle and hock. Note that the bones of the thigh (femur) and the gaskin (tibia and fibula) are shorter than in the leg having good angulation. In this sort of leg the hind pastern is long, therefore NOT placing the hock "close to the ground." "G" shows how trimming can minimize the faults of this leg somewhat by leaving well-carved long hair in front of the leg and in back of the pastern, and leaving a padding of hair on the buttocks. "H"—hindquarters having a steep croup and low tailset, due to sharper slope of pelvis. This sort of croup often accompanies a curved tails.

THE STANDARD ANALYZED

GENERAL APPEARANCE

The Airedale in the show ring and the Airedale in the field look often very different, but it could be the same dog. In the show ring it should present the stylish, sleek, well-polished, sophisticated dog on parade, while out in the field or at home in the backyard it presents the "teddy bear look." The additional hair makes its head look shorter and broader, and the extra coat may make it look fatter or lower to the ground. Not many people, including judges, can pick out the "best" dog just by the feel of his hands, so don't be deceived by hair and do realize that another person can make some unwelcome comments about a "hairy" dog. Many of us clip small puppies before offering them for sale so that the puppies will look like what the adult dog should look like. It is hard for a potential buyer to imagine how the "fuzzballs" should appear.

SIZE

Approximately twenty-three inches in height leaves room for a great variation in height. Most male Airedales measure about twenty-four inches at the shoulder with bitches twenty-two to twenty-three inches. It is felt that with our attention to vitamin-enriched "everything" our dogs today have heavier bone and much more substance as well as being slightly taller. The true test is the square, or as tall as the dog is in length. Weight varies entirely according to the bone structure; however, most males weigh in the sixties and the bitches in the fifties.

HEAD

The head should be well balanced with little difference between the length of foreface and the skull; however, a slightly longer foreface will accentuate the long, lean look with the top and side planes being flat, producing a brick appearance. The stop should be almost nonexistent. The temporal bones should feel flat to the touch and not rounded to give the curved appearance of other breeds. An Airedale should be well filled up under the eyes and not "dished" out, as this helps to achieve the long, lean look of the proper Airedale head. Cleanness of cheek means that the cheek muscle should not bulge out, making the dog's head appear as a triangle.

EARS

The ears should be V-shaped with a finger's width lift above the skull line folding over with the inside edge touching the dog's cheek. The ear does not point to the eye as in Fox terriers, rather it points to the outside corner of the eye. A proper ear looks like a triangle pasted on to each side of the dog's head.

EXPRESSION

The expression is the combination of the eyes, ears and the shape of the head and radiates the dog's spirit with the keen, hard-bitten look of the "King."

EYES

The eyes are oval, almond or even slightly triangular and as dark as possible. Remember, puppies' eyes have a bluish cast for several months, so don't be misled. The true eye color is not usually stable until a pup is several months old.

NOSE

The nose should be big and black. Some puppies at birth have pinkish noses that darken later and some dogs with less pigment will have what is called a "winter" nose; in other words, the nose gets lighter in winter when the sun rays are not as strong.

TEETH AND BITE

The teeth should meet in front with a scissors bite where the upper teeth overlap the lower teeth, or a pincer or level bite where all front teeth meet. The canine teeth, or the fangs, should fit closely along their length, thus keeping the mouth from being overshot or undershot. When examining teeth, look at the sides as well as the front to be sure the dog has full dentition.

NECK

The neck should present a graceful arch between the head and the shoulders with a clean throat line devoid of folds of loose skin.

A—A roached back. Otherwise the dog is of good conformation.

B—A weed of somewhat racy lines.

C—A thick-set, cloddy dog, with broad skull, low ears and round eyes. He also has a short gaskin and long back pastern. Though he has a straight backline it looks longer than it is, due to a complete lack of withers.

D—An angular dog, with "nothing in back of his ears." Neck is upside down, shoulders are straight and upper arm too slanted, and the front pastern "soft." Tailset is low and hindleg is very straight of stifle.

Conformation and Showmanship

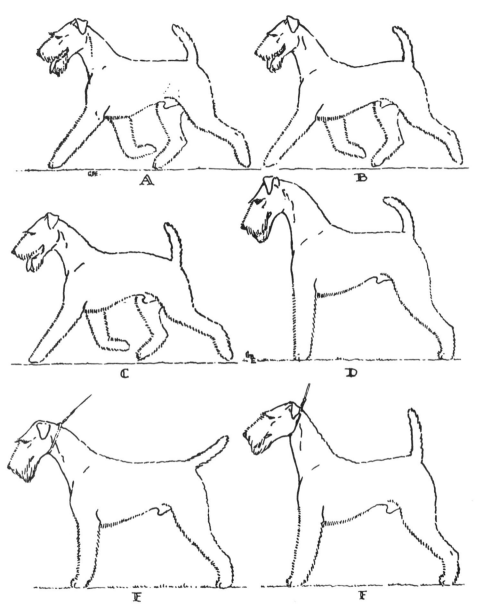

"A" is a dog with a good backline which stays straight when the dog trots. "B" is the usual result, a slight sag of the back, not evident when the dog is standing. "C" is an unpleasant roach, not noticed until the dog moves. This backline usually goes with very poor hind movement of the "rubber-legged" sort. "D"—A dog "on his toes" and showing off, on his own. "E"—Same dog, half asleep, making the backline seem much longer and the front less straight, especially notable in the slant of upper arm and pastern. "F"—Same dog, over-handled. Strangled by the lead, he "props" in self-defense, his hind feet come forward, and his back goes down. The neckline is far from the graceful arch the dog shows when allowed to spar against another dog.

FRONT, CHEST AND RIBBING

A proper Airedale front is moderately narrow with long, lean muscles and shoulders sloping toward the back. The theory that an upright shoulder causes base-wide or paddle movement is not necessarily so, as many a good mover has a shoulder more upright than is considered ideal.

The ribs of the Airedale are long and elliptical in shape, being flatter in front, thus giving the front legs freedom to move perpendicular to the body. The back ribs are "sprung" and curve upward toward the loin, thus permitting more lung expansion and giving the "well-ribbed-up" conformation. The withers that are prominent enough to help blend the neck cleanly into the back add an illusion of greater depth of chest and shortness of back.

BACK

The back is the short area between the withers and the loin and is often confused with the "backline," which includes the withers, loin and croup. The ideal backline is level and as short as possible. A roached back, a roller-coaster back or a sway or soft back are not pleasing to look at and are often covered by masterful trimming that can create the ideal look. The croup is the area from the point of the hipbone to the bone at the point of the buttocks both on the top and the sides. The slant or the levelness of the croup determines the tailset. The sacrum is the section of the vertebrae located directly in front of the tail and can rise when a dog pulls itself together as when sparring.

TAIL

A good set-on refers to a tail that is set so that it is positioned forward on the croup or rump. A dog that has a good set-on can squirrel his tail forward when excited due to tightening the backline muscling. The Airedale tail is docked usually level with the head and is done when the newborn puppy is three to five days old. The rule of the thumb is one-third off, but tails vary in length and thickness at birth, so no hard-and-fast rule can be set.

QUARTERS

The term "quarters" means the muscling in the thigh, usually only visible on the inside of the back leg since the outside is covered with the dog's furnishings or leg hair. A good bend of stifle or a well-angulated leg increases the length of stride and improves the dog's movement. Viewed from behind, the ideal rear could have an imaginary line drawn from the point of the buttocks down through the hock, the pastern and the foot. However, in a show

Effect of Stance on Conformation

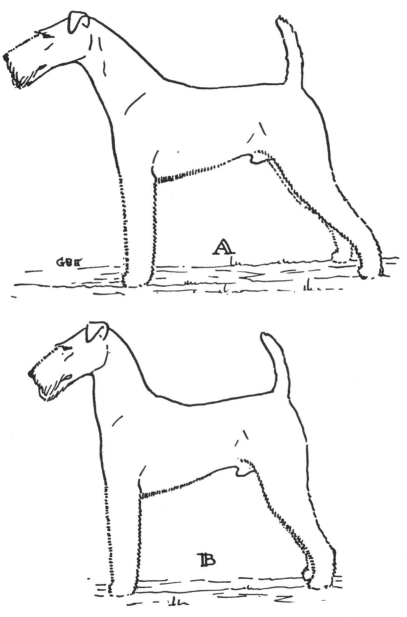

"A" shows a dog with rather plain neck and slightly high croup, posed to offset these faults. The neck is pulled forward by "baiting," and the hind feet are placed far apart to lower the croup, levelling the backline. "B," the same dog, improperly posed, with neck too upright, showing a bulge underneath; hind feet too far forward and close together, making croup appear even higher, and back consequently showing a dip.

Conformation

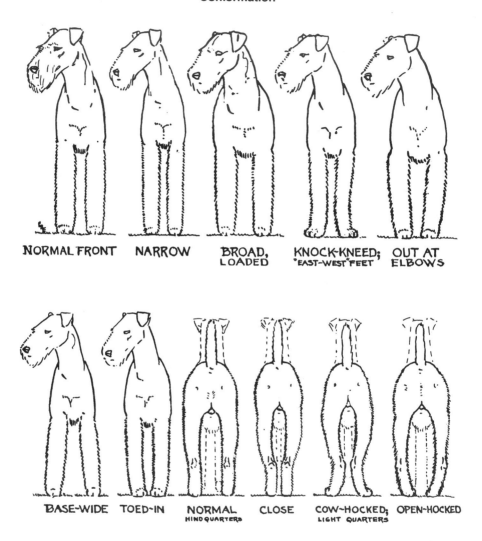

NORMAL FRONT   NARROW   BROAD, LOADED   KNOCK-KNEED; *EAST-WEST* FEET   OUT AT ELBOWS

BASE-WIDE   TOED-IN   NORMAL HINDQUARTERS   CLOSE   COW-HOCKED; LIGHT QUARTERS   OPEN-HOCKED

The normal front is "moderately narrow," and straight. Good hindquarters are broad, well-muscled, and straight, in rear view. The very narrow front is typical of the "pipe-cleaner" type of Airedale, and is undesirable, as are also the "broad," "knock-kneed," "out at elbows," "base-wide" and "toed-in" fronts. The "close" stance of the hindquarters is not necessarily the counterpart of the "narrow" front; it often occurs on otherwise good hindquarters. It is generally conceded that the "open-hocked" conformation is much less serious a fault than "cow-hocks."

186

Movement

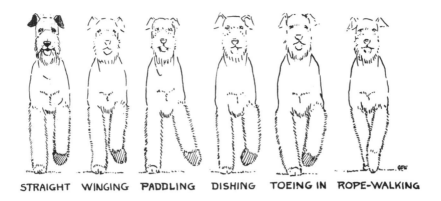

STRAIGHT WINGING PADDLING DISHING TOEING IN ROPE-WALKING

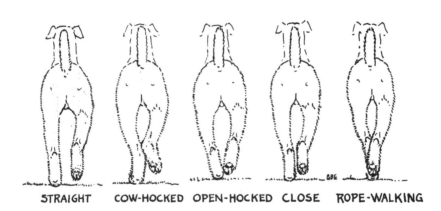

STRAIGHT COW-HOCKED OPEN-HOCKED CLOSE ROPE-WALKING

Correct and faulty movement, front and rear view. The faster the gait the more the leg inclines under the center of gravity.

stance the hind legs are spread a little farther apart to make the quarters look wider and straighten the backline.

LEGS AND FEET

The forelegs should be straight when looked at from all sides, including the pasterns, and should be heavy in bone and muscle. Dewclaws should be removed as they are useless and can cause problems when grooming the dog. In the rear leg the stifle joint should be well bent and the second thigh muscle should be long, making the hock joint close to the ground or "well let down." A dog "straight in stifle" moves with a stilted, stiff motion. The feet should be "cat-like" or small and compact, with high arched toes and deep pads. Keeping a puppy's nails short will help to keep the feet from spreading and becoming open between the toes.

COAT AND COLOR

A true Airedale coat should be hard, dense and wiry with a softer undercoat. The profuse furnishings and whiskers on the show dogs are the results of much conditioning, as a dog with a wiry coat often has leg and face hair that is wiry also and requires much attention to present the finished look of the show dog. The long goatee makes the head look longer and leaner, and profuse leg hair can cover minor faults.

A dog working in the field does not have the show trim, as the burrs and foxtails can get caught in the longer leg hair and cause the dog to be uncomfortable. Ideally, the dog has a black, black saddle and rich tan legs, head and underside. Some of the hardest coats carry a red diamond on the dog's back in front of the tail; this same red can be seen throughout the dog's coat and sometimes can be so profuse the coat is grizzled with no distinct saddle.

An Airedale puppy is born black with brown points, the hair coat is short and slick much as in a Doberman, Manchester or Welsh. The brown points are brown spots above the eyes and a brown bar on the chest, and the underside is brown. As the puppy grows, the black recedes, the ears become brown and the top of the head and then gradually the legs lose their puppy-coat black and the new hair comes in tan. A sheep-coated puppy can almost always be detected at birth as the black is sooty colored and the tan is a very light beige. These coats are not good for showing; however, a great deal of work can make them passable, but they usually retain some black in the back legs, on the ears and on the sides of the head.

MOVEMENT

Movement should be the true test of an Airedale. They should move free and fluid. A good-moving dog could carry a cup of water on its back and not spill a drop. The front legs should swing perpendicular from the body with a good reach out in front. The rear legs should move parallel to each other with a good amount of daylight showing between. The toes should point straight ahead on all four legs. The show dog is moved at a trot around the ring, and the tempo can be picked up when the dog is flowing in a smooth gait. The faster the dog is moved, the closer to the center of the body's gravity the feet will be placed to maintain balance. Please remember the Terrier front does not permit the acme of movement as demonstrated by the sporting dogs with an entirely different front.

"Single-tracking," "weaving," "plaiting" or "rope-walking" is a faulty form of travel and results when the dog places one foot directly in front of the one on the other side (both front or back). "Side-winding" is when the dog pulls away from the handler in front and moves at a diagonal down the ring in a crabbing motion.

Some Airedales will show off in the ring and paddle, pivoting against the lead and throwing their front legs, but if you can get them to settle down and quit playing, they will move in a true gait. A "hackney" gait is another way to show off and although it attracts attention, it is not proper for a Terrier.

Balance in a dog does not merely mean the all-over dog but means balance between the front end and the rear end so that the long, sloping shoulder and the great reach of the front legs are accompanied by a good bend of stifle and rear legs that reach out in the same length of stride. This movement is beautiful to watch.

Airedales for all ages—look-alikes—Charles Jackson of Jackson's Airedales.

190

14

Selecting Your Airedale and Starting Out Right

by Joanne Vohs, Jolee Aire

IF YOU'VE CHOSEN an Airedale as your friend and companion, you will want it to conform to the breed standard as set forth by the AKC.

Check to see the environment from which your puppy is coming. A reputable breeder will breed dogs that will enhance the posture of the Airedale in years to come and will possess a caring attitude for his dogs' well-being. His facility and animals will be clean and have a happy atmosphere. The breeder will be concerned after the sale as well as before, in helping you raise, train and care for your puppy. Ask what the health guarantee is; if the AKC registration and the pedigree are provided; if he furnishes shot and worming records; if he will be available to help you set the puppy's ears, if needed, to insure proper ear carriage. Remember, a few extra dollars are insignificant, spread over the lifetime of a dog, if you are buying what is practically a sure thing instead of a gamble.

Now that you've found a breeder you're comfortable with, the question arises: Should it be a male or female? Many people feel the male is as loving but a bit more devoted than the female. Contrary to the old wives' tale that males tend to run away more than females, the males actually are more likely to stay close and watch over you, while the females tend to be more independent. Both will wander, as will any dog that is not trained. Females will go

"Pick me."

John Abraham getting acquainted with two furry friends.

A basket of puppies. Look out world!

into season (heat) twice a year for three weeks unless spayed. Neutering for a male is sometimes less costly than for a female. Both sexes make wonderful companions for children as well as senior citizens.

If you are still undecided as to which sex you prefer, seek advice from your breeder as to which would best suit your life-style.

The next decision is whether to get a puppy or an adult dog. Contrary to popular belief, older Airedales adjust very well to a new home and environment. Don't hesitate to think about getting an older dog if you are not up to the rigors of raising a new puppy. If you work full-time and no one is home all day, if you want an instant companion to walk with, jog with or guard your home immediately, think about a mature Airedale.

Your breeder may have older kennel dogs with a little or a lot of training for sale for various reasons. Most reputable breeders want their dogs returned to them if their owners are not able to keep them because of divorce, death, relocation of family, etc. In any case, there often are wonderful adult companions available, sometimes through rescue efforts. The adults should be given a two-week trial to make sure they and their new owners are compatible. Request information on previous environment, the dog's good and bad habits, feeding instructions and general care.

While maintenance of an adult is considerably less than that of raising a puppy, you have to remember everything is new and different to him. At first, give him limited freedom of your home, and take your time getting to know each other; you'll have years of enjoyment as your reward for giving him a good home.

STARTING THE PUPPY OUT RIGHT

So, you've decided on a delightful bundle of puppyhood! A puppy will amuse, provoke, worry, please and love you. No matter what you have planned for your puppy's future, early training is the most important step toward its becoming an enjoyable adult.

Along with your puppy, you will need to purchase a *soft* nylon or leather collar, six-foot leather or nylon web leash, slicker brush, comb, toys, two stainless steel dishes and food. But *the most important purchase of all is a crate* (fiberglass or wire, not wood). Don't let anyone tell you it is cruel or unkind to put your dog in a crate. They are *wrong!* Left unattended, a puppy can cause extensive damage to your property and to itself. It is a source of amazement that so many people have trouble with adult dogs that they've raised from a puppy. However, in almost every case, the problem dog does not have a place in the home to call its own. The crate can be a sanctuary when the dog feels good or bad or tired, or just wants to be left alone for a while. A dog seldom stirs during the night except to get up, turn around and settle back down. If a dog is loose to wander, it will need to eliminate, investigate, and probably get into trouble. A dog used to a cage will be less demanding, less destructive, quieter, more trainable and generally a dog of better mental adjustment.

If puppy whines or barks at first, try playing soft music on the radio for company. Once used to being without littermates, it'll be fine. Leave the crate door open when puppy's not in it. You'll be surprised to find the the pup going in voluntarily to take a nap or play.

HOUSETRAINING

Start immediately! Think of a word to use—potty, make, whatever. Use the word and take puppy to the same place every time. If possible, leave a bit from last time to smell until puppy gets the idea. If the pup goes, praise enthusiastically and show how happy you are. Go out often at first—after waking up, after eating, after playing and before going to bed for the night. Remember this is a baby, and if left too long, puppy won't be able to hold it.

If the puppy eliminates in the house, take it by the back of the neck (like mother dog would), show it the mistake and say *"Bad Dog"* in a firm voice. Take puppy outside where it was supposed to go. Follow through with lots of praise when he goes in the right spot. Once puppies get the idea of where to relieve themselves, they will let you know they need to go outside, sometimes by just standing at the door. Keep a close watch so you learn to read the signs. If you're too busy to watch, put the puppy in a crate. We've known of some cases taking two days, and some taking several months; how long it takes you to housebreak your puppy will depend on how much effort you put into the task at hand.

Once the pup is housebroken and is four months or older, it is sufficient to put puppy out first thing in the morning, noon, suppertime and before you go to bed at night.

EARLY PUPPY TRAINING

A few words of caution about training: *Never* lose your temper. *Never* use a harsh command or correction on a young puppy. Your commands should be short and firm. Don't expect perfection overnight; patience and perseverance will pay off in the long run. Remember, your puppy's attention span is very short at this time, so keep training time to a minimum. You can work with puppy several times a day, but for only five to ten minutes at a time. As the pup gets older, you can increase your time up to twenty minutes, several times a day for an adult. Training should be fun and productive for both you and your dog. Never give a command that you don't follow through. Remember it is a *command,* not a request! Use the appropriate tone of voice. Be *consistent!* What is good is always good; what is bad is always bad.

One big tip on training dogs is that if they think they can get away with a little, they will try to get away with a lot more. They should be disciplined

194

Fancy and Marc Framke in a serious conversation.

"Let's play."

Doing what comes naturally.

every time it is needed, not just some of the time. Otherwise, they will try to have their own way, and you'll just be wearing yourself out being ineffective. You'll blame the dog for what you failed to convince it to do at all times . . . *behave!* Your puppy will be happiest when pleasing you. Be your puppy's best friend by training properly, and the pup will grow up to be *your* best friend.

If your puppy is afraid or cautious at first, don't worry. It will get to know you and your environment very quickly. If you have small children in the home, teach them to respect, love and care for this new baby. *A puppy is not a toy.* Encourage gentle and quiet play, and puppy will grow up to be gentle. If play is rough and tough, the pup will grow up to be a rough, tough and very active dog. *Teasing should not be allowed.*

The most important and first word you must teach your puppy is *"No";* the second is its name. As soon as your Airedale comes home, it will want to investigate and test everything. Your job is to lay down the ground rules. That puppy will mature at forty to sixty-five pounds. Jumping, biting, growling and barking are *not* traits you want in your Airedale.

When puppy touches something it shouldn't, say *"No."* If puppy doesn't listen, take the back of its neck, shake it and repeat *"No."* When puppy stops, tell it what a good pup it is. If puppy bites your hands, make it an unpleasant experience. Put your hand all the way back in its mouth or press down on its tongue with your finger—puppy will want your hand out of its mouth. When your hand is out, pet and stroke puppy gently on its face with praise. Pup will soon learn that not biting is more fun.

JUMPING

When puppy jumps on you, remember pup's going to get bigger. Gently put the dog down, say *"Off"* (*"Down"* means to lie down) and pet pup on the floor. Praise. Repeat as often as necessary. Be consistent. If this doesn't work, be more forceful. Knock puppy down with your knee, saying *"Off,"* follow down and pet pup. Praise a lot when puppy stays on all fours. When company comes, you should keep a leash on puppy at first. If puppy jumps on the company, jerk pup down, say *"Off"* and have the people reach down and pet puppy on the floor. Puppy just wants to be greeted, and needs to learn that four on the floor is the best way to get attention.

LEASH BREAKING

Leash breaking means that your puppy does not pull on the leash. The puppy doesn't have to be right at your side at first; heeling is trained at a later date. Your dog can have all or part of the six-foot leash, as long as it doesn't pull. Allowing the puppy to pull or strain teaches constant tension on the leash.

Gently tug, jerk or snap the leash toward you, saying the pup's name and praising all the while. *Do not drag*—tug or jerk, release, jerk and release, etc., until the pup's by you. Pet and praise. Repeat until the dog is following you everywhere. As soon as the leash gets taut, jerk. Never let there be tension. The dog will soon learn not to pull. A small child should be able to walk an Airedale that is leash broken. Do not be stingy with your praise; the puppy must know you are pleased.

BARKING

Some people think a good watchdog should bark at everybody and everything. Not so! If your dog is barking and carrying on all the time, how can you know when something is really wrong? Your dog will be much more effective if alert and thinking with mouth shut, ready to growl or bark if needed, than leaping hysterically and barking uncontrollably. So start on your puppy immediately. Growling and barking are not cute, and you won't stand for it. A sharp *"No,"* a shake if need be, holding the muzzle and saying *"Quiet,"* are some ways to correct this bad habit. Again, praise when your dog stays quiet.

SIT, DOWN AND STAY

To teach your puppy to "Sit," hold the puppy's collar with one hand. Take the other hand or lower arm and gently push in the puppy's back legs under its rear end. Make the puppy sit. Say the pup's name first, then give the command and sit your pup at the same time: "Buster, *Sit.*" Praise. If you wish, you can reward him now. Let the puppy up. Repeat, rewarding only if the pup sits. Do this several times a day for a few minutes. Once the puppy sits on his own, praise the pup lavishly.

Now you can introduce "Stay." With the dog in a sitting position, give the command *"Stay."* If the puppy moves, correct quickly with a jerk on the leash and a firm *"No."* Put the puppy's back in a sit and say *"Stay."* Repeat until the puppy stays for a few seconds. Praise! You can increase the time as the pup gets used to it.

To teach the puppy "Down" from a sitting position, put one hand on the pup's shoulders. With the other hand, take hold of the two front legs, gently. Slide the front legs forward while putting gentle pressure on the shoulders, pushing down at the same time. Praise and reassure the puppy all the while. If the pup resists, start over from a sitting position. Repeat until the puppy gets the idea of what you want. Once the pup is lying down when told, you can work on the "Down, Stay" using the same method as the "Sit, Stay."

To come when called must be the most important thing in your puppy's life. It also must be the most pleasant. *Never, ever call* the puppy to you for *punishment.* If you want the puppy to come and you know it won't, don't call. Never let the puppy loose if it doesn't come when called. Use a leash until you can be sure. When the puppy does come to you, make it the greatest thing ever. Praise lavishly.

To teach the puppy to come, put the pup in a "Sit, Stay" position. Walk to the end of the leash. Call: "Buster, Come!" Coax gently, jerking and releasing the leash until your puppy is right by you. Praise and repeat the process until your Airedale comes when called. You can then increase the length of the leash by using a soft clothesline or training lead twenty to thirty feet long. Work gradually, and soon your puppy will be coming every time you call.

Never leave your dog unattended or chained up. Lack of supervision and chaining outside could cause your dog to become a barker and possibly even strangle itself. Your local dog club may offer kindergarten puppy training classes and obedience classes for your older puppy or adult. We would highly recommend you take advantage of these classes.

CHEWING

Puppies need things to chew on for cutting teeth, to induce growth of permanent teeth, to assist getting rid of baby teeth, to assure normal jaw development and to settle permanent teeth solidly in their jaws.

An adult dog's desire to chew stems from the instinct for cleaning its teeth, gum massage and jaw exercise, and the need for an outlet for occasional doggie tensions, loneliness and spite.

You need to provide desirable chewing items that are safe for your dog to chew on or play with. The puppy should not be allowed to chew on anything you don't want it to have. Give the puppy plenty of its own things at all times, and the pup will be less interested in your things. The hard nylon toys, sturdy, squeaky latex or rubber toys, two old socks tied in a knot and a tennis ball tied in a sock are a few good toys. Use common sense when selecting play things for your puppy; don't give anything that will get gummy, slimy or sticky, or that will cake up in his coat. Stay away from items that will splinter or break off easily. Don't give anything undigestible or anything extremely abrasive that could damage the enamel on the teeth.

FOOD AND TREATS FOR YOUR NEW PUPPY

Feed your new puppy at first in a quiet place with no distractions, preferably in its crate. After the puppy develops good eating habits, you can feed your pup in the kitchen or any other desirable location.

The general diet (unless otherwise instructed) is to use a good name-brand (not generic) dry puppy food that has all the essential vitamins and minerals. We don't recommend canned foods, as they tend to coat the teeth

"Anyone for soccer?"

Pure bliss.

"Where's Santa?" asks Ch. Nipmuc Lord Philip, CD.

199

and the beard. Feed six- to twelve-week puppies three times a day as much as they will eat in fifteen to twenty minutes. Do not leave the bowl down between meals. Have water available at all times, except in the crate, and from mid-evening until wake-up time in the morning, until the puppy is housebroken.

When the pup is twelve weeks to twelve months old, feed twice a day. Remember to increase the amount of food as the appetite increases.

At one year you can go to feeding once a day, morning or early evening, whichever you prefer. You also can switch from puppy to adult formula. If you want to add oil to your puppy's food because of a dry coat, use one-half teaspoon peanut oil drizzled over dry food. You can increase the amount as the puppy grows, up to two tablespoons for an adult.

If your puppy has loose stools when you first bring it home, don't be alarmed. Among other things, change of environment or water can cause loose stools, as well as excitement or eating leaves, snow, sticks, grass or the myriad items a puppy can find. If the stool doesn't firm up in a day or two, seek advice from your breeder or veterinarian.

Treats can be a very controversial subject. Try limiting treats as much as possible, and use only for rewards, for training and for teaching tricks. Stay away from treats loaded with food dyes and chemicals. Use common sense, as you would in treating a child. Use healthy snacks, not junk foods. Pieces of the dog food and tiny pieces of cheese work very well.

Your puppy must be rewarded for a job well done with loads of praise and healthy treats.

PUPPY COAT MAINTENANCE

You must teach your puppy good grooming habits early, as the pup will need to be groomed all of its life. Use a gentle slicker brush with bent wires mounted in a firm rubber backing. The comb should be solid metal with a combination of coarse and medium teeth.

Brushing is essential for eliminating mats and tangles, removing dead hair, dirt and burrs and distributing the natural oils for a healthy, glowing coat.

First of all, you should select a proper working surface. The floor is your pet's playground so it should be used only as a last resort. Any solid nonslip work surface at a convenient height will work. Do not leave your dog unattended on this work surface.

A firm "No" should suffice when your pup tries to play or bite the brush or comb. Start in one area at a time. Don't allow the dog to twist and turn as you chase with the brush. Your pet eventually will win at this game, and you'll become exhausted and discouraged. Firmness counts.

Take the head in your hand and begin by brushing the face. Look in the pup's eyes and say "No" for misbehavior. Praise for good behavior. Brush the back, sides and tail, keeping the puppy in a standing position.

Move to the legs, which are probably the most neglected part of the grooming process. Hold the legs gently so as not to put undue pressure on the knee or hip joints. Lift front legs forward, toward you, and the back legs straight back.

Brush up and work in small sections down to the skin. Do the entire dog. Finish by combing the entire dog in the direction of hair growth. This whole process should only take about five minutes. If you're firm but gentle, and brush two to three times a week, your pet will soon look forward to these grooming sessions.

Start nail trimming at an early age so it isn't so traumatic for the puppy. Use a good sharp nail clipper and a file. Hold the puppy's feet (at the bottom of the leg) just above the toes. Avoid putting pressure or strain on his tiny toe bones and joints. Take off the curved end of the nails, praising the puppy all the time. Gently file the rough edges. You can do this on the table or with the puppy lying down on the floor. Do not panic if one of the nails bleeds a little. Have some Quick Stop styptic powder handy. Just dab a little on the bleeding nail, hold for a few seconds, and the bleeding will stop. Make the handling of your dog's feet a pleasant experience and your pet won't object in the future.

If you don't have the time or desire to brush your pet or clip nails, more frequent grooming by a professional is recommended. An Airedale, if clipped, should be groomed every eight to twelve weeks. Be sure to get your breeder to recommend a good professional groomer who knows how to make your Airedale look like an Airedale, not a Poodle or Schnauzer.

Do not bathe your puppy too frequently, as it washes out the natural oils and can cause dry skin. Your dog needs to be bathed only when clipped; but if you must bathe, use a very mild shampoo and make sure you rinse your pet thoroughly, removing all residue from the coat. Towel dry and brush the coat. Finish drying with a blow dryer before your puppy goes outside in cold weather.

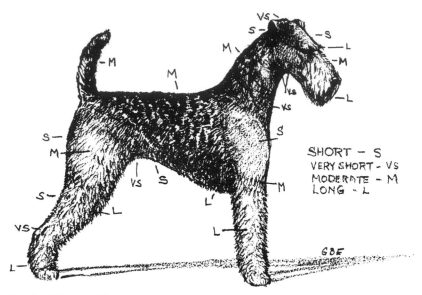

SHORT – S
VERY SHORT – VS
MODERATE – M
LONG – L

The final trim should appear as shown here. Body coat is about an inch long, that on the shoulders is from one-quarter to one-half inch in length, lying very flat. The "very short" areas are taken down as close as possible, "long" is never to give a lank or flowing effect.

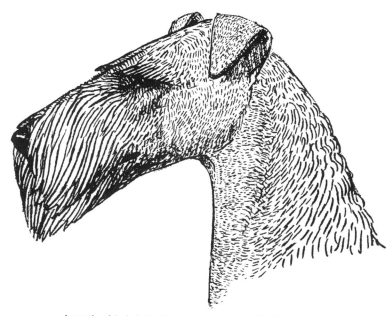

Length of hair is indicated by length of the lines.

15

Grooming the Airedale

THE WIRE HAIR of the Airedale coat is not constantly growing like human hair, but grows to a certain length, then dies. It does not necessarily shed as soon as it dies, but will cling half-heartedly until it is pulled out by the dog, by brambles or in the grooming process. Unlike other types of hair, it will pull out quite easily at almost any stage of growth. It is easiest, however, to strip the hard-coated dog when the coat is well "on the blow," long and open. Then a quick jerk on a tuft of hair will pull it out with gratifying ease, showing that it is "ripe" for stripping.

Wire hair is not ordinarily the same "caliber" throughout its length. It is fine near the root, coarse and stiff toward the end, with a tapered, pointed tip. There is variation in individual dogs as to the length of the wiry part before the hair fines down, which is one cue to the difference in even the best of coats, and in the time elapsed before certain coats need "topping," with the type having a short amount of hard portion not being adapted to proper topping at all. The fine portion of the hair, as a rule, is lighter color than the tip, although some coats are dark nearly to the skin. It is because of this change in both color and texture of each individual wire hair, plus the increasing presence of undercoat, that a clipped coat is ordinarily softer and quite unlike the normal, "garden fresh" new hair of the stripped coat. The thick, soft undercoat is completely different in makeup, never coarse at any time. On a clipped dog, cut portions of the outer coat can hardly be distinguished from undercoat. If a coat has been clipped repeatedly, it can take as long as a year (or even longer) to return to correct texture and color, hence the disrepute in which clipping is held.

When the coat has been properly stripped and is the correct length for show, there is little of the fine part of the wire hair yet grown out, so, except for the undercoat, only hard, wiry hair constitutes the coat. If a dog is clipped often, there are times when the coat will be reasonably hard, since, by the law of averages, there is bound to be a time when the dead hair was cut near the root, and if, through brushing, it has been removed, the new wire hair will come in. But, even so, there will be plenty of the cut hairs in view.

Condition of the dog will also affect the condition of the hair—a dull, lusterless, staring coat being one of the signs of ill health. But such things as washing too often, no care at all and the dog's swimming in salt water also affect the condition of the hair even though the dog is in good health.

Because dogs vary in the length of time it takes to grow a new coat, if it is at all possible, a dry run or two should have been made before the dog is to be prepared for show. Even this is not too accurate a guide, though, for condition, climate, age and many other unpredictable factors affect growth of a coat. The average time is eight weeks for a hard coat, but somewhat less for the sheep type, which is quick growing. Practice trims are beneficial in other ways, too, for a botched practice job will not be disastrous, though temporarily spoiling the dog's looks. And the beginner in the art will usually have learned a lesson from mistakes made in practice and will not repeat them when every hair counts.

WHAT TO EMPHASIZE

In grooming the Airedale coat, we want to emphasize the following: length of head, flatness of skull, cleanness of cheek and barrel-like muzzle; length and arch of neck; flatness of shoulders and moderate narrowness of front; levelness of topline; absolute straightness of front legs, with feet small and hardly visible beneath moderate furnishings, and the well-bent stifles of the hind legs, viewed from the side, and their well-muscled straightness, viewed from the rear. If the dog is good in the foregoing points, that is fine. But if he is not, then, even though we do not intend actually to fool anyone, we at least do not wish to emphasize a bad point through mistrimming.

GROOMING FOR SHOW

In grooming the Airedale for show, either of two methods of stripping may be used. One requires no tools, the thumb and forefinger doing the work, while the other is done with a dull stripping comb, preferably one made especially for the outer coat and coarse-toothed. Since the object is to *pull* out the hair, the first is the preferred method. Both the finger-and-thumb method and the tool-assisted stripping are loosely termed "hand stripped" to avoid confusion with clipping. In the restricted sense, however, hand stripped should

Trimming to Minimize Faults

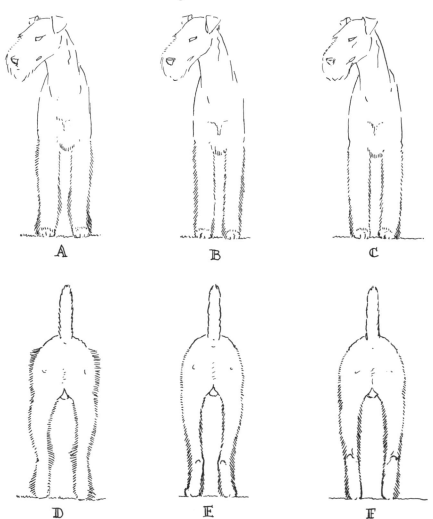

"A" Straight front appears splayed because of long hair in the wrong places. "B" Knock-kneed front made to appear more straight through trimming. "C" Bowed legs, which look more straight than if hair had been left the same length clear down to the feet. "D" Good hindquarters, improperly trimmed. Hair left on too high outside the legs, and too long. Cow-hocked appearance is given by the long hair inside the hocks and outside the feet. Short hair outside the hocks adds to the illusion. "E" Cow-hocked hindquarters, trimmed to minimize this bad fault though trimming cannot hide it. Hocks are taken down close on the inside, and the feet are trimmed close on the outside, the hair left long inside. "F" Bowed hindquarters. Long hair outside the feet and very short inside, helps disguise this fault slightly.

mean the finger-and-thumb method. In either method, the right way to remove the hair is with a quick jerk, not an actual pull at all, and only a small tuft is taken at once.

As an aid to hand stripping, the latex finger stalls obtainable at stationery stores work wonders. They not only ward off soreness, but also seem to have a magnetic effect in pulling out hair in that they "find" more fine hair than can the fingers alone. Scissors with blunted points, clippers, thinning shears and a razor-type stripping knife are available but the use of these tools is not recommended. The clippers ideally should be used only on the belly. In topping, the hair is roughed backward and a fine stripping knife is used to grasp the ends, thus pulling only a portion of the hair coat.

For a dog that has never been in show trim, or for one whose coat has not been kept in show trim, at least six months should be allowed from the beginning of the grooming process until the time the dog is to be shown. And the grooming should be done in distinct stages. As a prerequisite to the first stage the furnishings (leg and face hair) should be thinned drastically, preferably by plucking out the old hair by the finger-and-thumb method. This can immediately change the color of the furnishings to a surprising degree, as the light hair lightens the whole effect. The facial and leg hair takes longer to grow than does the body coat, so any time this is stripped down to the skin, at least six months should be allowed for regrowth. Again, the sheep coats may be the exception to prove the rule, due to their more rapid rate of growth.

First Stage: Approximately four months after the furnishings are plucked and eight to twelve weeks prior to the selected show, the coat must be taken off the entire body, clear down to the skin. In removing the coat at this time, it is recommended that a dull stripping comb be used for the top coat and a fine one for the fuzz.

It is the custom, also, to strip at this time the neck from behind the ears, down the back and sides of the neck, behind the shoulder blades, all of the back down the sides to the brisket hair that is usually tan in color and both sides of the tail, and round off the rear legs, leaving longer hair on the front edge tapering back over the leg muscle to skin. Pull hair to skin behind rear leg muscle and down the back leg to where the inner thigh muscle joins.

If the dog is a bit low in back and tailset, it is recommended that these two areas be plucked a couple of weeks before the rest of the body coat is done, giving a head start thereon, and making a thicker, longer fill when the time comes to straighten the topline in the final work-over.

Care During Intermediate Stage: After "Old Baldy" has been stripped, the dog can be bathed (unless bathed before the stripping was done). Stripping before bathing is preferable, unless the dog is very dirty, with oily hair.

After the bath, the skin should be rubbed with oil or a good lotion, and, of course, the dog kept indoors until thoroughly dry. Ordinarily, in cool or cold weather the dog should wear a blanket at night (and also during the day, if outside in very cold weather) until adjusted to the "skinless frankfurter" condition. If the furnishings are scanty, as on a young dog, and so hard they are inclined to break, any good lotion, cream or oil can be rubbed into the beard and legs by hand, or with a brush—a stiff one to increase the circulation. Consideration must be given to the fact that a dog whose coat is saturated with oil will be an unwelcome guest in the house. There are hair preparations that soften and improve the hair but which are not greasy, and it may be well to use one of this type. They may be a bit more expensive, but hardly so costly as a rug-cleaning bill or new upholstery. The softening effect of any hair preparation lasts only while the oil is on the hair. The oil should be washed out each week and replaced to keep the hair soft and silky.

As part of the routine of the dog's care, the coat should be brushed regularly, and, if necessary, superfluous undercoat kept raked out with either an undercoat comb or wire hound glove, and the coat should be checked for ragged hair and too rapid growth in certain areas.

Second Stage: Defuzz the previous stripped areas. Strip the head, the front and sides of the neck, the shoulders and the powder puff left on the rear (around the vent). This stripping is done two weeks after the first stage. Leave the ears for later as most dogs resent this area being stripped.

As the hair grows, the body coat should be shaped into the desired outline, leveling any high or low spots in the topline. During this growing period, the head, front and sides of the neck, shoulders, forechest, buttocks and back of tail should be kept very short and tight by going over these areas every week until show time. Since it is desirable that the chest look deep, the hair is left long on the brisket, shaping it like a ship's keel from the elbow in front tapering to almost nothing at the umbilical scar. However, if the dog is very deep of chest, this artful trimming is unnecessary.

Third Stage: The stripping for this third stage of the grooming should be done at least two weeks before the show. The hair on the skull, neck and shoulders should be again stripped down close. When hair is the ideal length for these parts, it looks like natural, rather short and wiry hair, averaging nearly a quarter inch in length on the shoulders. Cut or clipped hair can never stimulate new growth in color or texture, but some handlers do use a sharp stripping comb on these parts.

The skull is trimmed quite close from the eyebrows back, and the cheeks trimmed from the corner of the mouth to the jawline.

The hair under the throat should be very short, as are the cheeks. It will help to strip this short hair if chalk is rubbed into the hair to facilitate grasping the short hairs. The neck, to emphasize the arched effect, is trimmed very close underneath, less short on the sides and only moderately short on top, tapering into the shoulders and withers. It is trimmed shorter immediately in back of the head than at the crest.

The shoulder hair may be tapered into the leg hair at this time, or it may be done in the final stage, as preferred, but a more natural look is obtained if the tapering is done now.

If the backline shows need of remodeling, the work can be started at this time in order to have it perfect by show time. The high spots may either be

UNTRIMMED

BODY STRIPPED DOWN CLOSE
FURNISHINGS "TIDIED"

BODY STRIPPED, BUT
FURNISHINGS ROUGH

topped, by cutting off the tips of the hair, or they may be leveled by use of thinning shears. The latter is the better method, if done correctly, since only the underneath hair is cut, allowing the hair to lie flat, while topped hair will often stand up like stumps on logged-off land. Also, topped hair looks obviously cut and may cause the judge to be aware that the hair is shortened in that particular area to disguise a fault.

Since the buttocks should not be too short-haired, the sector below the tail should be taken down only moderately on the higher part, but close on the area inside the quarters. The furnishings along the back of the hind leg should also be fairly short, so that they outline the leg properly and do not look ragged, yet are not so freshly done that the leg looks half skinned.

Final Trim: This is done two or three days before the show and is no place for the amateur to practice, because the final work (especially the trimming of the head) can make or mar the dog's appearance. Since the head should look oblong, both from above and from the side, the trimming should emphasize that effect. A straight line from occiput to nose is desired, with only the eyebrows breaking the line. The beard is brushed forward (adding to the rectangular effect), all too-long hairs evened up and any part of the furnishings on the muzzle that interfere with the straight profile are leveled to the right height. If the cheeks need further flattening, they should be again worked over, but clipping at this late date is not recommended.

One point where novices usually fail is on the trim along the edge of the mouth. On most Airedales the hair should be trimmed close at the corner of the mouth, unless the muzzle pulls inward, as it would on the snipey type. The average person does not realize that the head will look different, even from the front, when the dog pants. But if any scraggly hair is left along the lower lip, at the corner of the mouth, the dog, when panting, will look like a grinning Cheshire cat or a fringe-whiskered sea captain. The straight outline (viewed from above) is, of course, destroyed by this billowing of untrimmed hair, so care must be taken to remove just enough to achieve a look of neatness when the dog's mouth is open, yet not so much that there will be an indentation of outline. Too much hair above the corner of the mouth also increases the "sea captain" effect, so the facial furnishings must be gradually tapered into the shorter hair of the head, and the hair below the eyes must never, under any circumstances, be scooped out, such over-industry being sure ruin to expression. It should always be remembered that the idea is to make the muzzle look as heavy as possible and well filled below the eyes. Viewed from the front (at a level with the eyes), the muzzle should appear cylindrical, not peaked, and especially not concave. Only enough hair should be removed from in front of the eyes to create this powerful-muzzle effect by rounding it off, assuming of course that a mass of fluff has not been left on the muzzle, *à la* Kerry, in which case the eyes could hardly be seen and some carving would be necessary.

Since long hair tends to lie flat, any hair beneath the eyes that has shown an inclination to become over-long and limp may be hand-plucked in the earlier stages of trimming so that by show time the hair will be new and of

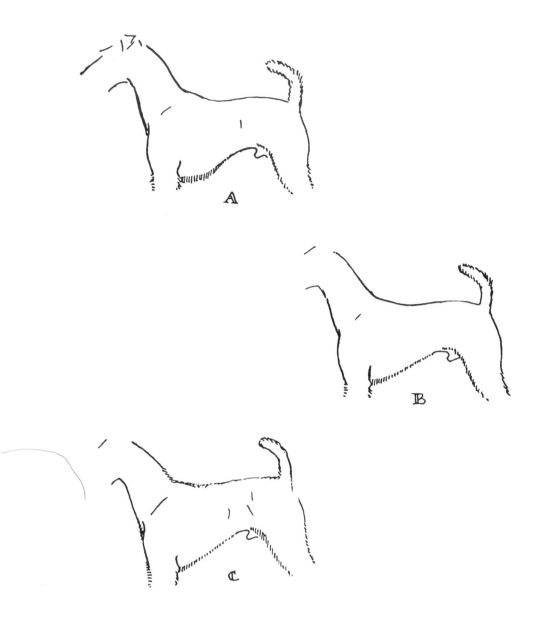

"A" shows a dog with a dip in back and low tailset, these faults accentuated by too much hair on the chest and curved underline. "B"—Same faults, but minimized slightly by a diagonal trim to underline. Tail is slightly squirrelled and made to appear more so by too much hair in the wrong places—under tip and at the outside bend of tail. "C"—Same dog trimmed to minimize all faults—topline levelled as much as possible by leaving hair long in the hollows and short over withers and loin. Neck blends into withers better due to longer hair at juncture of neck and withers. Neck improved by leaving more hair as it nears the chest, while too-angulated upper arm has longer hair in front to disguise this fault. Hair is left longer at flank and leading down to stifle.

210

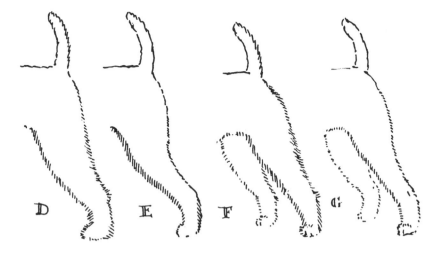

"D" and "E" show the illusion of a straight hindleg due to long hair along back of leg; also the disappearance of this effect by a closer trim along the back. "F" and "G"—Same thing, three-quarter view.

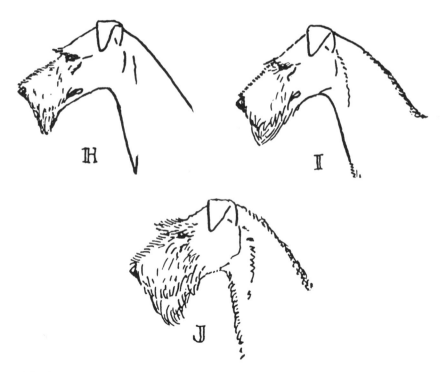

"H," "I" and "J" are the same head and neck over-trimmed; correctly trimmed; and not trimmed enough. Neck is angular, so hair along crest as on "I" gives effect of arch; while too much hair on neck makes it look thick in "J".

the stand-off type. However, even at a preliminary stage, the hair of the muzzle directly in front of the eyes should never be scooped out, for this makes the foreface look weak and dished. Only the long, flat-lying hairs should be taken out, and by the finger-and-thumb method, not with a stripping comb. Facial furnishings take a long time to grow—much longer than the body coat—and this fact must always be borne in mind with every tuft of hair removed. Hair on the top of and in between the eyes may be trimmed with the scissors, but only enough to make the topline of the head appear level.

The eyebrows are a tricky problem, and the art of trimming them must be studied firsthand to really learn it. Even then the first attempt or two may be bungled. The eyebrows are trimmed very close on the outside corner, longer on the inside corner, with the length varying according to the shape of the dog's head, the size (and color) of the eyes, etc. Longer brows are usually left on to help disguise light or large eyes, and the shape of the trim on the eyebrow also has some effect on the latter. The top of the eyebrow should blend into the hair of the head, the stripping comb doing most of this work, but scissors can be used, provided care is taken. The hair over the cheekbone and on the ridge below the eye should be shortened sufficiently for it to start the taper into the facial furnishings. If this hair is too short (as well as the hair on the muzzle just in front of it), the muzzle looks too light, so care must be taken here also.

The ears should again be checked for ragged hairs along their edges and underneath. Small ears that tend to fly can be aided a little by not clipping or stripping the hair at the tip too close and leaving enough hair underneath to weigh the tip down. It isn't necessary to leave much, and it must not be obvious. Ears that do not lie close enough to the cheek need not be trimmed so close along the inner edge, although very close on the outer edge, which will help slightly in fooling the eye. Naturally, while the edge need not be cut close on small ears, it must be trimmed to the skin on large ears.

The neck is given the once over again at this time, and if the neck is heavy underneath, it is again trimmed as close as possible at the bulging part—the center. If the dog is a bit "wet-throated," the hair at the throat also should be especially short. The neck should blend gradually into the withers, not coming in at an acute angle like a stovepipe.

The backline should be straight—in back of the withers—so a good deal of attention should be given this area if it needs any artful carving. The dog should be viewed on the ground as well as on the trimming table, and preferably sparring with another dog, for this will change the outline. The higher viewpoint will show up any uneven spots that may have been missed, and since the withers will rise somewhat when the dog tightens, it should be especially noted whether additional hair need be taken off, even though the withers are not too high when the dog is relaxed. Any further retouching on the "straightening" process already started a couple of weeks earlier will have to be done, and all stray hairs that will not lie flat when brushed should be topped or pulled.

The tuck-up should be clipped at this time, and the lower line should be evened up. Shallow-chested dogs need a fair amount of hair on the brisket, but too much will call attention to their deficiency. Dogs that are unusually good in this department are usually taken down quite close on the chest to show the world that the depth is all theirs, not merely a hirsute adornment.

The shoulders, by this time, should have a close, new crop of hair, as will also the upper arms. The problem now is to blend in the leg furnishings with the coat of the upper arm, with no sudden billowing out of cowboy chaps. This means that the hair on the elbow, both on the outside and on the point of the elbow, will have to be trimmed close, and the forearm will also need attention, especially if well muscled; otherwise, the dog may look a bit out at the elbow when moving, for a surplus of hair on this section will fluff out when the dog trots and spoil the clean outline. Consequently, the dog should not be trimmed from the table's-eye view only, but should also be checked for incorrect trim (or conformation) as he trots toward you. A knock-kneed dog will have to have a bit more hair taken off the inside of the knees than would a straight-legged dog.

The forelegs should be, if possible, absolutely straight from any angle. The Cocker-type feathering around the foot should be taken off completely, and the foot stripped close around the lower edge and nails, although the back of the pastern may curve gradually up to the rest of the furnishings rather than straight, if desired. Any long hair between the pads should be cut out, and the nails filed as close to the quick as possible. Although the furnishings should be moderately heavy, they should by no means be in Afghan-like profusion, nor should they be ragged. Again, remember the straight lines. The hair on the forechest should also blend gradually into the hair of both the chest and the upper arm, with no noticeable tufts, and should be very short.

The coat should come down over the hips, mingling with the leg furnishings at the top of the thigh muscle. The furnishings should never be allowed to extend above this point, as is done on Dutch-cut Poodles, although that is of course exaggerated. Neither should the furnishings be taken down so close on the hindquarters that they seem to be nonexistent. The hair inside the quarters is trimmed short to show the strong muscling.

A first-class conditioner of hard-coated Terriers can keep a dog in show coat for months at a time by going over the dog nearly every day, using the finger-and-thumb method, pulling out any dead hairs. This keeps replacements growing in—a sort of "rotation of crops" idea—and it works. The hair is then always bright and new, very different from the hacked-off, blunt-ended appearance of topped hair, even though topped hair may have been tapered by singeing. This last is an art that is strictly for those who know how, with speed and dexterity the first requisites.

GROOMING THE PET DOG

Although clipping is considered unethical, it is nevertheless being done, even by Airedale exhibitors, who, no longer showing a dog, do not have time to keep it in trim otherwise. Clipping also eases the problem for pet owners who want their Airedale well groomed in appearance but who have not been able to find the time (or the person) to strip the dog.

The general effect of the clipping job is similar to that obtained in grooming for show, but is much easier. There is no worry about a gouge in the wrong place, and the job is done all at once, too—no waiting for the hair to grow at different times in various places, although, as was pointed out before, the coat will not appear so crisp and wiry as when stripped.

Keeping in mind the general effect achieved through stripping, the dog is clipped on that part of the head normally stripped, on the neck and on the body. The furnishings are tapered down to the clipped hair with a sharp stripping comb, freed of dead hair and thinned and shortened enough so they can be readily combed without snagging or snarling.

The clipped area should extend down the ribs and under the flank, but not under the chest, for there the hair should be blended into the coat with the sharp stripping knife. Thinning shears or the clippers themselves can be used for this tapering process, easing the latter into and then out of the longer hair. The No. 10 blade is commonly used, but a higher-cutting blade, called the stripping blade, may be used if it is desired that the coat be longer from the beginning. The ears are better clipped with a finer blade, such as No. 15.

Since clipping can cause a sore known as clipper burn, oil or lotion should be applied to the skin afterward, especially under throat, jaw and tuck-up. If the dog is bathed after clipping, the oil should, of course, be applied after his coat has been thoroughly dried.

BATHING

Some Airedales can be bathed the day before a show and not have the coat curl in places, but some cannot, so it is well to know the characteristics of the dog's coat. A dog that has been well brushed during the pre-show period will need no washing at show time unless the coat has become dirtied to an unbrushable degree. The furnishings, however, are normally washed just before the day of the show, for the more they stand out and fluff up—in a crisp way, of course—the better.

If the dog's entire coat must be washed just before it is shown, the coat should always be dried by rubbing a towel with the lay of the hair, never against it. If the dog is toweled in a back, forth and whirlwind fashion, the coat will look as if it had been combed with an eggbeater. The furnishings, however, should be rubbed every which way—to make them stand out as much as possible.

214

A booklet entitled *Grooming the Broken-haired Terrier,* complete with text and drawings, is available from the Airedale Terrier Club of America for a nominal fee. This booklet is authored by the late Mrs. Arden Ross of Wire Fox Terrier fame and was originally published in installments in the *Terrier Type* magazine by editor Dan Kiedrowski. This booklet can be a guide for both stripping the show Airedale and clipping the pet dog.

16

Showing the Airedale

THE CONFORMATION or breed classes at dog shows are essentially beauty contests. The dog which most nearly fits the official breed Standard as interpreted by the judge is the winner. The Standard is the word picture of the "perfect dog," and the same words can mean different things to different people. This is why various judges will select separate winners from among the same group of dogs competing on the same weekend or circuit of shows.

LEAD BREAKING

How do you go about showing a dog? First the dog must be lead broken. This means walking briskly and under control on a lead, neither pulling nor lagging behind. The dog must literally put the best foot forward. The easiest way to accomplish this is to put a string lead on a young puppy and encourage the pup to move along with you. Great patience is the most essential asset in lead breaking a puppy—make it play and not work. Children often are more successful than adults when it comes to introducing a young hopeful to the lead. A child probably makes it more fun for the puppy and has more patience than most adults.

Many times the initial attempt at lead breaking results in a puppy that refuses to move, as well as a frustrated owner. You want the puppy to walk, but you should not resort to dragging. It is often helpful to entice the puppy with a bit of boiled liver, chicken, cheese, cracker or some other tasty morsel to get cooperation. Any lesson, successful or not, should never last longer than five or ten minutes. Young puppies have a short attention span, so prolonging lessons is a bad mistake. The best show dog is the one that enjoys the spotlight; this association should be imprinted early in the dog's life.

When the puppy will walk nicely on the lead on the handler's left, it is ready for the second step—stacking.

STACKING

Some people call it "stacking"; others say "posing," "setting up" or "standing for examination." However you refer to the exercise, stacking means getting the dog to stand in such a way as to approximate the breed Standard as closely as possible. An Airedale that is properly stacked will be standing with its front legs straight down from the shoulder and its front feet pointing forward. The rear legs are set back until the vertical line from the hock point to foot is perpendicular to the ground. Ideally, his pose should also show a straight topline. However, if you find your puppy roaching his back a trifle, as most will, move the rear legs slightly further back, or spread them slightly further apart to improve the picture.

As with lead breaking, lessons in stacking should start early. Many breeders will start posing their puppies when they are able to stand. It helps to begin stacking lessons on a table, as puppies will be more manageable off the ground. Early lessons in stacking are always worthwhile, especially with a male puppy. A full-grown male Airedale that never has been taught to stack will not appreciate having a stranger handling his parts, especially his testicles, and will actively resist the attempt to do so. In the show ring, a judge will physically handle every part of your dog from head to toe. The dog that resists the judge will have almost no chance of winning despite any merits it has; while the dog who stands well can be properly evaluated. It is not unusual for a better dog to lose to a lesser rival because the latter made the most of itself, while the former did not.

Many people find it beneficial to stack the dog in front of a mirror; it shows how the puppy will look to the judge, and tells you if any adjustments are needed. Stack the dog holding the lead above the head in your right hand, with your left hand holding the tail up if necessary.

Your puppy should be taught to stand quietly, once properly stacked. As mentioned earlier, the judge will examine the dog all over and the dog must not move nor come unglued during the examination. Most good handlers, professional and amateur, will move around the dog as the judge examines it, holding the head as the judge moves to the rear. A proficient handler will carry some boiled liver or other bait into the ring to tempt or "bait" the dog while the judge is performing the inspection ritual. A dog thus baited often forgets all about the stranger's examination. The dog will raise its ears and tail, pull together and be the picture of Airedale alertness. Your dog may even quiver

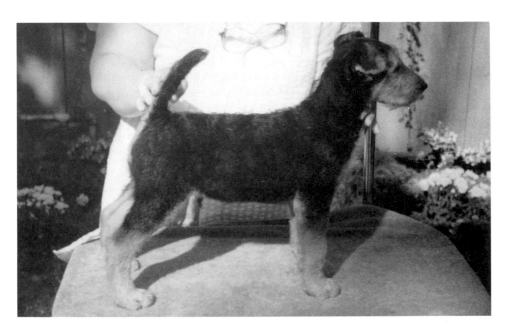

Puppy being "stacked" on a table.

a bit when baited, but so long as the desired picture is presented, keep the liver in play. Another bait for the unhungry dog is a squeaky toy hidden in a pocket or hand and squeaked at the most advantageous time. A dog that baits well can always be in the proper position exhibiting a keenly alert look when the judge looks at him, whether close-up or from a distance.

AT THE SHOW

To be eligible to enter a dog show held under AKC rules, your Airedale must be at least six months old on the day of the show, and must either be registered with its own AKC number or be from a litter registered with the AKC. To enter your dog in a show, obtain an official entry form from the show superintendent. Fill it out and return it with the proper entry fee to the superintendent prior to the published closing date. Shortly before the show you will receive the Schedule of Judging and your exhibitor's pass in the mail. The schedule will show the approximate time of judging and the number of dogs entered in each class in each breed.

As an exhibitor, it is your responsibility to get to the show on time and to have your dog groomed and ready at ringside when your class is called. Dog shows go on whether you get there or not, no matter what the weather, so allow enough time for travel, grooming and normal snafus.

Once at ringside, check in with the steward who will give you an arm band printed with your dog's catalog number. Check to make sure no mistake has been made. Wait, with your dog, a short distance from the ring entrance; then when your class is called, you enter the ring with the dog on your left and line up as the judge directs. At times you are permitted to enter randomly; at other times the judge will specify catalog order, which means the lowest number first.

IN THE RING

Usually the judge will have all the dogs gaited around the ring together in a large circle; you move your dog at a trot counterclockwise around the judge, always keeping the dog between you and the judge. Try to move the dog at the speed that shows your dog's movement to advantage, but don't run over the exhibitor ahead of you.

When the judge signals the class to stop, you do so, stack your dog and wait for your turn to be examined. Try to keep your dog stacked and reasonably alert while you are waiting. The judge will conduct a detailed examination of each dog, and will check general conformation, coat, teeth, bite, testicles (male dogs must be entire), eye color and anything else according to the standard. Following this examination, the judge may ask that your dog be moved, or may go on and check the next dog, saving movement testing for later.

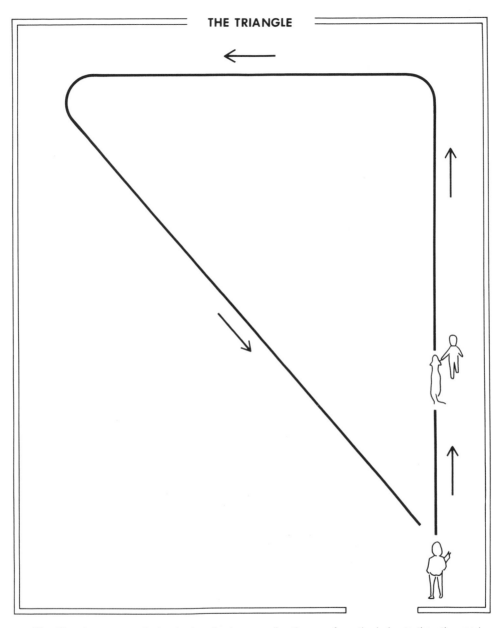

THE TRIANGLE

The Triangle pattern calls for the handler to move directly away from the judge to the other end of the ring, turn left at a 90° angle, go to the other corner, turn left and return to the judge.

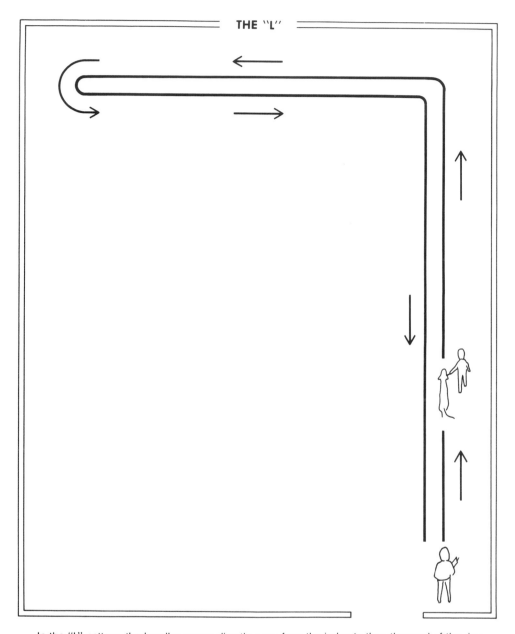

In the "L" pattern, the handler moves directly away from the judge to the other end of the ring, turns left, goes to the other corner, and then makes a complete turn and retraces the pattern back to the judge in the form of an "L."

Regardless of this procedure, the judge will want to see your dog gait in a pattern used for all dogs in the ring. Many judges use the "triangle," in which the dog is to move straight away down the ring, across to the opposite corner and back to the judge on a diagonal. Another popular pattern is the "L." Here the dog is moved straight away down the ring, across to a corner, back to the center and back to the judge. In the "T," the dog moves straight away down the ring, across to one side of the ring, back across to the other side of the ring, back to the center and then returns to the judge. "Up and back" is just what the judge says: straight away down the ring and straight back to the judge.

When you are completing your individual gaiting pattern and are just a few feet away from the judge, have the liver or a small squeaky toy ready to alert the dog, thereby presenting your dog in the best possible manner. At this point, most judges will thank you and send you to the end of the line, going to the next dog to repeat the same procedure. The sharp handler will be watching the competition to see if it can be outshown. Learn to keep one eye on the competition, one eye on your own dog and an "extra" eye on the judge. The name of this game is dog *show,* so teach your dog to *show* on command. You won't be sorry.

After all the dogs in the class have been examined and gaited, the judge may have the class move again in a circle in order to take a final look. Sometimes judges want to compare a few dogs by bringing them into the center of the ring to "face" them off. This is also known as "sparring." When Airedales face off, they become alert and everything tightens up, including their tempers, *so keep a secure hold on the lead and do not let your dog get out of hand.* After deciding, the judge will send the first four placings to the designated markers, mark the judge's book and distribute the awards. When all the dogs have left the ring, the next class enters and the whole procedure will start again. You are expected to take your wins or losses graciously. Good sportsmanship is very important in the dog shows, as in any other competitive activity.

If your Airedale has won first in its class, you must return for the judging of Winners. This class is composed of all the first place winners in the regular classes for one sex, and is judged immediately following the judging of all the classes for that sex. It is this class that carries the championship points; thus, if your male is designated Winners Dog, he receives points toward a championship. The number of these coveted points will depend on the number of other dogs in the regular classes present and competing. A second best in the sex, or Reserve Winner, also is chosen in the event the Winners Dog is disqualified for any infraction of the rules. In that event, the Reserve would then move up and be credited with the Winners points.

After judging for Reserve Winners Dog, all bitch classes are judged in the same way. When judging has been completed for Winners Bitch and Reserve Winners Bitch, all champions entered will compete for Best of Breed. This class is composed of champions of record, dogs that have completed their championship points but have not yet been officially confirmed by AKC, the Winners Dog and the Winners Bitch. The judge will examine this class as all others and will select Best of Breed, Best of Winners and Best of Opposite Sex.

The Best of Breed Airedale then will be eligible to compete in the Terrier Group against the Best of Breed winners from all the other Terrier breeds for a Group placement. The dog chosen first in the Terrier Group competes against the other six Group winners (Sporting, Hound, Working, Toy, Non-Sporting and Herding) in the last competition of the day for the coveted Best in Show.

BECOMING A CHAMPION

Championship points are awarded in each breed to the Winners Dog and the Winners Bitch. The number of points won, from one to five, depends on the number of dogs of the same sex actually present and competing in the classes. The required number of dogs for a given point rating will vary from one part of the country to another, depending on the number of dogs usually shown in that breed in that region during the previous year. The AKC revises the point schedule in May of each year, and this is printed in every dog show catalog.

To become a champion, a dog or bitch must acquire fifteen points under at least three different judges, and two of these wins must be "majors" worth three points or better. A dog's major points must be won under different judges. A technical point sometimes difficult for the beginner to grasp is the computing of points for Best of Winners. The Best of Winners is awarded points equal to the higher rating in either sex for the breed. For example, if the Winners Dog earned four points by beating a large entry of males and the Winners Bitch earned two points by beating a smaller entry of females, if the Winners Bitch goes Best of Winners (defeating the Winners Dog), she wins four points instead of only two. There is a maximum possibility of five points per show.

MATCH SHOWS

Most experienced breeders routinely take their puppies to match shows for ring education long before they are old enough or mature enough for serious competition. Matches are held in many areas nearly every weekend, and many are open to all breeds. They are run along the lines of championship shows, but no points are offered and the atmosphere is pleasant and relaxed.

The match show is intended as a training ground and is a good place for you and your puppy to learn show procedure; it gives you a chance to compare your puppy with other puppies in the same age group. It is an opportunity for comparing your grooming and conditioning with the serious breeders. It also is a place to acclimatize you and your puppy to the activity of other dogs and people.

Most all-breed clubs and regional breed clubs hold training classes for ring showing (conformation), as well as obedience classes. Inquire from your regional breed club about the sanctioned match that must be held to qualify the club to hold a specialty show.

Most entry fees at match shows are very reasonable, and entries can be made on the day of the match when you arrive on the grounds. Many of the exhibitors will be helpful to newcomers, explaining the procedures and giving encouragement as needed. Match shows also are training grounds for aspiring judges, so don't let yourself be too elated or too deflated by their placements. You will find a great deal of additional helpful information in *The Forsyth Guide to Successful Dog Showing* by Robert and Jane Forsyth, as well as in *Dog Showing: An Owner's Guide* by Connie Vanacore (both published by Howell Book House, New York, NY).

OBEDIENCE TRIALS

Obedience trials are an entity unto themselves. This is where your dog shows off his brains—and his training. Obedience trials are held in conjunction with most all-breed (conformation) shows, and sometimes as separate events by dog training clubs. In obedience, the dog and handler work as a team; the trials have grown to be popular, well-supported events.

Many Terrier owners claim obedience and Terrier temperament do not mix, but as you have seen earlier in this book, many Airedales have achieved great success in obedience competition. Also, more then a few with obedience degrees are bench champions.

In obedience work it is only the dog's work that scores, not looks. The dog can be trimmed or untrimmed, fat or thin, young or old; however, most exhibitors take pride in their dogs and try to have them looking like typical breed representatives while working for a top score. It is pleasing when your Airedale is both bright and beautiful.

THE PROFESSIONAL HANDLER

If you feel your own bumbling efforts at first might hurt your dog's chances, you can obtain a professional handler. Employing a handler, at least occasionally, gives you the opportunity to see your dog compared to the competition, much better than if you actually are in the ring. It can be a lesson to see this contrast. It can also be either encouraging or discouraging, depending on the quality of the competition and how they are showing.

After you are as expert as your dog, you can do your own handling, right up to Best in Show if you have what it takes. But if you decide to have a professional handler show your dog, go to several local shows and observe the handlers. There are all-breed handlers and those who specialize in certain groups, such as Terrier handlers. Usually your dog is boarded, conditioned and shown by the handler. Quite often dogs behave better for a handler than they do for mama or daddy, much as a child does better for the teacher than for you.

It should be emphasized that all long-legged Terriers of the Airedale stamp are assisted by the handler as to tail carriage. Usually when a dog comes to a stop, it relaxes a little and the tail goes somewhat down or back. The tail doesn't relax much, but just enough to make the back appear longer. When a dog will show, especially when sparred against another dog, the backline tightens up; this automatically pulls the tail head further forward also. In the lineup, most dogs will get a little bored, so the handler pushes the tail forward to improve the picture. The same is true when taking photographs, although at that point several people are trying to make the dog alert. This still is not the same as when challenging another dog, so the tail may be held at 45 degrees instead of straight up; consequently, when you see all those pictures of dogs beautifully posed but with the handler pushing the tail forward, t'aint necessarily so that they *need* that assistance at any other time.

The best of all worlds is having a dog that does not need to be handled at all—except to be holding the lead while you move around the ring as the judge directs. This ideal is the stylish Airedale that does all its own showing, striking a proper stance with neck arched, ears alert and tail held up under its own power.

AN IMPORTANT REMINDER

Puppies change from week to week, and some very promising ones end up as "also rans." On the other hand, some "ugly ducklings" turn into real "swans." So keep your sense of humor and remember that showing dogs is a sport. If you lose today, tomorrow will bring another show with a different judge and it may be your day. Most of all, *never* blame your dog if you don't win. A dog is only as good as you have presented it. Your confidence or lack of same goes down the lead; your dog reflects your state of mind. Borrow a motto from the Boy Scouts, and "Be Prepared."

17

Breeding the Airedale

THE TIME HAS COME to think about breeding your Airedale bitch. By her second or third heat, you have either shown her to her Championship and in so doing have had several AKC judges' opinions of her quality, or if showing is not for you, experienced Airedale people have compared her to the Standard for the Airedale Terrier and have determined that she exemplifies the qualities required of a good specimen of the breed. Now you must look for the best possible mate.

BREEDING STRATEGIES

There are three breeding strategies: outcrossing, linebreeding and inbreeding. Outcrossing is just that. You select a mate that has different ancestry from your bitch, and the resulting puppies will reflect this. Puppies from an outcross may all look different; some may favor the sire, others may favor the dam and some may embody qualities of both.

Linebreeding involves selecting a mate that has many of the same ancestors as your bitch. That is, the two families, or lines, behind the sire and dam of your bitch are closely related to the family lines behind your chosen stud. The advantage of linebreeding is that offspring will be quite uniform in size and appearance.

Inbreeding is only for the very experienced, since it is risky and should be done with considerable caution. Inbreeding involves mating mother and son, father and daughter or brother and sister. While this is done only to "set" outstanding features (e.g., extremely good heads, good movement, good fronts), it carries certain risks. The good puppies can be very good, but the bad puppies can be very bad, since you are genetically doubling up on bad qualities as well as on good ones. Also, hereditary defects are more likely to show up.

After deciding on a general breeding plan, you must still select a specific mate. You can choose a dog that is strong in the same qualities in which your bitch is strong; this is breeding through strength. Or you can select a dog that can complement your bitch and strengthen her weaker attributes.

STUD SERVICE AND PLANNING

After much study and discussion, you make your selection. When you approach the owner or handler of the selected stud to inquire about the stud fee, also ask what tests the owner of the stud may require. Tests for brucellosis (a bacterial disease that has implications for reproductive failure) or X-rays for hip dysplasia may be required for your bitch. Hip dysplasia does occur in Airedales, and X-rays can indicate that certain stock would be a poor breeding risk because the disease does appear to have a genetic component.

The stud fee is an agreed-upon amount of money, which is paid at the time your bitch is serviced. While the stud fee is not a guarantee of puppies, most stud owners will give a return service during the next heat if your bitch fails to conceive. Another form of payment is to allow the stud owner to select the puppy of his or her choice, the "pick of the litter." If you choose to relinquish the "pick" to the stud owner, the time of selection should be determined prior to the mating. To avoid later misunderstandings, most stud owners formulate these conditions in a contract drawn up prior to the breeding. Do remember that once you give up the right to have first "pick," you must honor the stud owner's choice, even if he or she selects the only puppy of one sex born.

Hopefully, all of these arrangements and negotiations are completed before your bitch comes into season. When she shows "color" (bloody discharge), notify the owner of the stud. Together you will make arrangements to have her bred between the tenth and the fourteenth days of her cycle, since this is usually the most fertile time. By this time, the swollen vulva will have softened somewhat, and the discharge will have lost its bright red color and will appear pink or straw-colored. Your bitch will begin "flagging" with her tail, which is laying her tail to one side when touched from the rear. In general, she will become quite solicitous of males.

STUD SERVICE: THE BREEDING

During the mating, it is wise to muzzle the bitch and hold her head to prevent her from biting the male, especially with a maiden bitch, who may become confused by and unsupportive of initial mating efforts. After the sexual "tie" is made, the male is turned so that the dog and bitch are facing in opposite directions. This is done to relieve the bitch from having to sustain the male's weight during a tie that may last twenty minutes or more. After the tie breaks and the two dogs separate, the bitch is often crated briefly. After the first breeding, most breeders skip a day before the second (insurance) breeding, thus allowing a broader exposure of the fertile period since sperm can remain active for twenty-four hours within the bitch's body.

Another method is artificial insemination with sperm taken from the male and inserted directly into the bitch using fresh, cooled or even frozen sperm that can be shipped or stored.

PRENATAL CARE

The gestation period for puppies is approximately sixty-three days, so mark your calendar to expect puppies nine weeks after the first breeding. Since some bitches go off their feed during the first weeks of pregnancy, it is important to insure that they eat, even if you have to resort to bribery. During the pregnancy, feed your bitch her usual healthy diet, but supplement it with a prenatal vitamin. After the fifth week, when you are reasonably sure that your bitch is pregnant, it is wise to offer her an additional light feeding. Many breeders give their bitches a daily tablespoon of raw liver (chopped); most bitches relish this treat.

THE WHELPING BOX

During the final few weeks, build a whelping box in which the bitch will deliver her pups. For an Airedale, the whelping box should be approximately three feet by four feet. The lining of the box should be a material that is easily scrubbed, such as Masonite or urethane-treated wood. A whelping box that has sides and a door that opens and closes will keep your bitch from wandering away from her puppies when she gets bored. An inner rail (two or three inches from the sides and bottom) will provide the protection that puppies occasionally may need when a bitch lies close to the side of the whelping box and unintentionally exposes them to the danger of being smothered. An ingenious design for whelping box railings uses plastic sprinkler-pipe inserted through predrilled holes in the whelping box. This allows for easy cleaning of the railings and for quick removal when they are no longer required.

Since most Airedales are very curious and eager to be a part of the family, relegating them to a quiet and secluded place invites boredom. It may result in the bitch jumping up at every noise to see what is going on in the household. It is easier on everyone to put the whelping box in the den or kitchen, so that the bitch can be in the center of things and still be a mother. The room should

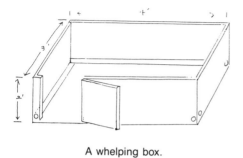

A whelping box.

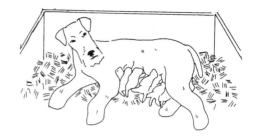

Mother and litter.

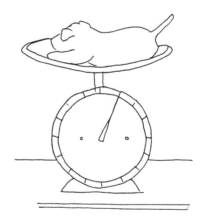

Puppy in the sac with placenta attached.

Weighing the puppies.

be about 70 degrees and comfortable for the bitch; her body heat warms the pups. If you decide that a heating pad is necessary for warmth, take precautions to insure that the cord cannot be chewed. The cord can be inserted, for example, through a length of garden hose. The bitch should be introduced to the whelping box several days before the anticipated whelping date. Give her newspapers to use during whelping because they can be changed easily and quickly.

THE WHELPING

As the whelping time approaches, there are several signs to watch for. The puppies will move back in the bitch's body, and her rib cage will begin to look less expanded, with her waistline becoming nonexistent. Her normal temperature of 101 degrees will drop, often to as low as 97 degrees, which may make her shiver. Often she will not eat, or if she does, she may vomit. When she starts to go into labor, the first sign may be a cycle of panting, stopping for a few seconds and then panting again. The intervals during which she stops panting are when she is having her first contractions. Contractions are not timed as they are in human births. In the early stages, you will not observe strong body contractions, but rather only the cessation of panting. Sometimes the bitch will get a glazed, faraway look in her eyes. As labor progresses, the bitch will start bearing down with obvious muscle contractions, and she will hook her tail into an inverted "U"-shape. She may labor heavily for minutes or as long as several hours. If the hard, bearing-down labor extends much beyond two hours, this may indicate problems with the delivery, and your veterinarian should be consulted. After the hard contractions, you will begin to see a bulge appearing between the anus and the vulva. Following a few more contractions, you should see the sac containing the puppy emerge from the vulva. The bitch's body may also excrete fluid, sometimes a bloody discharge and other times a blackish green fluid; this is normal. However, the excretion of large amounts of bright red blood may indicate an internal hermorrhage, and the discharge of yellow fluids may indicate a possible infection. Consult your veterinarian without delay.

The puppy sac is an opaque membrane attached to a placenta by an umbilical cord. Have paper towels nearby in case the bitch needs your help when the sac emerges. Since the sac is wet and slippery, a paper towel will give you a better hold. The puppy in the sac, the cord and the placenta should be expelled at the same time. If the bitch does not seem to recognize this "package," you may have to tear open the sac and stimulate the puppy's breathing by rubbing it vigorously with a terry towel. If the puppy appears to be full of fluid, "swing" the puppy to allow gravity to aid in clearing the lungs. Swinging means literally to turn the puppy from head up to head down several times. This is done to clear fluid from the breathing passages, but care must be taken to support the puppy's head so that the neck does not snap. The easiest way to accomplish this is to place the puppy between your hands (as if you were praying) and to turn your hands from fingers pointing upward to fingers pointing downward. Another way to clear the lungs is to put the puppy on your lap, with the head lower than the body, and rub the puppy with a towel. Experienced breeders can use a rubber syringe, as is done for human infants.

Do not give up prematurely on efforts to get the puppy to begin breathing; puppies can come around and begin breathing a long time after being born. A limp puppy may suddenly gasp and start trying to breathe. Put the puppy in an incubator or make an incubator with a cardboard box that has a heating pad under it and a towel covering it. The heating pad should be turned low so that the puppy cannot get burned. A puppy slow to start breathing may also be slow to nurse, but do not give up; This puppy may catch up quickly to the others and even turn out to be your best puppy.

Check the puppy's mouth for any sign of a cleft palate. This can appear as a small pink hole or as a groove that extends the length of the roof of the mouth. A puppy with this defect should be destroyed since it will never be able to eat or drink properly, and often there is a linkage among birth defects. Do not be heroic and attempt to save this puppy; most often you will later regret it.

With the first cry or wail, the bitch will suddenly realize that a puppy is hers and will want to take over her responsibilities. Very efficient mothers will expel the puppy, neatly bite off the cord, eat the placenta (which resembles a five-inch piece of raw liver) and begin to stimulate its circulation and breathing by licking the puppy. This licking should cause the puppy to expel the merconium, a black stool that is within the puppy at birth. When the bitch is satisfied that the puppy is doing well, she should push it back to a nipple to nurse. For the less efficient mother, you will dry the pup, cut the cord, throw away the placenta and put the puppy on the bitch to nurse. Nursing helps the bitch to continue laboring and stimulates the movement of the unborn pups down to the birth canal and through it. However, if your bitch is one who jumps up to deliver in a standing position, or one who curls up nose to tail, watch that nursing pups are not scattered around the box or stepped on.

Since Airedale litters can be large, it is a good idea to keep a record on paper of how many placentas have been expelled; there should be one for each pup. Placentas can be expelled between pups or with the birth of the next pup. It will be most helpful to your veterinarian to know how many placentas have been expelled since retained placentas can be a source of infection.

With all going well and six or seven puppies successfully delivered, your bitch may suddenly want to go out, or perhaps even want to eat or drink. Do not be misled—this could be the "seventh-inning stretch," when she gets her second wind to finish the job. If she wants to go out to relieve herself at night, take a flashlight and go out with her, as many a pup has been born in the yard. To illustrate, Ch. Anfeald Moses got his name after being found in the daylight lying under the lawn sprinkler. While your bitch is on her feet, gently press her sides from the ribs back; any lumps you feel are more pups. An injection of oxytocin, a pituitary hormone, may be given by your veterinarian to stimulate the uterus to contract and thus expel any remaining pups or missing placentas. This injection is usually given within the first twenty-four hours and will help the bitch to bring in milk.

POSTNATAL CARE

After the litter has been born, your bitch and her whelping box should be cleaned. Put fresh papers in the box and place fabric on top of the papers to give the pups better footing while they nurse. The decupitus pads made for human hospital patients are perfect for puppies. The pads look like synthetic white lamb's wool but they function like disposable diapers—the tops stay dry and the pads give an excellent footing. They are comfortable for long naps, and best of all, they can be washed and dried easily. This material is designed to be autoclaved, so it is tough enough to withstand Airedales.

After cleaning the dam and her bed, give her a drink of water or broth (for added protein, dissolve a packet of unflavored gelatin in the liquid). Check to be sure that the puppies have settled down to nursing. If your litter numbers more than seven puppies, it is easier to separate them into two groups. While one group nurses, the other can sleep happily in your cardboard incubator. Rotate the groups every hour so all puppies are getting enough nourishment, and be sure that smaller pups do not get pushed aside. Remember that a noisy nurser is an inefficient nurser, so watch that each pup is ingesting enough milk.

The bitch should lick the puppies' genitals to stimulate them to urinate and defecate and to keep them clean. Not every bitch likes this chore, so it is wise to check all pups each morning and night to be sure that she is doing her job. If not, you will have to step in. You can imitate the bitch's actions by using a piece of cotton dipped in warm water and gently rubbing the genital area. It helps to apply Vaseline or A & D ointment to this area, since the bitch will both stimulate and clean the pups in her efforts to remove the ointment.

Be sure to take the dam out periodically to relieve herself and to stretch her muscles. Often a new mother will lie very rigidly for fear of disturbing her puppies. Give her water, broth or milk to drink, as the more fluid she takes, the more milk she will produce. Most of the time she will want to be fed her meals while lying in the whelping box. Several meals spaced throughout the day and night will often be better than a single large meal that will overload her stomach and make her uncomfortable while lying still. At first you may have to tempt her appetite, but get her back on her regular diet as soon as possible, since a good diet is important for milk production.

Check your bitch's temperature every day, and if it is over 102 degrees, consult your veterinarian. Be sure to wash off any discharge around the vaginal area or on her legs, as this can result in skin irritations. The discharge will continue during nursing but decreases after a few days.

Puppies should be weighed every day to insure that each is gaining

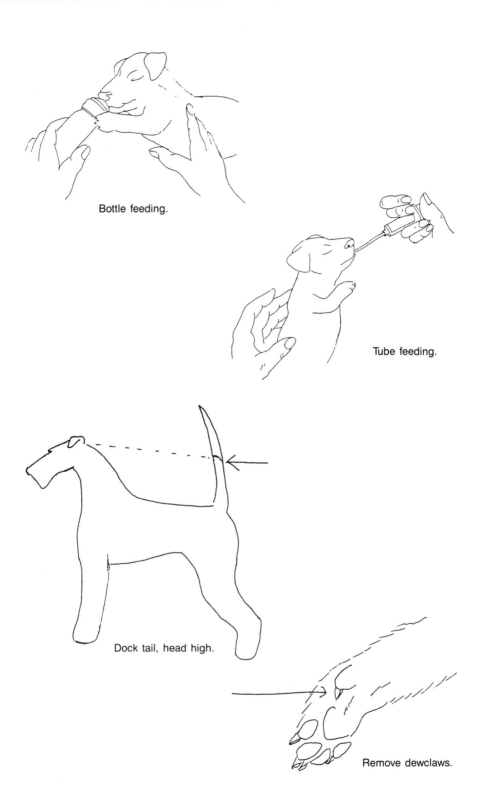

Bottle feeding.

Tube feeding.

Dock tail, head high.

Remove dewclaws.

weight. Their nails should be cut every few days with a man's nail clipper (cut off the little hooks on the end of the nail). Healthy, happy puppies have shiny, glossy coats, and they seldom cry. They eat, sleep, twitch and creep around.

BOTTLE FEEDING AND TUBE FEEDING

Weak puppies (mark them with a dab of nail polish on head) can be helped with supplemental feedings. Use a regular baby bottle with a soft "preemie" nipple for bottle feedings or use a human infant feeding tube (#8 French, 15 inches long) for tube feeding. There are canned formulas available that can simulate bitch's milk, or goat's milk (canned) diluted with equal parts of Pedialyte can be used. Regular canned milk can be used but the sugar content can cause diarrhea. A good formula recommended by a nutritionist is: one-half goat's milk to one-half Pedialyte, 1 egg yolk, 1 teaspoon corn oil; strain and heat to skin temperature. For bottle feeding, position the puppy on its stomach, either on your lap or on a table covered with a towel, and give the puppy the tip of the nipple. It is helpful to make an "O" of the forefinger and thumb of the left hand; by then encircling the pup's muzzle, you can help it to hold on to the nipple and make suction.

To use the stomach tube, first measure the pup from the nose to the last rib and mark the tube for this length. The tube must be inserted so that it bypasses the windpipe and enters the esophagus, which leads to the stomach. Soak the plastic tube in warm water to make it flexible and dip it into the warmed formula. Attach a regular syringe (without the needle) to the lock on the end of the tube. Draw the formula up through the tube and into the syringe; the number of cc's of formula required will be determined by the size of the pup. Slide the tube gently down the pup's throat and into the stomach going as far as the mark you previously measured. Usually, after the first time, the pup will taste the formula and swallow the tube. Slowly empty the syringe, sending the formula through the tube and into the pup's stomach. The pup's sides will expand immediately. Gently withdraw the tube. Feed puppies at five-hour intervals, unless a puppy is extremely weak or small. Check for dehydration by pinching a fold of skin directly in front of the tail. If the fold returns immediately to normal, the puppy is not dehydrating, but if the fold remains in the pinched-up position, the puppy is in need of fluids. To increase liquids, you can also use Pedialyte, an electrolyte solution, which can be administered orally by tube or bottle between milk feedings. Pedialyte is packaged in ready-to-use bottles and is stocked in the baby section of most markets and drugstores. If the puppy does not respond to this, the veterinarian can inject fluid under the skin.

WEANING

The puppies' ears will unseal first, and at approximately fourteen days their eyes will open. By now they are scooting all over the whelping box. Puppies can be started on solid foods during the third week. You can use a mixture of baby cereal, a small amount of lean ground meat and canned bitch's milk (Espilac or Unilac) or canned goat's milk formula. Each puppy should be fed individually until it gets used to lapping the food.

During the fourth week, give the mixture to the puppies in a shallow dish or an aluminum puppy pan (one kind resembles a giant hubcap with an elevated center surrounded by a two-inch trough, which is big enough for the puppies' heads but not for their bodies). It will be easier for the puppies if you elevate the pan to chin level. The first meals are messy, and your bitch gets many additional calories just from cleaning her puppies after each meal. You may want to help with a damp, warm washcloth. When the puppies are eating well, begin to add wet kibbled dog food that has been put through a blender. Use one-half as much water as kibble, and measure the amounts before blending. As you add the kibble, subtract the baby cereal. Pups should be given four daily feedings and should have fresh water available in a shallow dish that cannot be overturned. Initially, the puppies will wade through the water but will soon learn that water is for drinking. At this time restrict the bitch's nursing time so that the puppies will be interested in the solid food.

DOCKING TAILS AND REMOVING DEWCLAWS

At three to five days of age, tails are docked and dewclaws are removed, either by a veterinarian or by an experienced breeder. If the tail docking is done by your veterinarian, be sure that he or she is aware of the correct tail length for an Airedale. When the puppy is held in an upright position (as if it were standing on its four feet with its head and tail up and its neck extended), the tail should be docked at the point where the tail and head are even. A guideline is to leave two-thirds of the tail remaining; however, tails vary in length and thickness so guidelines have to be modified.

The dewclaws are like "thumbs" and are always removed on Airedales. Be sure to check the rear legs, too, since occasionally a pup will have a rear dewclaw. Because there is very little feeling at this age, the pup will cry mainly because you are holding it tightly. To stop any bleeding, use Monsel powder or the clotting powder used for nail cutting.

INOCULATIONS

Check with your veterinarian for the recommended schedule of inoculations, as many have different suggested plans. Have a stool sample examined for the presence of worms, and, if needed, have the puppies wormed.

Chow down.

Ready to go.

One of these puppies is Ch. M.J.'s Stone Ridge Chosen One and another is Ch. Stone Ridge Shannon O'Regent. Can you tell which ones are the champions? The breeder couldn't.

AKC REGISTRATION

To register your litter, obtain a form from the AKC. After supplying the required information of the sire and dam (registered names and registered numbers), you will sign as owner of the dam and the stud owner will sign as owner of the sire. After AKC receives this form and the specified fee, they will send blue registration slips (one for each puppy) to you. A blue slip is filled out, signed and given to each purchaser of a puppy, together with a copy of the pedigree of the sire and dam and information about feedings, shots and worming, as well as the name of your veterinarian.

Weary as you and your bitch may be, you can look at each other and think, "Together we did it, a tough job well done." And you share with pride the happy, bouncing puppies that are ready to take on the world as only Airedale puppies can. All you can think of now is "Look out world—Here they come!"

Ready for the world.

18

The Airedale in Art

HAUNTING THE ANTIQUE STORES, swap meets and junk stores has yielded many older figurines and collectors' items from days gone by. Some are expensive and some are strictly trinkets that express the love of the Airedale by many people. The figurines produced by Royal Doulton (England) in various sizes are sought after, bringing a good price, as are those bearing the Royal Copenhagen (Denmark) mark.

Many of these old figurines are found executed in glass, carved wood, fabric, yarn, metal (both pot and previous metals), porcelain, bisque, bronze, clay, rhinestones, diamonds—and some of undetermined materials used in the Art Deco period.

The Airedales appear in a variety of poses. One sees heads, busts and figures standing, sitting, sitting up, playing, taking naps and doing all the things that come naturally to the breed. They guard books as bookends; appear on door knockers; hold the master's pipe; guard house slippers (and eat them, too); appear as automobile hood ornaments; protect the logs in the fireplace as andirons; serve as boot scrapers; decorate boxes, glasses, dishes, wall plaques, wall hangings, rugs, stuffed toys, wind chimes, jewelry, lapel pins and rings, and are depicted on magnets, watch faces, clocks and as fabric designs. Look closely; you will find Airedales everywhere.

The Airedale has appeared in many paintings, including those by Arthur Wardle, reproduced as give-away cigarette cards, now highly collectible. An interesting painting hangs in the Whitney Gallery of Western Art in Cody, Wyoming; it features an Airedale and two mountain men pausing for a rest on a rugged trail against a background of mountain peaks and sky. This

A *Saturday Evening Post* cover from 1918 found in an antique store.

Antique brass airedale (two feet tall).

Antique bronzes from the
Framke Collection.

Cups, ale bottle, candle,
soapstone from the Framke
Collection.

Ceramic by Ed Klein.

Wood inlay by Diane Hartjes from the Framke Collection.

Etching of Ch. Clarkedale Joy D'Evalynn.

242

Painting (oil on canvas) "Hunters with Dog," artist Philip Goodwin (1822–1935). Courtesy of Buffalo Bill Historical Center, Cody, Wyoming.

243

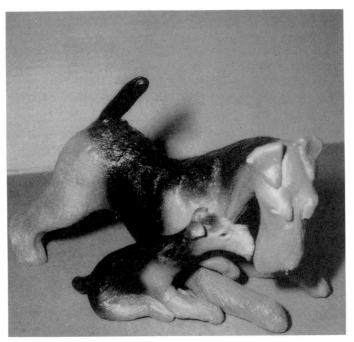

Airedale Mother and Baby—Dannyquest Designs (artist J. Dutcher).

Watercolor by L. Smith (Framke
Collection).

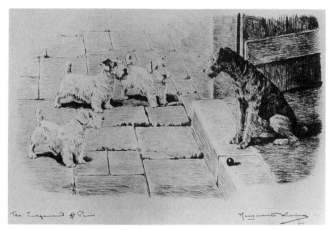

Marguerite Kirmse etching "The Judgement of Paris."

'Mend your speech a little,
Lest it may mar your fortunes.'

King Lear. I. 1. 96

Persis Kirmse etching "Mend your speech a little,/Lest it may mar your fortunes." (*King Lear* I.1.96)

Marguerite Kirmse etching "The Young Visitor."

245

Oil painting of Ch. Sunnydale Coppercrest Dinah by Frances Miller, noted watercolorist.

Hand-painted porcelain plate by Daisy Austad.

painting is by Philip Goodwin and was painted for the Winchester Rifle Company.

Recent motion pictures have had Airedales as performers. Often we see them featured in advertising for dog foods, fashion clothing and bed sheets, and even accompanying a young woman to a handy automatic bank teller.

The "Dopey Dale" cartoons of Paul Clarke of New Zealand show many of the joys and hazards of living closely with our favorite breed.

There are children's books of the now time frame that rival the older stories from Jack London. Through the years one stumbles on charming books featuring the Airedale in fiction.

Just lately three Airedales of Anne Curtis's Victorianne breeding have become cover girls by gracing the popular slick magazine *Connoisseur,* accompanied by an extremely well-written article by Chip Brown of New York. A recent *Better Homes and Gardens* cover pictures an Airedale statue on a bedside table. So watch wherever you travel, and Airedales will be there for your enjoyment both in the flesh and in the many forms of art.

Appendix

Direct tail-male line of descent from the founder of the breed.

CHART I

Airedale Jerry 1888
  Ch. Cholmondeley Briar
    Briar Test
      Ch. Master Briar
        Ch. Clonmel Monarch
          Clonmel Chilperic
            Ch. Master Royal
              Ch. Midland Royal
              Ch. Midland Rollo
                Requisition
                  Wadsworth Royalist
                    Cragsman King
                    Cragsman Dictator
                      Eng. & Am. Ch. Warland Ditto 1919
                      Ch. Moorhead Marquis 1921
                      Ch. Warland Whatnot 1921
                        Ch. Warland Waterman 1924
                      Clonmel Monarque 1921
                        Ch. Clee Courtier 1925
                          Ch. Junemore Bonnie Boy 1929
                          Ch. Matador Supreme
                          Ch. Warbeck Eclipse (Chart 1-A)
                          Walnut King Nobbler 1930 (Chart 1-B)
                          Ch. Matador Mandarin 1929 (Chart 1-C)

CHART 1–A

Ch. Warbeck Eclipse
Bighorn Duke
  Ch. Rusty Dusty, UDT
    Sierradale Lone Indian
      Sierradale Indian Buck
        Int. Ch. Sierradale Medicine Man
          Ch. Ruff-Out
            Sergeant Staff Art
              King Hobo
                Ch. Hobo'Shanter
                  Ch. Ko'Jak de AAA
                    Ch. Aldee's Navajo de AAA
                      Ch. Safari's Serengeti
                        Ch. Safari's Jack Armstrong
                        Ch. Safari's Archangel of Dabob
                        Ch. Safari's Highpoint Ardsley
                        Ch. Safari's Handsome Boy
                        Ch. Safari's Saharan

CHART I–B

Walnut King Nobbler
  Tri. Int. Ch. Cotteridge Brigand
    Ch. Rockley Robin Hood
    Ch. Fallcrest Harry
    Eng. Ch. Monarch of Tullochard
    Ch. Rockley Roasting Hot
      Ch. Royel Hot Rock
      Ch. Eleanore's Brigand
      Ch. Eleanore's Royalty of Lionheart
        Ch. Lionheart Copper
          Ch. Studio Top Brass
            Ch. Studio Liontamer (Chart II-A)
  Eng. & Am. Ch. Cast Iron Monarch
  Ch. Walnut Clipper of Freedom (Chart II-B)
    Ch. Freedom Freelance
      Ch. Freedom Full Force
  Ch. Lamorna Prince Nobbler
  Ch. Turkish Western Guard (Eng.) (Chart II-C)
  Ch. Llanipsa Toreador (Chart II-D)

CHART I–C

Ch. Matador Mandarin
  Ch. Stockfield Aristocrat (Eng.)
    Ch. Waycon Aristocrat (Eng.)
      Waycon Designer (Eng.)
        Can. Ch. Murraysgate Monty
          Holmbury Murraysgate Merrijack (Eng.)
            Eng. Ch. Son of Merrijack (Chart III)
    Ch. Wolstanton Bostock (Eng.)

Berrycroft Atoppa (Eng.)
    Ch. Wyrewood Aristocratic of Harham
    Ch. Holmbury Bandit (Eng.)
    Solo Aristocrat
        Ch. Rural Aristocrat
            Ch. Rural Wirewood Apollo (Eng.)
                Ch. Searchlight Defiance
                Ch. Collipriest Stormer (Eng.)
                    Ch. Bengal Collipriest Diplomat (Eng.)
                    Ch. Bengal Sabu (Chart IV)
                Ch. Riverina Siccawei Phoebus (Chart V)
    Ch. Broadcaster of Harham
    Ch. Chathall Wostan (Eng.)

CHART II-A

Ch. Studio Liontamer
   Ch. Hilltop's Rocky Top Notch
      Hilltop's Blitzkrieg
         Ch. Town Girl's Challenge
            Ch. Buckshot III
            Ch. Thunder's Playboy
               Ch. Airewyre's Big Ernie
                  Ch. Ernie's Jack Flash
                     Ch. Loc Aire's Maestro
                     Ch. Loc Aire's Virtuoso
                        Ch. Fresh Aire Meistersinger Loc
                        Ch. Cedarcrest Star Contender
                     Ch. Kinetic Brooke's Image
                     Ch. Stone Ridge Union Jack
                        Ch. Stone Ridge Regal Mac
                           Ch. Briggsdale Flying Ace, CD
                     Ch. Kinetic Self Sufficient
                     Ch. Kinetic Jack Be Quick
                       Ch. Tobaire's Flash Gordon
                     Ch. Kiryat Sampson's Tartan
                       Ch. Tartan's Mr. Sage
                         Ch. Arista Darbaire Diable
                       Ch. Tartan Bannochburn Drummond
                   Ch. Blackheath Dragonslayer
                   Ch. Scottshire Rimfire Rusty
                   Ch. Brisline's Sassenach Tristan
Coppercrest Brandy
   Siouxaire's Chief Duff
      Ch. Love's Stoney Burke
         Ch. Love's Gabriel of Coppercrest
            Ch. Papago of Indianaire
         Ch. Carboncrest
         Ch. Coppercrest Iron Dynamo
         Ch. Geronimo of Indianaire
            Ch. Moesonof Indianaire
         Ch. Despot of Dominaire
            Ch. Coppercrest Ruddy Rogueaire
            Ch. Quincy Christopher Murase
         Ch. Coppercrest Jonathan Swift
            Ch. Scatterfoot Lysander
            Ch. Coppercrest Mr. McTavish
            Ch. Coppercrest Tornado
            Ch. Coppercrest Little John
         Ch. Geoffrey Earl of Stratford
            Ch. Jerilee's Jumping Jericho
               Ch. Jamboree Secretariat
            Ch. Brown's Jigsaw John
               Ch. Katiaire's Avenger
               Ch. Drou R Shawndee's O'Henry
               Ch. Crofter's Rebellious Rascal
               Ch. Kingsmen Buckden Pike
               Ch. Kingsmen Lord of the Rings

Ch. Cripple Creek Frodo Baggins
Ch. Cripple Creek Bilbo Baggins
Ch. Gingerbred's Spice of Life
Ch. Kingsmen Baron Nickolaus
 Ch. Kingsmen Dexter Darcy
 Ch. Kingsmen Maxwell Arthur
 Ch. Gingerbred's Britain
Ch. Shadrak Tellas Kingsmen
Ch. Kingsmen's Sergeant Saxon
 Ch. Ragscroft Alexis Stardust, CD
 Ch. Gemstone Indiana Jones
 Seneca Major Motion, CD
 Ch. Kingsmen Lord Chancellor
 Ch. Gemstone Last Starfighter
 Ch. CVO Hackberry's Prince Andy
 Ch. Kingsmen Midnight Magic
 Ch. Tellas Tristan Should
Ch. Jolabar Lowers the Boom
Ch. Kaktus Kunte Kinte de AAA
 Kaktus Kunta of Flint de AAA
 Ragscroft Roscue, CD
Ch. Coppercrest Contender
Ch. Coppercrest Conqueror
Ch. Sunnydale Durango Kid
Ch. Sunnydale Doc Holiday
 Ch. Rudigan Robear
 Ch. Waggin Aires Jeremiah
  Ch. Sullivan's Buttonnose Tiger
 Ch. Dandyaire Dixie Jazzman
  Ch. Se-aire Runnin with the Nite
  Ch. Se-aire Man of Distinction
  Ch. Taryn Indiana Jones
  Ch. Dandyaire Earl of Blackburn
  Ch. Bridgedale's Dallas Cowboy
 Ch. Waggery's High Country
  Ch. Good Medicine Renegade
  Ch. Good Medicine Ri of Brocaire
  Ch. Waggery's Nitty Gritty
 Am. & Can. Ch. Morgan, Earl of Stratford
Ch. Good Medicine Golliwog Jake
 Ch. Golliwog's Kasanova
 Ch. Altena's Flintrock Loverboy
Ch. D'Aires Bat Masterson
Ch. Sunnydale Holmes
 Westmoor's Ding Dong Daddy
 Ch. Jolee Aire Alexander Dumas
 Ch. Deanridge Clayton
 Happydaze Casey
 Ch. Bright Monarch of Cragcrest
Ch. Sunnydale's Wichita Lineman
 Ch. Sunnydale's Tanglewod Ted
 Ch. Sunnydale's Triton
 Sunnydale Pendragon
  Ch. Coppercrest Un Poco Loco

Ch. Coppercrest Sunnydale Pico
Ch. Lay Dee Ayr's Starlight Gambler
Ch. Brisline's London Fog
Ch. Brisline's Lady's Man
   Ch. Santana's Santamente
   Ch. Harringon's Kantankras Kyna
   Ch. Dandyaire Gambler of Aireham
     Ch. Royalcrest Crown Prince
   Ch. Santana Sancho
   Ch. Talbert's Lord Lancelot
   Ch. Talbert's Lord Tristan
Ch. Sunnydale Osage Devil
Ch. Tellas California Holiday
Ch. Sunnydale's Quartermaster
   Ch. Blackdale's Dauntless
   Ch. Blackdale's Storm Warning
   Ch. Blackdale's Lord Baronington
   Ch. White Rose Amadeus
   Ch. White Rose Doc Watson
Ch. Woodhue Joint Venture
   Ch. Woodhue's Preferred Stock, CDX
Ch. Woodhue of Buckingham
Ch. Wildtree Sunny Doc
Ch. Brisline's Norbert Holiday
Ch. Woodhue Traveling Man
Ch. Talbert's Lord Tristan

CHART II–B

Ch. Walnut Clipper of Freedom
  Ch. Freedom Freelance
    Ch. Freedom Full Force
      Ch. Freedom's Great Pride
        Ch. Rek En Nad's High and Mighty of Freedom
        Ch. Rek En Nad's Hitting Away
          Ch. Rek En Nad's Mainliner
        Ch. Rek En Nad's Sir Richard

CHART II–C

Ch. Turkish Western Guard (Eng.)
  Turkish Western Dictator (Eng.)
    Talena Majestic (Eng.)
      Cont. Ch. Brineland Bonny Boy
      Lineside Marquis of Burdale (Eng.)
      Ch. Barton of Burdale
        Ch. Kresent Samuel (Eng.)
        Brunel of Mynair (Eng.)
      Eng. & Am. Ch. Sanbrook Sandpiper
      Ch. Jerejan Beau Blade
      Ch. Pine-Aire's Sandboy
      Sanbrook Senator

Ch. Seabrook Senturian
Anfeald Royal Grundy's Britt
Ch. Anfeald Brandywine
Anfeald Hot Spur
Am. Can. Ch. Anfeald Moses
Aust. Ch. Mr. Smith of Burdale

CHART II–D

Ch. Llanipsa Toreador (Eng.)
Westhay Alliance (Eng.)
Ch. Riverina Reunion (Eng.)
Ch. Riverina Tweed (Eng.)
Ch. Riverina Tweedsbairn (Eng.)
Aust. Ch. Riverina Mandarin
Aust. Ch. Siccawei Remus

CHART III

Eng. Ch. Son of Merrijack
  Ch. Bengal Bahadur of Harham
    Ch. Danhow Farouk
      Ch. Talyn's Tom Tom
        Ch. Talyn's Man About Town
          Ch. Jolabar's O'Donnell Aboo
          Ch. Jolabar's O'Shaughnessy
          Ch. Loujeannes Rock of Gibraltar
          Ch. Jolabar's O'Flynn
    Ch. Buccaneer Rocky Mount
    Ch. Dets Wind Storm
    Aireline Hallmark
      Ch. Wraggletaggle Checkmate
        Ch. Wraggletaggle Ebenezer
          Ch. Golliwog's Guy Fawkes
        Ch. Dandyaire Cinnabar Gremlin
        Ch. Caper
        Ch. Barbate Excalibur
          Ch. Anfeald Sam I Am of Britham
            Ch. Britham Bourguignon
        Ch. Jumping Jack Flash
      Ch. Lay Dee Ayr Nicodemus
        Ch. Lay Dee Ayr Happy Go Lucky
        Ch. Conair Detention
        Ch. Lay Dee Ayr's TNT of Karengary
          Ch. Karengary's Rocket of Sujawe
          Karengary's Upper Bunk
            Ch. Sujawe's Teddy Bear
        Ch. Lay Dee Ayr's Apollo of Edane
          Ch. Centurion's Janus
        Ch. Lay Dee Ayr's Hay Maker
          Ch. Talranjac's Mister Hobnob
          Ch. Justice P Coppercrest
          Ch. Lay Dee Ayr's Astronomer
  Ch. Benaire Queen's Ransom
    Ch. Erowah Command Performance
    Ch. Benaire Erowah Crown Prince
      Ch. Benaire King's Counsel
        Ch. Cyndale Smiling Sam
          Ch. Cyndale Sam's Son
      Ch. Benaire Courtney's Duet
        Ch. Benaire Argus Blackjack
        Ch. Argus Checkmate
          Ch. Argus Mr. C. J.
            Ch. Clintwood Busby
              Wagtail Me N My Arrow
        Ch. Benaire Argus Atlas
          Ch. Dariare Yosemite Sam
          Ch. Valaire Barbate Fra Diabolo
          Ch. Rivendell Oakenshield
            Ch. Crissie's Wrigbee-Dee
            Ch. Edgemere's Robinhood

Ch. Querencia's Bengal Diplomat
    Ch. Querencia's King Little
Blackheath Exchequer
  Ch. Toprock's Blackwood
    Ch. Airegard's General Mudd
    Ch. Toprock's Odin's Image
    Ch. Weathers Rowdy of Toprock
    Ch. Glenaire Alister
      Ch. Pequod Sea Bird
        Ch. Pequod T'Gallant Royal
          Ch. Pequod Salt Horse
            Ch. Pequod Blackbeard the Pirate
          Ch. Harry of Pequod
          Ch. Pequod's Torpedo
          Ch. Pequod Marlinspike
          Ch. Accabonac Barbarossa
            Ch. Accabonac Desiderio Gramary
          Ch. Accabonac Capi Di Tutti Capi
          Ch. Pequod's Mizzen Mast
Can. & Am. Ch. Aireline Star Monarch
  Ch. Dandyaire Cottage Commando
Blackheath Inquisitor
  Ch. Captain Chris
  Ch. Dandyaire Friend Freddy
  Ch. Dandyaire Flint Fire
  Ch. Chancrest Topper

CHART IV

Ch. Bengal Sabu
  Ch. Bengal Bladud of Harham
    Eng. Ch. Kresent Brave
    Eng. Ch. Bengal Fastnet
      Eng. Ch. Siccawei Baronet
     Aust. Ch. Tjuringa Foxy Felix
     Eng. Ch. Siccawei Ransom
       Eng. Ch. Lancastrian
        Eng. Ch. Bengal Tarquin
       Bengal. Turith Comet
        Ch. Bravo True Grit
         Ch. Finlair Tiger of Stone Ridge
          Ch. Stone Ridge Murphy C
          Ch. Rubicon's Lord Richelieu
          Ch. Trevorwood Otis Orme
          Ch. Stone Ridge T Bear, CD
          Ch. Stone Ridge Baxter Ladd
          Ch. Trevorwood Upton
          Ch. Good Medicine Gaucho
          Ch. Dig 'M Instigator of Edgemont
            Ch. Maximilian Trump
          Ch. Dig 'M Devlin Bullgator, CD
            Ch. RAA Diamond Jim Jazzman
          Ch. Windom's Run for the Roses
          Ch. Oxford Highwayman, CD
          Ch. Brisline's Blockbuster
          Ch. Waggin-Aire's Jonah
          Terrydale's Admiral Drummer
            Ch. Terrydale's Avenging Angel
            Ch. Terrydale's Heaven Kan Wait
              Ch. Terrydale's Overboard
          Ch. Brisline's Brass Ring
          Ch. Epoch's Time Out for Kenaquhar
          Ch. Moraine Bold Goldsmith
            Ch. Moraine Lone Ranger
            Ch. Moraine First Edition
            Ch. Kopperas American Express
          Ch. Counselor Constellation
          Ch. Mistyaire's Lancer of Tiger
          Ch. Britham Finlair Benjamin, CD
        Ch. Eden's Brass Bamboo
         Ch. Lynaire's Southern Cross
         Ch. Plum Creek's Artful Dodger
        Ch. Briggsdale Bear Claw
      Ch. Stone Ridge Strongbow
       Ch. Accabonac Indelicato
       Ch. Redcoat's Zak the Fifer
       Ch. Forepaugh Pinball Wizard
       Ch. Forepaugh's Prudential
         Ch. Seneca Newcomers Chance, CD
       Ch. Jolee Aire William Tell
         Ch. Nipmuc Lord Philip, CD
         Ch. Nipmuc Lord Theodore

258

Ch. Santeric Tony the Tiger
Ch. Santeric Tru Grit of Warwick
Ch. Windward's Stonehenge
Ch. Briggsdale Boss of Stone Ridge
   Ch. Briggsdale Gaucho Grande
   Ch. Waggin-Aire's Gideon
   Ch. Settle-Aire's Southern Comfort
   Ch. Spindletop's Supertanker
Ch. Tartan's Oil Patch Poppa
Ch. Tartan's Texas Ranger
   Ch. Piccadilly's Ring Master
   Ch. Piccadilly's Semper Fi
Ch. RicRac's City Slicker
   Ch. Lay Dee Ayr's Yankee Doodle
Ch. Tartan's Black Gold
Ch. Tartan's Liquid Gold
Ch. Tartan Lariwinkin
Ch. Epoch's Nineteen Eighty-four
Ch. Finlair Lyon of Stone Ridge
   Ch. Bryn Hafod's Willie Boy
Ch. Chado's Whistle-N-Flute
Ch. Evermay Jodee's Artful Dodger
   Ch. Jodee's Knight of Excalibar
Ch. Finlair Intruder of Wie
Ch. Cripple Creek Carib v Frisch
Ch. Kingsmen Simon Brode
Ch. Stone Ridge Dickens
Ch. D'Aire Whirlwind
Ch. Finlair Imperial Trent
Ch. Riva Elijah of Waggin-Aire
Ch. D'Aire Energizer
Ch. D'Aire Eveready
Ch. Stone Ridge Fame of Fireside, CD
   Ch. Stone Ridge American Storm
   Ch. Royalcrest New Generation
   Ch. Royalcrest Oldham's Aquila
Ch. Prize Gang Buster
Ch. Brisline's Ace in the Hole
   Ch. Trevorwood Captain Absolute
   Ch. Trevorwood Hole in One
   Ch. Hi-Tail Amazing Jake
Ch. Fireside Fiery Sinbad
Ch. Blackjack's Grand Slam
Ch. Blackjack's Doubledown Danny
Ch. Stone Ridge Jigsaw G-Man
   Ch. Stone Ridge Wild Bill Cody
Ch. Stone Ridge Bucko Bravo
Ch. D'Aire Watch Out for Dig'M
   Ch. Ad Lib Dig'M's Little J
      Ch. Ad Lib's Lonesome Jubilee
      Ch. Ad Lib's Benim Bashari
Ch. Bravo Star Buck
   Ch. Briardale's Main Event
      Ch. Rustiaire's Sam Spade, CD
   Ch. Cisseldale's Cocky Corkie

Ch. Cisseldale's Charlie
Ch. Cisseldale's Casey
Ch. Cisseldale's Redsky Montgomery, CD
Ch. Blackjack's Mighty Samson
Ch. Royalroads King of Blackjack
Ch. Blackjack's Nostradamus (Top Sire in England 1988 & 1989)
Ch. Richlin's Topgun
Ch. Country-Aires Royal Flush
Am. & Arg. Ch. Blackjack's Ringo Starr
Ch. Blackheath's Sam's Son
Ch. Belleterra Intrepid Ares
Ch. Dandy Boy of White House
Ch. Reffal Samson
Ch. Moraine Mausser-Reg Bernabee
Ch. Sheer's Dandy Sam
Ch. Lancelot W's Sebastian
Ch. Roulette of White House
Ch. Safari Blueacre Rocket, CD
Ch. Castalia's Panama Jack
Ch. Rainbow Warwich Samuel Pepys, CD
Ch. Bishop's Mitre
Ch. Moraine Bold Quarterback
Ch. Safari's Titan of Blue Acres
Ch. Dabob's Pride of Piccadilly
Ch. Evermay's Harry Winston
Ch. Aldee's Chubaca
Ch. Aldee's Gizmo
Ch. Highpoint Bold Star
Ch. Monfort Victorianne Whodunit
Ch. Safari's Brush of Birchrun
Ch. Britham Duke of Tarragon
Ch. Britham Maximillian
Ch. Tartan's Buck Rogers
Ch. Bacchus' Star Contender
Ch. Kinetic Lucky Lucifer
Ch. Cisseldale Sanger Sam II
Ch. Bravo Comet's Streak
Ch. Hayrob's Jolly Jeremy
Ch. Turith Country Cousin
Ch. Maximus of Meadow Creek
Ch. White Rose Concert Master
Ch. Pudding Hill Zachary
Ch. White Rose Rocka My Soul
Ch. Victorianne's Piece of the Rock
Ch. Forepaugh's Rock of Ages
Ch. Forepaugh's Rock of Gibraltar
Ch. Forepaugh's Rockin' Robin
Ch. Seneca Stony Stone Bandit, CDV
Ch. Seneca Cornerstone
Ch. Stirling's Silver Duncan
Am. & Can. Ch. Stirling's Country Thane
Am. & Can. Ch. Lindar's Last Laugh
Ch. Jolabar's Andy of Talyn
Ch. Allegro Vivace

Ch. White Rose Nickelodeon
Ch. Birchrun Six Boys Amos
Ch. Reginald Man of War
Ch. Tartan's Chief of the Clan
Ch. Tartan Southern Chieftan
Ch. Tartan King of the Mountain
Ch. Tartan's Country Bumpkin
Ch. Seneca Country Sport
Eng., Am., Can., Ger. & Dutch Ch. Jokyl Bengal Figaro
Ch. Reffal Prince Figaro
Ch. Jokyl Supreme
Ch. Wraggletaggle Marksman
Ch. Bryn Hafod Kings Ransom
Ch. Pendragon's Amos of Plunkett
Ch. Harbour Hill Naugahyde
Eng. Ch. Jokyl Space Leader
Loudwell Dandino
Ch. Loudwell Mr. Universe
Ch. Anfeald J. C. Superstar
Ch. Jokyl Superior
Ch. Briardale Duke of Windsor
Ch. Argus Knight Watch
Ch. Argus Fast Heat
Ch. Valaire's Argus Kidnap Ransom
Eng. & Am. Ch. Jokyl Kenlucky Sam
Jokyl Chippinghey Kestrel
Ch. Jokyl Prince Regent
Ch. Senator of Whitehouse
Ch. Talyn's Limited Edition
Ch. Breezewood Beat the Band
Ch. Birchrun Surgeon
Ch. Moraine Bold Regent
Ch. Arelsh Fireball MacDougall
Ch. Moraine Bold Ringmaster
Ch. Rippledale's Mr. Barnaby
Ch. Glo-Nels Mr. R. B. Barnaby
Ch. Glo-Nels Pudgy Reggie
Ch. Milchin's Konrad Gustav
Eng. & Am. Ch. Jokyl Superman
Ch. Lay Dee Ayr's Wakanda
Ch. Sasha Alexander
Ch. Reffal No Nonsense
Ch. Reffal Big Casino
Ch. Marydale's Fame & Fortune
Ch. Kingsmen Tiger Grand Slam
Ch. Kingsmen Tiger Pennant Pace
Ch. Kingsmen Tiger Power Hitter
Ch. Kingsmen Tiger League Leader
Ch. Kingsmen Alexander Conal
Ch. Lay Dee Ayr's Avenger
Ch. Quirnus Legacy of Loyalty
Ch. Starboroughs Socrateaser
Ch. Lay Dee Ayr's Aristocrat
Ch. Lay Dee Ayr's Witchdoctor

Ch. Marydale's Headliner
  Ch. Sea-Aire Marydale's Avenger
    Ch. Sea-Aire Avenger's Replica
  Ch. The Tornado
    Ch. Reffal Tombill's Tornado
      Ch. Sea-Aire's Irish Connection
  Ch. The Ring Master
  Ch. The Sting
    Ch. The Flying Dutchman
    Ch. Richmark's Gigolo
  Ch. The Pac Man
  Ch. Ringtrue Rifle
Ch. Suzark Open Sesame
  Ch. Suzark Watch
    Ch. Afton's Applejack
Ch. Harbour Hills Klark Kent
  Ch. Harbour Hills Drummerboy
  Ch. Harbour Hills Orion
    Ch. Harbour Hills Loyal Lad
      Ch. Territage Bestseller
      Ch. Territage Calculated Risk
        Ch. Territage Game Plan
      Ch. Territage Eli Tamerlane
    Ch. Harbour Hills Autumn Ace
Ch. Dandyaire's Quickfire
  Ch. Titekotes Helfyre
  Ch. Dandyaire's Blazing Son
    Ch. Harrington's Casey Jones
Ch. Dandyaire's Quite a Guy
  Ch. Aireland's Fearless Freddy
  Ch. Waggery's Favorite Son
    Ch. Copperfire Dandydale
Ch. Lay Dee Ayr's Wardance
  Ch. Centurian Brother Bruce
Ch. Moraine Forest Fire
  Ch. Revere Sir Lancelot
Ch. Waggery's California Comet
Ch. Jokyl Supermaster
  Ch. Stone Ridge Son of Supermaster
  Ch. Stone Ridge Brass Tacks
  Ch. Stone Ridge Dino
    Denver von Guenzburg
      Grovenay Bingley Barrister, UD
  Ch. Argus Stone Ridge Hunky Dory
    Ch. I and M's Mannix Airedale Farm
    Ch. Stone Ridge Jack Daniels
    Ch. Stone Ridge Seventy-six
      Ch. Hijinx Madcap Marauder
      Ch. Stone Ridge River Shannon
Ch. Jamboree Don Juan
  Ch. Jamboree Maygan Tigreto
    Ch. Juliet's Alexander Warwick, CD
  Ch. Jamboree El Cordobles
Ch. Redaire Clarkedale Sailor

Ch. Eden's Spring Hepatica
Ch. Eden's Sal Senecia
Ch. Eden's Sal Sorbus
Ch. Hamm's Smithfield of Eden
Ch. Piccadilly's Tom Sawyer
Ch. Shawndee's Jackpot
Ch. Shawndee's Red Alert of Drou-R
Ch. Starmist Supercharger
Ch. Eden's Jacobina
Ch. Afton's Spectacular Kid
Ch. Cymbeline Leaping Lizzard
Ch. Sunnydale's Kensington Earl
Ch. Eden's Summer Sambucus
Ch. Accabonac Garofano
Ch. Tropic Aire's Energizer
Ch. Accabonac Ayatolla
Ch. Eden's Peperomia
Ch. Finlair Eden ET Phone Home
Ch. Bravo Bravo of Eden
Ch. Bravo Exchequer of Eden
Ch. Dellaires Peter Pan Maxwell
Ch. Lancelot Lord Cedric
Ch. Ajay's Stone Ridge Super Chief
Ajay's Lee Jax Magnifique, CD
Ch. Stone Ridge Gingerbred Man
Ch. Stone Ridge Trash Masher
Brulyn's Baha-Dur
Eng. & Am. Ch. Optimist of Mynair
Ch. Krislyn's Oliver Cromwell
Ch. Krislyn's Sargent Major
Ch. Tucker's Marine Gunner
Ch. Moraine Bold Ruler
Ch. Stone Ridge Last Knight
Int. Ch. Oscar of Mynair
Dan. Ch. Loudwell Mayboy
Loudwell Battleship
NZ. Ch. Loudwell Krisp
Aust. Ch. Loudwell Viewpoint
Ch. Strongfort Saturn
Ch. Sunnydale's Satellite
Ch. Coppercrest Dinah's Jason
Ch. Sunnydale's Viva Zapata
Ch. Sunnydale's Schweppes
Ch. Coppercrest Queen's Counsel
Ch. Tjuringa Yahoo
Ch. Bandar's RJ Just Terrific
Ch. Oak Forts Hugger McDuff
Loudwell Stratford
Eng. & Aust. Ch. Loudwell Whispers
Ch. Bengal Flyer
Ch. Aristocrat of White House
Ch. Rockledge Come-Along Clancy
Ch. Harbour Hills Iroquoi
Ch. Harbour Hills Indian Ink

Ch. Harbour Hills Millhouse
 Ch. Harbour Hills Fumigator
 Ch. Pepperidge Ready for Phreddy
Ch. Talyn's You Betcha
Ch. Talyn's Yankee Clipper
Ch. Talyn's Yohorum
 Ch. Elroy's Sir Oliver
  Ch. Max-Aire's Great Spirit
  Ch. R. G.'s Major Domo
 Ch. Rockdale's Arab
  Ch. El-Ef's Arab Emir
  Ch. Rek En Nad Bold Challenge
   Ch. Deaknabe Frac of Dar V Jo
 Ch. Talyn's Sound Your A
 Ch. Matte's Regent of Agincourt
 Ch. Talyn's Usadit
  Ch. Dob-N-Aire Little Gem
Eng. Ch. Bengal Gunga Din
 Ch. Bengal Mowgli
  Sw. & Nor. Ch. Kresent Quartermaster
   Sw. Ch. Ragtime Colombo
    Sw. Ch. Gay Gordon's Christmas Box
     Int. Ch. Bengal Gay Gordon's Pomp & Circumstance
     Ch. Bengal Rajaraja
      Ch. Sequoyahs Derby Days
     Ch. Loudwell Fife & Drum
      Ch. Botarus Keyboard
   Copperstone Field Fairfax
    Sw. Ch. Copperstone Hannibal Hayes
    Aust. Ch. Mynair Keep in Touch
  Bengal Buldeo
  Eng. Ch. Bengal Flamboyant
   Ch. Angevin Lord Argyle
   Ch. Bengal Galahad
   Ch. Bengal Saladin
    Int. Ch. Bengal Sahib
     Mex. & Am. Ch. Stone Ridge Bengal Bravo
     Ch. Stone Ridge Montgomery Bravo
     Ch. M. J.'s Stone Ridge Chosen One
     Ch. Anfeald's Supernatural
     Ch. Stone Ridge Padric O'Rorke
     Ch. Stone Ridge Tornado Watch
  Eng. Ch. Siccawei Galliard
   Eng. Ch. Perrancourt Pirate
    Eng. Ch. Stargus Sea King
     Eng. & Am. Ch. Florac King of Scotts at Stargus
   Ch. Turith Brigand
    Ch. Glentop's Krackerjack
     Ger. Ch. Gay Charlie of Glentops
      Ch. Golf Vom Wissel
     Happy Chance of Glentops
      Ch. Glento's Yentl
       Ch. Stone Ridge Traveler
   Aust. Ch. Drakehall Dragoon

Ch. Jokyl Cinerama
  Ch. Tropic-Aire Alter Ego
    Ch. Tropic-Aire First Class
      Ch. Tropic-Aire Jet Fighter
    Ch. Tropic-Aire Archibald
  Ch. Harbour Hills Ultimatum
    Ch. Harbour Hills Olympian
  Ch. Harbour Hills Warlock
Ch. Turith Adonis
  Ch. Scottshire Roger Boy
  Ch. Altaire Bubbling Cauldron
  Ch. Greenfield's Arrogante Thor
  Ch. Scottshire Sir Vival
  Ch. Apollo of Whitehouse
  Ch. Cadet of Whitehouse
  Ch. Sir Xavier Bachman
  Ch. Belleterra Bacchus
  Ch. Turith's Adonis Plum Duff
  Ch. Scottshire's Jock Scott
  Ch. Edambs Boston Bouncer
  Ch. Greenfield's Greek God
  Ch. Serendipity Red Adonis
  Ch. Blackjack's Tom Terrorific
  Ch. Birchrun Brittania
    Ch. Trevorwood Rough Rider
  Ch. Westmoor's Warlock
    Ch. Clarkedale Hat Trick
    Ch. Westmoor's Wizard of Mattamy
      Ch. Holly Oak's Sugar Bear
      Ch. Stone Ridge Start Your Engine
  Eng. Ch. Jokyl Gallipants
    Ch. Jokyl Hillcross Hot Rod
    Ch. Shadli Fantom
      Ch. Shergar of Shadli
  Ch. Jokyl Speedy Bairn of Eden
    Eden's Bailwick Snap To It, CD
  Ch. Turith Forester of Junaken
    Ch. Blazoncrest Spitfire Kato
Ch. Saredon Military Man
  Ch. Belleterra Ganymede
    Ch. Colonel Jack
  Eng. & Am. Ch. Turith Echelon of Saredon
    Ch. Santana's Wild Bill
    Ch. Scottshire's Ambassador Toby
    Ch. Bravo Echelon of Santeric
      Ch. Scottshire's Black Bart
    Ch. Meadow Creeks Kinetic Comet
    Ch. D'Aire's Upper Echelon
      Ch. D'Aire's Whistlin' Dixie
        Ch. D'Aire's Stonewall Jackson
        Ch. Brisline's Colorado Cowboy
        Ch. D'Aire Doctor Who
    Ch. Berrypatch's Mister Macho TT
    Ch. Bravo Ironman of Santeric

265

Ch. Berrypatch's Mikey Ate It
Ch. Blackheath SS Sir Chumley
Can. Ch. Fonaire Franklin
Am. & Can. Ch. Fonaire Iron Ancistrodon
Ch. Firethorn Intrepid
Ch. Firethorn Indigo Blue
Eng. & Am. Ch. Jokyl Spic N' Span
Ch. Piccadilly's Patent Pending
Ch. Piccadilly's Hurly Burly
Ch. Firethorn Folle A Deux
Briardale Shshown Indian
Int. Ch. Shshown Que Forte, CD
Ch. Shshown's Alli Caramba
Ch. Epoch's Chauncey Jerome
Ch. Epoch's Hallmark of Time
Ch. Shshown's Kublai Khan
Am. & Can. Ch. Harrington's Hercules
Ch. Shshown Ivies Fitzwater
Tally-Ho's Glory Seeker
Ch. Forepaugh's Jolee Aire Macho Man
Ch. Forepaugh's Whatagoodboyami
Ch. Eden's Leucojum
Ch. Hijinx Great Expectations
Ch. Solaire Midnite Masquerade, CD
Ch. Tally-Ho's Galant Invader
Ch. Highpoint King Midas
Ch. Highpoint Humptey Dumptey
Ch. Flintkote Galahad
Ch. Stone Ridge Simonize
Ch. Stone Ridge Inspector Clouseau, CDX
Ch. Winsom's Grand Ragazzo
Ch. Winsom's Che Ane Mooch
Ch. Schaire's Ajax
Ch. Schaire's Doctor Jokyl, CDX
Ch. Schaire's Rubber Duck
Ch. Schaire's Face
Ch. Schaire's Country Bumpkin
Ch. Birchrun Country Squire
Ch. Ballinden Zigtweed Highland
Ch. Schaire's Jonathan Hart
Eng. Ch. Jokyl Smart Guy
Ch. Jokyl Smart Set
Ch. Jokyl Fair Play
Ch. Data Bank Buster
Ch. Droffats Breaker Morant
Ch. Semper Fi's Jeremy
Ch. Piccadilly's Tuff Turf
Ch. Piccadilly's Ace Barnstormer
Ch. Jokyl Supercopy
Ch. Reffal The Duke of York
Ch. Denbryl's The Black Prince
Ch. Tucker's Sargent Major Graf, CD
Ch. Rorke's Prime Rib
Ch. Rorke's Canned Heat

Ch. Bengal Nevasa
Eng. & Sw. Ch. Bengal Brulyn Sahib
Ch. Searchlight Tycoon
   Ch. Searchlight Cocksure of Tanworth
      Ch. Flintkote Cocksure Mustang
      Ch. Flintkote Cocksure Sandman
      Ch. Flintkote Cocksure Bengal
Ch. Querencia's Suerte Brava
  Ch. Ringtrue Mr. Wonderful
  Ch. Querencia's Man O' War
  Ch. Querencia's Little King
    Ch. Querencia's Red Baron
    Ch. Talyn's Have At Em
      Ch. Dob N Aire Little Joe
        Ch. Al Fran's Euphonious
  Ch. Querencia's Lord Teddy
  Ch. Prince Caspian
Ch. Elroy's Yankee Tweedsbairn
Ch. Buckey
Ch. Talyn's River Rogue
Ch. Corgaire's River Rogue
Ch. Dandyaire's Mephisto
  Ch. Golliwog's O'Malley
Ch. Dandyaire's Matthew
Ch. Dandyaire's Monarch
  Ch. Dandyaire Oil Producer
Ch. Talyn's Kaywin Chester
Ch. Five Star Commando
Ch. Talyn's Ironclad Leave
Ch. Foxdale's Super Jet Stream
Ch. Cyndale Challenger
Ch. Birchrun Bartender
Ch. Blackburn's Baronof Brutus
  Ch. Blackburn's D'Bruno Magruder
  Ch. Arrowood's Case Ace
  Ch. Blackburn's Danadan Elessar
  Ch. Blackburn's Orcus
  Ch. Blackburn's Othello
Ch. Buccaneer's Copper Crown
Ch. Buccaneer's Swashbuckler
  Ch. Buccaneer's Border Lord Hamish
Ch. Birchrun Bash 'em
Ch. Birchrun Sebastian
Ch. Birchrun Prizefighter
Ch. White Rose Act

CHART V

Ch. Riverina Siccawei Phoebus (Eng.)
  Ch. Mayjack Briar (Eng.)
    Ch. Lanewood Lysander (Eng.)
      So. Afr. Ch. Bengal Skipper of Limebell
      Ch. Bengal Leprechaun
        Ch. Bilmar Bengal Fere of Barbate
        Barbate Chiparoo
          Ch. Rivendell Angus
            Ch. Anfeald Irish Whiskey
          Ch. Britham Cayenne
            Ch. Britham Captain America
          Ch. Britham Lord of the Rings
            Ch. Britham Croissants
         Ch. Circle's Bengal Brigadier
           Ch. Airmont's Bengal Buccaneer
        Barbate Chorister
         Barbate Dante
           Ch. Barbate Henchman
            Ch. Brisline's Bamboozle
            Ch. Codelly's Chapper
            Ch. Barbate Jackpot
            Ch. MacDougall de AAA
      Ch. Birchrun's Most Happy Fella
        Ch. Jackson's Conquistador
        Ch. Jackson's Lord Lashbrook
        Ch. Jackson's John Paul Jones
          Ch. Meadowlark's Aristotle
        Ch. Jackson's Calculator
          Ch. Jackson's Sir John Falstaff
        Ch. Sir Terry of Indianaire
      Bengal Leander
        Ch. Bengal Havildar
          Ch. Eden's Dandelion
          Ch. Coppercrest Cosmopolitan
          Ch. Eden's Jon-Quil
          Ch. Eden's Zwart Narcis
          Ch. Eden's Dutchman of Senoj
           Ch. Samson of Senoj
    Eng. & Am. Ch. Jokyl Bengal Lionheart
      Ch. Cyrano Admiral's Alert
      Ch. Cyrano Apollo
      Ch. Lion Hill MacDuff
      Ch. Tibsen's Skipper's Hercules
      Ch. Tibsen's Diamond Jim
      Ch. Lionheart Gladwyn
        Ch. Alii of Cicadasong Hilla
      Ch. Flintkote Jokyl Krackerjack
        Ch. Flintkote Jack's Red Alert
        Ch. Flintkote Jack's Lord Byron
      Ch. Scatterfoot My Boy Sam
      Lionheart Ute
        Ch. Lionheart Factor

Ch. Ironsides Pek's Bad Boy
    Ch. Ironsides Pacific Station
    Ch. Ironsides Skipper
    Ch. Ironsides Scuttlebutt
      Ch. Ironsides Battle Station
    Ch. Golliwog's Ichabod Crane
    Ch. Golliwog's Infidel
  Ch. Blazon Lionheart Victor
  Ch. Blazon Lionheart Fax Favour
Ch. Briardale Charlie Brown
  Ch. Briardale Kung Fu
    Ch. Harrington's Go For The Gold
    Ch. LocAire's Blazing Comet
    Ch. Brandyaire A Jumbi Norton
  Ch. Finlair Banquo
  Ch. Briardale's Prodigal Son
  Ch. Corgaire's Foxfire
  Ch. Hubbard's Corgaire's Gator
    Ch. Hubbard's Garnet Ray
Ch. Winstony Exceptional
  Ch. Coppercrest Rifleman
    Ch. Terragate Adobe Red
      Ch. Devonshire's Brick Red Alert
      Ch. Adobe Brick O'Sullivan
      Ch. Cymbeline Richmond Rascal
    Ch. Brigand of Coppercrest
    Ch. Coppercrest Tempest
  Ch. Roy-Al Coppercrest (exported to Japan)
  Ch. Coppercrest Redstone Rufus
  Ch. Coppercrest Ramrod
    Ch. Coppercrest Courier
  Ch. Sierradale Warbow
  Ch. Sierradale El Jefe
Ch. Loudwell Kommando
  Loudwell Outlaw
  Loudwell Quest
Ch. Kresent Golden Boy
  Ch. Kresent Red Ribbons
    Ch. Bilmar Knight of Knights
    Ch. Triumph's Ribbon Repeat
    Ch. Breezewood Bozo
    Ch. Millaire's Clintwood Crescent
      Ch. Millaire's Clintwood Chaucer
Reffal All American
  Ch. Reffal Galant Guy
  Ch. Reffal Zoom Zoom

Glossary

AKC. The American Kennel Club.

ALMOND EYE. The shape of the skin around the eye.

AMERICAN KENNEL CLUB. The body that registers all purebred dogs in the United States and handles all litter and individual registrations and transfers of ownership. It keeps all dog show and obedience records, issues titles earned and licenses all dog show and obedience trials and recognized match shows. It makes and enforces all rules, regulations and policies of breeding, raising, exhibiting, handling and judging of purebred dogs in the United States.

ANGULATION. The angles formed by the bones between the shoulder and upper arm in the front and the stifle and hock in the rear.

APPLE HEAD. Roundness of the top-skull.

ATCA. Airedale Terrier Club of America.

BAD BITE. Wryness of the jaw or faulty dentition.

BAD MOUTH. A mouth in which the teeth do not meet correctly.

BALANCE. A well-balanced dog is one where all of the parts appear in correct ratio to each other.

BEEFY. Overdevelopment of the shoulders or quarters or both.

BENCHED SHOW. A dog show that requires the dogs to be kept on benches when not being shown.

BEST IN SHOW (BIS). The dog or bitch chosen as best representative of any dog in any breed from the Group winners at an all-breed show.

BEST OF BREED (BOB). The dog judged best of any competing in its breed.

BEST OF OPPOSITE SEX (BOS). The dog or bitch that is selected as the best of the opposite sex to the Best of Breed.

BEST OF WINNERS. The dog or bitch selected as the better between Winners Dog and Winners Bitch.

BITCH. The female of the species.

BITE. The way the upper and lower jaws meet.

BONE The size in width of a dog's leg bones.

BRACE. Two dogs or two bitches, or a dog and a bitch, similar in size, markings, color and general appearance, moving together in unison.

BREED. Purebred dogs descended from mutual ancestors refined and developed by man.

BREEDER. A person who breeds dogs.

BRISKET. The front of the body between the forelegs and beneath the chest.

BROOD BITCH. A female dog used for breeding.

CANINE TEETH. The four sharp pointed teeth at the front of the jaws, two upper and two lower, often called fangs.

CASTRATE. To neuter a dog by removal of the testicles.

CAT FOOT. A short-toed, round, tight foot similar to that of a cat.

CD. Companion Dog (Obedience degree).

CDX. Companion Dog Excellent (Obedience title).

CH. Champion.

CHAMPION. A dog or bitch that has won a total of fifteen points, including two majors, under at least three different judges. (See Major.)

CHARACTER. Appearance, behavior and temperament of the breed.

CHEEKY. Cheeks that are overly rounded or bulging.

CHEST. Rib cage.

CHISELED. Clean-cut below the eyes.

CHOKE COLLAR. A chain, leather or nylon collar that gives control over the dog by tightening or relaxing the pressure.

CLODDY. Thickset

CLOSE-COUPLED. Short in the loin.

COARSE. Lacking elegance.

COAT. The hair covering of the dog.

COMPANION DOG. The first obedience degree.

COMPANION DOG EXCELLENT. The second obedience degree.

CONDITION. General health. A dog in good condition is carrying the right weight, has a coat that is alive and glossy and shows an appearance of well-being.

CONFORMATION. The structure of the dog.

COUPLING. The loin of a dog, such as close-coupled or short in the loin.

COW-HOCKED. Hocks turned inward at the joint.

CROSSING. Front feet cross over each other.

CROUP. The back above the hind legs.

CRYPTORCHID. An adult dog with testicles not descended.

DAM. Mother of a dog or bitch.

DENTITION. Teeth.

DEWCLAWS. Extra claws on the inside of the legs, sometimes removed according to breed standards.

DISTEMPER TEETH. Discolored, stained or pitted teeth associated with a history of distemper.

DOCK. To cut the tail.

DOG. A male of the breed.

DOG SHOW. A competition where dogs have been entered for an evaluation and the opinion of a judge.

DOG SHOW, ALL-BREEDS. A dog show in which all breeds are judged.

DOG SHOW, SPECIALTY. A dog show featuring only one breed.

DOMED. A top-skull that is rounded.

DOUBLE COAT. A coat consisting of a hard outer coat with a soft, short undercoat.

DOWN-FACED. Muzzle slanting down from eyes to nose.

DOWN IN PASTERN. Weakness of the pastern.

DRIVE. The powerful action of the hindquarters.

DRY NECK. A firm neckline.

DUAL CHAMPION. A dog that has won both confirmation and obedience titles.

DUDLEY NOSE. Flesh-colored nose.

ELBOW. The joint of the forearm and upper arm.

ELBOW, OUT AT. Elbow out from the body rather than being held in close to the body.

EVEN BITE. Exact meeting of the front teeth.

EWE NECK. A concave curvature of the top of the neckline.

EXPRESSION. The typical expression of the breed as one studies the head.

EYETEETH. The upper canine teeth.

FANCIER. A person active in the sport of purebred dogs.

FLANK. The side of the dog at the loin area.

FLYER. A promising young dog.

FLYING EARS. Correct ears that stand up or out occasionally.

FOREFACE. The muzzle.

FRONT. The head, forelegs, shoulders, chest and feet as viewed from in front.

GAIT. The way a dog moves.

GAY TAIL. Tail carried high and over the back.

GET. Puppies.

GROOM. To bathe, brush, comb and trim the dog.

GROUPS. Refers to the variety groups in which the breeds of dogs are divided.

HACKNEY. High lifting of the forefeet.

HANDLER. A person who shows dogs in competition.

HAW. A third eyelid.

HEAT. A period when the bitch can be bred, usually evidenced by a discharge, sometimes called "in season."

HEEL. A command for the dog to walk closely at the left side.

HINDQUARTERS. Rear legs of the dog.

HOCK. The joint between the second thigh and the foot.

HOCKS WELL LET DOWN. Hocks are low to the ground (not elongated).

IN SEASON. Same as Heat.

INCISORS. The small front teeth between the canine teeth.

INT. CH. International champion.

JUDGE. Person making the decisions at a dog show or obedience trial.

KENNEL. The building where dogs are housed. Also a person's collection of dogs.

KNEE JOINT. Stifle joint.

KNITTING AND PURLING. Crossing and throwing of forelegs as the dog moves.

LAYBACK. The angulation of the shoulder.

LEATHER. The ear flap or the skin of the nose.

LEG. in obedience, a qualifying score of at least 170 out of a possible 200 points, including over fifty percent of every exercise required.

LEVEL BITE. The teeth of both jaws meet exactly.

LEVEL GAIT. A dog moving smoothly with the topline carried level.

LIPPY. Lips that do not fit tightly.

LOADED SHOULDERS. Shoulders with excessive muscular development.

LOIN. Area of the sides between the ribs and the hindquarters.

LUMBERING. An awkward gait.

MAJOR. A win in either dogs or bitches, carrying with it three, four or five championship points. (See Champion.)

MATCH SHOW. An informal dog show usually held for puppies and young dogs. No championship points are earned at matches.

MATE. To breed a dog and a bitch to each other. Littermates are puppies born within the same litter.

MILK TEETH. Baby teeth

MOLARS. Four premolars are located at either side of the upper and lower jaws. Two molars exist on either side of the upper jaw, and three on either side below.

MONORCHID. A dog with only one descended testicle.

MUZZLE. 1) The part of the head in front of the eyes. 2) A device over the mouth to prevent biting.

NOSE. The dog's organ of smell, also his talent at picking and following a scent trail.

OBEDIENCE TRIAL. A licensed obedience trial is one held under AKC rules where it is possible to gain a "leg" toward a dog's obedience title.

OBEDIENCE TRIAL CHAMPION. A dog that has gained a specified number of "legs" to qualify for a title.

OCCIPUT. Upper point of skull.

OFA. Orthopedic Foundation for Animals.

ORTHOPEDIC FOUNDATION FOR ANIMALS. An organization of certified radiologists that certifies the existence or lack of hip dysplasia.

OUT AT ELBOW. Elbows away from the body.

OUT AT THE SHOULDER. Shoulder blades that jut out from the body.

OVERSHOT. Upper teeth overlap the lower teeth.

PACING. A gait in which both legs on one side move concurrently; rolling gait.

PAD. The covering of the bottom of the foot.

PADDLING. A gait in which the front legs swing forward in a stiff upward motion.

PASTERN. The area of the foreleg between the wrist and the foot.

PEDIGREE. Written record of the dog's ancestors.

PIGEON CHEST OR CHICKEN BREAST. A short, shallow breastbone.

POINTED. A dog that has won points toward its championship.

PUT DOWN. To prepare a dog for the show ring.

QUALITY. Excellence of type and conformation.

RACY. Lightly built or slender.

RANGY. Excessive length and shallow body.

REACH. The distance to which the forelegs reach out in gaiting.

REGISTER. To record your dog with the AKC.

REGISTRATION CERTIFICATE. The paper issued by the AKC giving the breed, assigned name, names of sire and dam, date of birth, breeder, owner and assigned number of the dog.

RESERVE WINNERS. The dog or bitch selected as second to the Winners Dog or Winners Bitch.

ROACH BACK. A convex curvature of the topline.

SCISSORS BITE. The outside of the lower front teeth touch the inside of the upper teeth.

SECOND THIGH. The back leg between the hock and the stifle.

SEPTUM. The skin between the nostrils.

SET UP. To pose your dog for examination by the judge; stack.

SHELLY. A body lacking in substance.

SHOULDER HEIGHT. The height of the dog from the ground to the highest point of the withers.

SIDE WIND. A dog moving with its body at an angle rather than coming straight at you.

SIRE. The father.

SKULLY. An expression used to describe a coarse skull.

SLAB SIDES. Flat sides with little spring of rib.

SOUNDNESS. Mental and physical stability.

SPAY. To neuter a bitch by surgery.

SPECIAL. A dog or bitch entered in a show for only Best of Breed competition.

SPECIALTY CLUB. An organization devoted to an individual breed of dog.

STANCE. The natural position of a dog standing.

STANDARD. The official description of the ideal specimen of a breed.

STIFLE. The joint of hind leg such as a person's knee.

STILTED. The choppy gait of a dog lacking in correct angulation.

STOP. The indentation at the juncture of the skull and foreface.

STRAIGHT BEHIND. Lacking angulation in the hindquarters.

STRIP. Method of grooming consisting of pulling the hair out to the skin using either thumb-and-finger or a stripping knife.

STRIPPING KNIFE. A serrated knife used to assist in pulling the hair coat out. Coarse, medium or fine are used on different parts of the body. Many different kinds are used by individual groomers.

STUD. A male dog used for breeding.

STUD BOOK. The official record kept on the breeding particulars of recognized breeds of dogs.

SUBSTANCE. Bone size.

SWAYBACK. Downward curvature in the topline between the withers and the hip-bones.

SWEEPSTAKES. Competition at shows for young dogs, usually up to twelve or eighteen months of age, sometimes with money prizes.

TAILSET. The way a tail is placed on the rump.

TD. Tracking Dog degree.

TDX. Tracking Dog Excellent degree.

TEAM. Usually four dogs being shown together.

THIGH. Hindquarters from the stifle to the hip.

THROATINESS. Loose skin at the throat; wet neck.

TOPLINE. The dog's back from withers to tail.

TRACKING DOG. A title for dogs who have completed requirements of a licensed Tracking Test.

TRACKING DOG EXCELLENT. An advanced tracking degree.

TRAIL. To hunt by following a trail scent.

TUCK-UP. The shallowness of the body at the loin creating a small-waisted look.

TYPE. The combination of features that makes a breed unique from other breeds.

UD. Utility Dog (title).

UDT. Utility Dog Tracker (title).

UNBENCHED SHOW. Dog show at which dogs must arrive in time for judging and may leave anytime after the judging.

UNDERSHOT. When the front teeth of the lower jaw reach beyond the front teeth of the upper jaw.

UPPER ARM. The front leg between the forearm and the shoulder blade.

UTILITY DOG. Obedience degree (advanced).

UTILITY DOG AND TRACKER. A double title for a dog that has earned both utility and tracking titles (Utility Dog Tracker).

UTILITY DOG AND TRACKER EXCELLENT. A double title indicating a dog that has earned both utility and advanced tracking degrees.

WALK. The gait of a dog.

WEEDY. Lacking sufficient bone and substance.

WELL LET DOWN. Short hocks.

WET NECK. Superfluous loose skin on neck.

WINNERS BITCH OR WINNERS DOG. Dog or bitch chosen first from the winners of each class and the one receiving the points toward its championship.

WITHERS. The highest point of the shoulders, behind the neck.

WRY MOUTH. When the lower jaw is twisted and not properly aligned with the upper jaw.

The End—We take our rest.